Teach
Yourself
MICROSOFT®
INTERNET
EXPLORER 4

in 24 Hours

Teach Yourself

MICROSOFT®
INTERNET
EXPLORER 4

in 24 Hours

Noel Estabrook
Maxine London

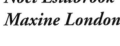

201 West 103rd Street
Indianapolis, Indiana 46290

Copyright © 1997 by Sams.net Publishing

International Standard Book Number: 1-57521-233-1

Library of Congress Catalog Card Number: 96-71215

2000 99 98 97   4 3 2

Interpretation of the printing code: the rightmost double-digit number is the year of the book's printing; the rightmost single-digit, the number of the book's printing. For example, a printing code of 97-1 shows that the first printing of the book occurred in 1997.

Composed in AGaramond and MCPdigital by Macmillan Computer Publishing

Printed in the United States of America

Trademarks

President   Richard K. Swadley
Publisher and Director of Acquisitions   Jordan Gold
Director of Product Development   Dean Miller
Executive Editor   Beverly M. Eppink
Managing Editor   Jodi Jensen
Indexing Manager   Johnna L. VanHoose
Director of Marketing   Kelli S. Spencer
Product Marketing Manager   Wendy Gilbride
Marketing Coordinator   Linda Beckwith

Acquisitions Editor
Beverly M. Eppink

Development Editor
Scott D. Meyers

Production Editor
Susan Pink

Indexer
Johnna L. VanHoose

Technical Reviewer
Kelly Held

Editorial Coordinators
Mandie Rowell
Katie Wise

Technical Edit Coordinator
Lorraine E. Schaffer

Resource Coordinators
Deborah Frisby
Charlotte Clapp

Editorial Assistants
Carol Ackerman
Andi Richter
Rhonda Tinch-Mize
Karen Williams

Cover Designer
Tim Amrheim

Book Designer
Gary Adair

Copy Writer
David Reichwein

Production Team Supervisors
Brad Chinn
Andrew Stone

Production
Carol L. Bowers
Jenaffer Brandt
Chris Livengood
Tim Osborn

Overview

Contents

Part V   NetMeeting and Chat   237

Hour 17   Understanding Live Online Communications   239

Hour 18   Chatting with Microsoft Chat   253

About the Authors

Noel Estabrook is currently the technical coordinator of two programs in the College of Education at Michigan State University. He has created over 20 Web sites for private, education, government, and rehabilitation organizations. He is heavily involved in delivering Internet training and technical support to educators, professionals, and beginners. He also runs his own training and Web consulting business (www.oesystems.com) in addition to writing. Most recently, he authored *Teach Yourself the Internet in 24 Hours* (Sams.net Publishing). You can contact him at noel@oesystems.com.

Maxine London is a ten-year veteran of the computer software industry. She is the author of nine computer books and hundreds of magazine articles on computer technology, especially the Internet.

Dedications

To my children, Adam and Eden, who will know more than I do about computers by the time they're teenagers.
—Noel Estabrook

I would like to dedicate this book to

- ☐ *Noel, for being a perfect partner*
- ☐ *The editorial and production staffs at Sams.net, who are the best in the business*
- ☐ *Microsoft Corp., for almost getting it right this time*

—Maxine London

Acknowledgments

After a dozen books, I find myself thanking the same people over and over. Well, I'm going to do it again. I want to thank my wife, Anita, and my acquisitions editor, Beverly Eppink—two women who somehow manage to put up with me year after year. And, of course, I have to thank my Lord, the Author of the only Book that really matters.

—Noel Estabrook

Tell Us What You Think!

As a reader, you are the most important critic and commentator of our books. We value your opinion and want to know what we're doing right, what we could do better, what areas you'd like to see us publish in, and any other words of wisdom you're willing to pass our way. You can help us make strong books that meet your needs and give you the computer guidance you require.

Check out our Web site at http://www.mcp.com.

JUST A MINUTE

> If you have a technical question about this book, call the technical support line at 317-581-3833, or send e-mail to support@mcp.com.

As the team leader of the group that created this book, I welcome your comments. You can fax, e-mail, or write me directly to let me know what you did or didn't like about this book—as well as what we can do to make our books stronger. Here's the information:

Fax: 317-581-4669

E-mail: mset_mgr@sams.mcp.com

Mail: Beverly M. Eppink
          Comments Department
          Sams Publishing
          201 W. 103rd Street
          Indianapolis, IN 46290

Introduction

Twenty-four hours. What can you do in 24 hours? It takes me the first 24 hours of each week just to think about what to do with the remaining 144 hours. Then again, having spent 24 hours on a bus once (Boston to Chicago—don't ask), I know that 24 hours can seem like forever. I guess time passes slowly or quickly depending on how you spend it.

This book offers the quick kind of 24 hours. In that short span, you can become a highly proficient operator of Internet Explorer 4 for Windows.

CAUTION

> Readers are strongly cautioned not to attempt to complete this tutorial in a single, marathon 24-hour session. Sure, we wrote it in a single, marathon 24-hour session, but do as we say, not as we do. Thank you.

Becoming proficient in Internet Explorer means much more than it used to. Sure, Internet Explorer is a *Web browser*, a program for surfing a part of the Internet known as the World Wide Web, or Web for short. (You knew that already, didn't you?) But when accompanied by its optional components, Internet Explorer 4 is also a program for

- ☐ Exchanging e-mail
- ☐ Participating in Internet newsgroups
- ☐ Joining in live voice or video conversations with folks the world over
- ☐ Subscribing to *channels*, special Web pages that deliver information to you automatically
- ☐ Creating and publishing your own Web pages

You learn how to do all of this here, with Internet Explorer and its components, in 24 easy hours.

Actually, you learn all that stuff in only 20 hours. There's one more thing about Internet Explorer 4: It changes Windows. After you install Internet Explorer, lots of things in Windows look and act differently, even when Internet Explorer is closed. For example, you can single-click to do stuff that used to require double-clicking, and you can use your Start menu and the toolbars on folders in new and exciting ways. In this book, you learn to operate the new, Internet Explorer 4-enhanced Windows in just four hours, roughly the time it takes to watch the restored cut of *Lawrence of Arabia*, or to watch four reruns of *Law & Order*.

By the way, I'm Maxine London, your co-tutor on this expedition. My estimable partner, Noel Estabrook, and I have developed this book to make you highly proficient in Internet Explorer 4 very quickly, and to offer you as much fun along the way as we can. We hope you enjoy learning Internet Explorer.

And for those of you who are wondering, yes, Noel is a man, but no, we are not a couple. In fact, we've never met. We co-wrote this book by communicating with one another—and with our publisher—almost exclusively through the Internet. That's just a taste of the productivity potential in the skills you discover here.

How to Use This Book

Computer book publishers always think you need to be told how to use a book. I always wonder what Shakespeare would have put at the start of *Hamlet* if he'd sold it to a computer book publisher: "Start with the part where everyone is alive, read the acts in order by number, and when almost everyone is dead (especially Hamlet), stop reading."

So before I give you the required version, I'll offer you Maxine's: Start reading at the beginning, do what we say as you go along, skip over anything you couldn't care less about, and when you reach the end (or when you know everything you wanted to learn), stop reading. Simple, No?

Here's the other version: Each chapter is this book is designed so that you can read it and perform any activities described in an hour or less (we leave a little extra time for snacks). You don't have to follow the book in order (nobody's watching), but you'll find that your skills develop much more effectively if you do. To a varying degree, each hour builds on those that came before it.

At the start of each hour, you'll see a brief introduction and a list of things you'll learn in the hour. If, after reading the list, you decide that a particular hour covers stuff you don't care about, feel free to skip it. Completing every hour isn't really necessary.

Special Highlighted Elements

Along the way, you'll see a family of special elements broken out from the main text. These elements are completely self-explanatory, and will be automatically and intuitively understood by anyone who can read above a sixth-grade level. So without further ado, I'll now explain each in detail. (See what I said earlier about computer book publishers.)

To Do: Sections flagged by a "To Do" heading offer the exact steps needed to accomplish a task or practice a new skill.

NEW TERM **Term:** We try to introduce new terms as little as possible in this book. But when we first use a term that not everyone understands, a New Term icon appears next to the definition. That way, if you already understand the term, you can easily skip the definition, but if the term is new to you, you can't miss the definition.

TIME SAVER

These boxes offer tips and tricks for doing more with the skill at hand, doing it better, or (especially) doing it faster (which is almost always the same thing as doing it better).

JUST A MINUTE

These boxes alert you to crucial information that you shouldn't miss. They're not meant to be scary; they're just here to say, "Hey, be sure to pay attention to this."

CAUTION

These boxes focus your attention on problems or side effects that can occur in specific situations.

Q&A, Quiz, and Activity: Each hour concludes with a brief question and answer session, in which we respond to questions that may or may not have occurred to you during the hour. In the Q&As, you can learn about stuff that's interesting but usually not required for understanding or using Internet Explorer.

Following the Q&A, you can take a brief quiz to test your knowledge. The questions in the quiz pertain directly to the hour you just completed. More importantly, the questions and answers are sometimes pretty funny, so taking the quiz can actually constitute a fun little break. And most importantly, the answers to the quiz immediately follow the questions, so you can check your knowledge—or cheat.

Following the quiz, you'll find a wholly optional activity that offers you a chance to practice, reinforces or expands on what you learned in the hour, or prepares you for the hour to come.

Ready to start learning Internet Explorer? Start the clock, and move ahead to Hour 1.

PART

I

Orientation

Hour

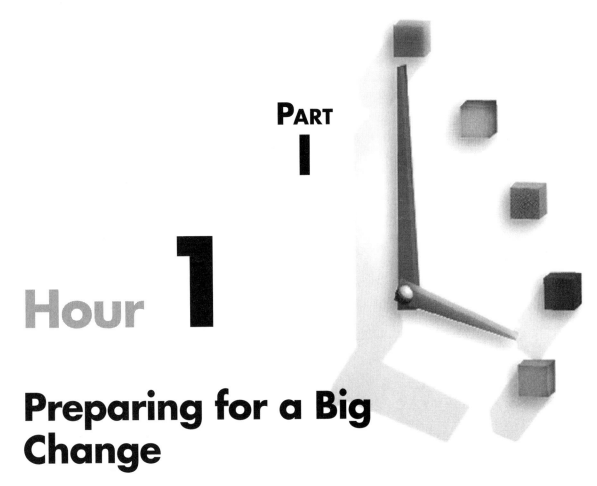

Hour 1

Preparing for a Big Change

No matter who you are or what you already know, Internet Explorer 4 will confound your expectations—at first. If you have any experience with Windows 95 or with Web browsing, Internet Explorer changes many of the rules you're familiar with. If you're a true Windows 95 and Web beginner, you'll discover Internet Explorer's rules from scratch—and have the advantage of starting with a clean slate.

You'll find that Internet Explorer makes most Windows activities—whether Web-oriented or not—more natural and consistent. But first you have to become accustomed to the way Internet Explorer changes things. In this easy hour, you briefly meet Windows and Web browsing in the post-Internet Explorer 4 world, to prepare you for the nuts and bolts in the hours to come.

JUST A MINUTE

To help current Windows 95 users begin adapting their skills to Internet Explorer, this hour mentions a lot of Windows 95 stuff and how it has changed. If you're just learning Windows 95, don't let this information throw you. As this book proceeds, you'll be told exactly what you need to do, whether it's a Windows 95 technique, an Internet Explorer technique, or a stew of both.

This hour introduces you to the major changes you'll discover as soon as you install Internet Explorer 4. At the end of the hour, you'll be able to answer the following questions:

- ☐ Why did Microsoft build Internet Explorer to change the way Windows looks and acts?
- ☐ After Internet Explorer has been installed, how will the icons in Windows look different than they do now?
- ☐ How will I use my mouse buttons differently?
- ☐ What's the big rectangular bar Internet Explorer 4 puts on my Windows desktop?
- ☐ How does Internet Explorer 4 change my Windows folders, desktop, and Programs menu?
- ☐ How will my Windows taskbar change?

JUST A MINUTE

Keep in mind that this hour merely orients you to the changes you can expect in Windows after you install Internet Explorer. You learn how to use and make the most of those changes in later hours.

What's the Big Change?

Before Internet Explorer 4, Internet Explorer was only a Web browser, just like Netscape Navigator, Mosaic, and other Web browsers you may have heard of. Folks used Internet Explorer to access, open, and display stuff published on Web sites all across the Internet.

NEW TERM   **Web browser:** This is a program used to access and display Web pages.

Previous versions of Internet Explorer came equipped for all activities Web surfers commonly needed. For example, using Internet Explorer, you could

- ☐ Access and display Web pages
- ☐ Jump from one page to another by clicking on a link

 Link: A link is text or a picture in a Web page that you can click on to jump to a different page, usually one containing information related to the page you jumped from.

☐ Jump backward to previously visited pages by clicking a toolbar button called Back

☐ Display and play a variety of computer files found on the Web, such as documents, video clips, and sound clips

☐ Create a list of Web pages you like to revisit often, called favorites, so that you can easily jump to any of your favorites' pages by clicking its name in the list

 Favorites: Your favorites are Web pages you like to visit often. When you visit a page that you'll want to revisit, you create a favorite for it. The next time you want to visit that page, all you have to do is choose it from a list of favorites.

Internet Explorer 4, shown in Figure 1.1, still lets you do all these things. But at your option, Internet Explorer can add to Windows a feature called the Active Desktop, sometimes also called Web Integrated Desktop or Desktop Update (Microsoft can't make up its mind). The *Active Desktop* changes Windows 95 so that accessing and opening files and programs on your own PC or local network is just like accessing and opening a Web page on the Internet. In effect, Internet Explorer makes all of Windows 95 behave a lot like the Web.

Figure 1.1.

Internet Explorer, still a browser after all these years.

For example, with Internet Explorer 4 installed on your PC, you can click on links not only to jump around the Web, but also to open files and programs on your PC. You can click a Back button to jump back to a Web page you've visited previously, and you can click a Back button to revisit a file, folder, or program on your PC.

TIME SAVER

In general, Internet Explorer 4's changes to Windows 95 are optional. You can switch them off (so Windows 95 behaves normally) and still use Internet Explorer as your Web browser.

Why the Big Change?

Although you may not think of it this way, what you do on the Web is not that different from what you do on your PC or local area network. Table 1.1 shows how online activities (those you perform through the Internet) and local activities (those you perform on your PC) are really very much the same.

On a PC (local activities)	On the Web (online activities)
You navigate to programs and files by clicking folders or clicking through a directory provided by Windows Explorer.	You navigate to programs and files by clicking links in Web pages and by clicking through directories of links.
Sometimes, you navigate to a file by specifying its location, for example, by entering a disk letter and path (such as C:\Programs). You open programs and files by double-clicking their file icons or names.	Sometimes, you navigate to a file by specifying its location, for example, by entering an Internet address (such as http://www.mcp.com). You open programs and files by clicking links, which may be pictures (icons) or text (names).

Because so many of the things you do locally match similar activities on the Web, why not retool Windows and a Web browser so that you do everything the same way? Why learn two different ways to perform the same basic task, just because one file is on your PC and the other is on a Web site in Kansas? A file is a file, right?

With the Active Desktop installed, you navigate among files and folders, and open files and programs, the same way whether the file is local or on the Web. You needn't learn two different ways of getting around, and in many cases, you won't even have to think about whether the file or program you want to use is on the Web or on your PC.

In effect, Internet Explorer 4's Active Desktop merges your PC with the Web so you can use the resources each contains in a consistent way. After you get used to it, that consistency should improve your productivity and your ability to exploit whatever you find online and at home.

1

Exactly What Changes?

In Part II, you learn all about using the Active Desktop. But just to give you an idea of how completely Internet Explorer 4 can remodel Windows 95, here's a summary of most of the changes you'll notice in Windows.

File Icons Become Links

The Active Desktop makes into a link every file icon, program icon, and folder icon in a Windows folder, in Windows Explorer, and on the desktop. Observe in Figure 1.2 that the icon's label is underlined (just the way a link is underlined in a Web page) and that the pointer turns into a pointing finger when on the icon.

TIME SAVER

> Depending on your configuration, the underlining on icon labels may appear at all times or only when you point to an icon. You learn how to choose between these modes in Hour 8.

Because of the link formatting, to open a file, a folder, or a program, you don't have to double-click the icon, as you have always had to do in Windows. Instead, you point to the link-like file icon and click once, just as you do to activate a link online. Also, you no longer have to click at all to select a file icon when moving, copying, or performing another such operation on it. Just point to the icon and wait a second, and the icon is selected.

Figure 1.2.

Internet Explorer 4 changes file icons to links and adds a channel bar to your desktop.

File icon

Channel bar

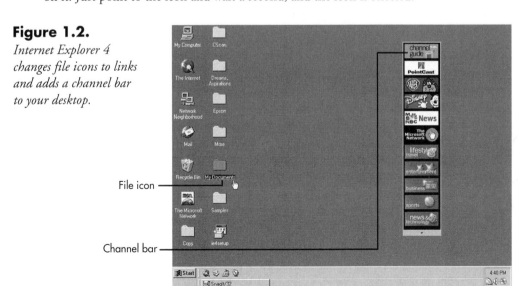

The Channel Bar Appears

On your desktop, you'll immediately notice a rectangular box. This is the channel bar (see Figure 1.2), and it has a powerful purpose, as you'll discover in Hours 7 and 12. You will eventually fill this box with new buttons that open channels to online information you want to keep apprised of. The buttons you will see right after you install Internet Explorer 4 are samples Microsoft has given you, to help you get started with channels. After you create your own buttons, you can delete Microsoft's if you want to.

 Channel: A channel is a Web site that automatically sends updated information, such as news and scores, to your PC at regular intervals or whenever the information changes.

Don't let the channel bar throw you. Until you learn how to use it, you can just ignore it.

Your Folders Turn Webby

The appearance and behavior of all your Windows folders changes (see Figure 1.3). As mentioned earlier, file and folder icons become links, but there's even more webbiness than that. You can now get from place to place in a folder just like you get around the Web, by using the browser-like toolbars on every folder window and in Windows Explorer. You'll also see a number of other enhancements to folders, such as the nifty title and graphic in the folder shown in Figure 1.3.

Figure 1.3.

All Windows folder windows change so that using them is just like using a Web page.

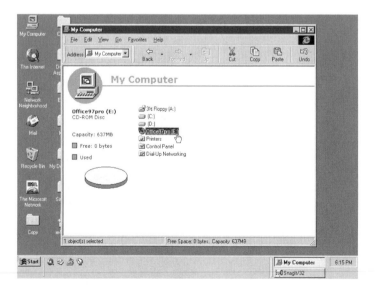

Windows Explorer Turns Webby

People often get confused when I talk about Windows Explorer—the file management system built into Windows 95 (see Figure 1.4)—because they think I'm talking about

Internet Explorer, the browser. If you ask me, Microsoft deliberately made the names similar to confuse everybody so we wouldn't notice when they changed the name of the next major Windows release from "Windows 97" to "Windows 98."

Perhaps in part to eliminate the confusion, Microsoft has more or less merged Internet Explorer 4 with Windows Explorer. You now use a very browser-like window (see Figure 1.5) to do all the stuff you used to do in Windows Explorer: display and navigate among disks, folders, and file lists; create, copy, move, and delete files; and open files and programs.

Figure 1.4.

The Windows Explorer file manager before Internet Explorer 4.

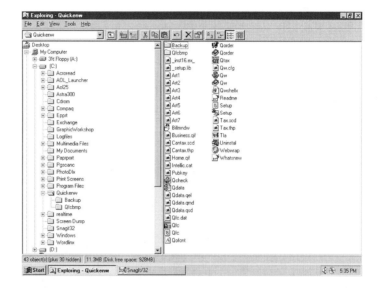

Figure 1.5.

The Windows Explorer after Internet Explorer 4: It's webby!

The Programs Menu Sprouts Favorites

If you've used the Web before, you probably know about favorites, also known as bookmarks in some browsers. The Active Desktop puts your Favorites list right into your Windows Start menu (see Figure 1.6). Choose a favorite, and Internet Explorer 4 opens automatically to take you there.

TIME SAVER

In addition to opening the Favorites list from the Programs menu, you can open it in any folder window or in Windows Explorer by choosing Favorites from the menu bar.

Figure 1.6.

Internet Explorer 4 puts your Favorites menu right in the Windows 95 Start menu.

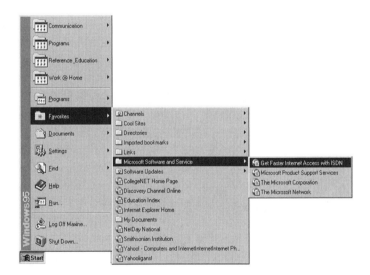

The Taskbar Gets New Power

The Windows 95 taskbar—the bar with the Start button that usually serves as the starting point for a Windows session—becomes a far more powerful tool with Internet Explorer 4.

As Figure 1.7 shows, the taskbar has grown to two rows (although you can adjust the size) and you can now put folders into your taskbar, ready to be opened on top of any other activity on your screen. You can even put your desktop icons or the contents of your Documents menu in the taskbar.

Also, the left end of the taskbar gets a new row of buttons—quick launch buttons—that offer you instant access to browsing the Web, using e-mail, and a few other activities.

1

Even better, you can make some Internet Explorer 4 toolbars appear within the taskbar, for fast access. For example, Figure 1.8 shows the Internet Explorer address bar right in the Windows 95 taskbar.

 Address bar: The Internet Explorer 4 address bar is the toolbar you use to type the address of a Web page you want to visit. You learn how to use the address bar in Hours 6 and 9.

Figure 1.7.

With Internet Explorer 4, the taskbar has new quick launch buttons, and can host folders and desktop icons.

Figure 1.8.

The taskbar can also host any Internet Explorer 4 toolbars, such as the address bar shown here.

How You'll Change

When you get become accustomed to the ways Internet Explorer 4 changes Windows, you might find that you work more quickly and more intuitively. Whenever your brain must jump back and forth between two skill sets (an activity called *code switching*), your productivity suffers. When you can do all things with one set of skills, your brain can focus on the task at hand, not on the techniques that accomplish it.

With Internet Explorer 4, you'll deal with all files and programs the same way, whether they're online or local. This streamlined way of working may also make you more comfortable working with online resources, so you'll get more out of the Web.

Summary

As it was before version 4.0, Internet Explorer remains a capable Web browser, one you can use to surf the Web and exploit all you find there.

But in this first of your 24 hours, you began to discover the ways Internet Explorer 4 goes beyond its Web browsing role to change the way you do almost everything in Windows. These changes enable you to apply one set of computer skills to both online and local activities, which may make you more productive and, well, happy.

Q&A

Q **I'll have to decide whether to use the Active Desktop when I install Internet Explorer 4. But until I've experienced it, I really can't decide whether I want it or not. What do I do?**

A You're right; it's a confusing call. But as your parents told you when you first confronted asparagus, you should always try something first before deciding whether or not you like it. Also, if you choose to use the Active Desktop when setting up Internet Explorer 4 (as described in Hour 3), you can always switch the Active Desktop off later (which you learn to do in Hour 8).

So for the purposes of this book, you might as well let Internet Explorer 4 change Windows the way it wants to, and then explore the new Windows features in Part II. After Part II, if you think you prefer old Windows 95 better, you can switch back—and by then, you'll know how.

Q **You say that with Internet Explorer 4 installed, I can treat files on my PC and files online as if they were all local. But my PC is not connected to the Internet 24 hours a day. When I access an online resource, I must first dial the Net and open my browser. So getting to online resources is always different from using local ones.**

A True, true. But two things are erasing that difference. First, the popularity of the Internet has resulted in the availability of local access numbers almost anywhere, and in unlimited usage accounts (see Hour 2) being the norm. People connect to the Internet more spontaneously than they did in the past because doing so no longer costs extra.

Second, Internet Explorer 4's new connect dialog and other enhancements make connecting to the Internet more automatic than before. In most configurations, you can access Internet resources with one click from anywhere in Windows. True, when Internet Explorer 4 must dial the Net to access a resource, getting that resource takes more time than opening a file on your PC. But the effort on your part is identical; you click and go.

Q **Just when I got the hang of Windows 3.1, I had to switch to Windows 95. Now I'm finally comfortable with Windows 95, and you want me to change the way I work again. What assurance do I have that the Powers-That-Be won't pull the rug out from under me again?**

A In devising how you would accomplish things in Windows 3.1 and Windows 95, Microsoft was all powerful. But the Web-style steps—such as single-clicking links or using a Back button—Internet Explorer 4 adds to Windows have evolved over time, by popular consensus, from the best of the many approaches tried by different browser makers.

1

In other words, Microsoft didn't design most of the steps you'll use in Windows now; it borrowed them from Web tradition. That bodes well for their long-term usefulness. Although a new Windows is due in 1998, these Web techniques have become so prevalent that the new Windows will likely still support them.

In fact, if current reports hold true, the changes the Active Desktop makes to Windows 95 will show up as a standard part of Windows 98. That means the skills you learn now with Internet Explorer and the Active Desktop may actually train you for using Windows 98.

Quiz

Take the following quiz to see how much you've learned.

Questions

1. To use the Internet Explorer 4 Web browser, you must also use the Active Desktop, the ways Internet Explorer 4 changes Windows 95.

    a. True

    b. False

2. Internet Explorer 4 makes all of Windows work more like the Web because

    a. Internet Explorer carries a powerful mutant virus that makes everything webbish.

    b. Users will be more productive and learn new tasks more quickly if they can apply a single set of skills to both online and local activities.

    c. The Web is rad, dude.

    d. The Vice President has spearheaded an initiative to make all things more Web-like by the new millennium, beginning with pastry.

3. Among the changes Internet Explorer 4 makes to Windows, it allows you to add to your Windows taskbar:

    a. Folders

    b. Desktop icons

    c. Internet Explorer 4 toolbars

    d. All of the above

Answers

1. a. You can switch the Active Desktop on or off whenever you feel like it. So there.

2. b. The other choices are silly.

3. d. Any of Internet Explorer 4's toolbars can be added to the taskbar. (You learn how in Hour 6.)

Activities

As you perform tasks in Windows 95 (between now and Hour 3, when you install Internet Explorer 4), think about the steps you perform to accomplish basic tasks. Observe that you must double-click to perform many basic activities, and that folder windows provide little in the way of toolbar help for everyday tasks. Would any of this be easier if done Web-style?

Hour 2

Getting Your Internet Account

You may already have an Internet account—and if so, feel free to skip this hour. (However, make sure you waste a whole hour somewhere along the way so that you come out at an even 24 hours and we don't have to change the book's title.)

If you don't have an Internet account yet, it's best to get one before you install Internet Explorer. During installation, you have to supply Internet Explorer with information about your account, such as the number to dial to reach your Internet provider and your e-mail address. Getting your account first means you'll have this information at hand when you set up Internet Explorer 4 and you can go right online as soon as you finish installing Internet Explorer.

In this hour, you learn the basics of finding and choosing an Internet supplier, sometimes also known as an Internet service provider, or ISP.

| NEW TERM | **Internet service provider (ISP):** An ISP is a company that supplies Internet connections to subscribers. |

At the end of the hour, you'll be able to answer the following questions:

- ☐ What types of connections can I use to connect to the Internet?
- ☐ From which types of companies can I get an Internet account?
- ☐ How can I find an ISP?
- ☐ What questions should I ask before choosing an ISP?
- ☐ How can I get space on a Web server, so I can publish my own Web pages?

JUST A MINUTE

> As you learn in Hour 3, while installing Internet Explorer you'll be offered an option that connects you to a special service at Microsoft, through which you can choose an ISP. Because of this option, it is not absolutely necessary to choose your ISP before installing.
>
> However, Microsoft's service does not list all ISPs that may be available to you. To be sure you have a wide range of ISP options from which to choose, and to make an informed choice, I recommend that you use this hour as a guide for finding and signing up with an ISP *before* installing Internet Explorer 4.

Types of Connections

Your first decision to make before choosing an Internet supplier is to decide what type of connection you want. Different connections require different hardware, and different Internet providers support different connection types.

Dial-Up Modem Connection

The most common Internet connection for a PC is called a dial-up connection, in which you use a modem in your PC to dial an Internet provider over a regular phone line.

 Modem: A modem is an electronic device that converts computer data into audio signals. These audio signals can then be transmitted over a normal phone line. At the receiving end, another modem converts the audio signals back to computer data.

The speed of a modem is measured in kilobits per second (Kbps). The most common modem speeds for Internet connections are 28.8 and 33.6 Kbps. A few providers offer 56.6 Kbps connections, the fastest possible connections available through conventional phone lines. Note, however, that 56.6 Kbps modems are costly and that because of a variety of factors that influence speed—such as the responsiveness of servers—you may notice little or no difference between a 56.6 Kbps connection and a less expensive 33.6 Kbps connection.

2

ISDN

ISDN stands for Integrated Services Digital Network. ISDN lines are special telephone lines that transmit digital signals instead of analog signals. With digital signals, data can be transmitted at a much faster rate than with a traditional modem. To use the Internet over ISDN, you need a special ISDN modem for your PC, an ISDN line from your telephone company, and a special ISDN connection with your Internet supplier. Note that ISDN modems are very expensive compared to other options, and that both your ISP and your phone company charge significantly more for ISDN than for the use of a regular phone line. Also, ISDN is not available everywhere, particularly in rural areas.

Despite these caveats, ISDN lines have a number of advantages. You can get much faster Internet access through an ISDN line; it's more than twice as fast as a 28.8 Kbps modem. In addition, ISDN connections support multiple simultaneous communications channels, so that you can speak on one channel, send a fax on another, and connect to the Internet over another—all at the same time.

Cable Modem Connection

Wouldn't it be great to have the connection speed found in large companies available to your home PC? Enter the cable modem, the next great leap in at-home connection solutions.

With a cable modem, your computer is hooked not to your phone line but to your coaxial television cable. Cable modems are targeted toward the Internet enthusiast with the need for speed. According to some accounts, the fastest cable modems will be capable of receiving data at 10 Mbps and sending it at 768 Kbps.

The suggested fee for that cable-modem service might be $30 to $40 monthly. Including the $600 price tag on the modems themselves, this will be one substantial upgrade.

Getting your hands on the hardware may be the easy part. Only certain areas are experimenting with the use of cable modems, but their use is rapidly expanding. Contact your local cable company to see whether it is planning to carry Internet access with cable modems.

T1 and T3

A T1 line is a high-speed digital connection capable of transmitting data at a rate of approximately 1.5 million bits per second. A T1 line is typically used by small and medium-sized companies with heavy network traffic.

This line is large enough to send and receive large text files, graphics, sounds, and databases instantaneously, and it works at the fastest speed commonly used to connect networks to the Internet. Sometimes referred to as a *leased line*, a T1 line is basically too large and too expensive for individual home use.

A T3 line is a super high-speed connection capable of transmitting data at a rate of 45 million bits per second. This connection represents a bandwidth equal to about 672 regular voice-grade telephone lines. A T3 line is wide enough to transmit full-motion, real-time video and very large databases over a busy network.

A T3 line is typically installed as a major networking artery for large corporations and universities with high-volume network traffic. The backbones of the major Internet service providers, for example, are made up of T3 lines.

Types of Internet Suppliers

You can get your dial-up Internet account from three general sources: online services, national ISPs, and local ISPs. Each is described in this section.

Online Services: AOL, CompuServe, MSN, and Prodigy

If you've recently bought a computer magazine, chances are it came with ads (and probably software) for one or more of the major national online services: America Online (AOL), CompuServe, Microsoft Network (MSN), or Prodigy. The online services are ISPs, but they also offer unique activities not accessible to the rest of the Internet community.

One of the selling points of these services is their sign-up process. Connecting to them is usually simple: You install the free software they provide, follow the onscreen instructions, and you're connected. In addition to giving you access to the vast resources of the Internet, these services give you access to content that is not available to people who don't use the services. These services have their own chat rooms, newsgroups, online shopping, special-interest groups, and searchable references that only subscribers to the service can use.

The national online services have recently adopted pricing policies that are generally competitive with the local and national ISPs, although you can almost always get a slightly better deal from a regular ISP than from any online service. More importantly, the online services—AOL, especially—have earned a reputation for getting overburdened, offering slow and unreliable Internet connections, or even confronting subscribers with busy signals (rather than a connection) when too many subscribers want to connect at the same time. (To be fair, some regular ISPs suffer from overcrowding, too.)

Still, the online services are continually improving both their pricing and their capacity, and they're worth considering. Also, if you travel a lot, keep in mind that the national online

2

services offer local access numbers almost anywhere, so you can connect to the service from wherever you travel without having to make a toll call.

Here's a rundown on the services as they stand now. Note, however, that pricing and other policies change often. Check with the services for the latest information.

JUST A MINUTE

Regardless of your choice for an ISP, make sure the company offers a dial-up number for connecting to the Internet that is a local call from your PC's location. Otherwise, you'll end up paying long-distance fees to the phone company in addition to whatever your ISP charges for Internet access.

In most cities, finding local access numbers is no problem—any local ISP, national ISP, or online service will have a local number you can use. In some suburbs and many rural areas, finding a local number gets more difficult. Often your best bet in such circumstances is to find a local ISP or to see whether your local telephone company offers Internet access (many do).

Note that some services offer an 800 number that you may use to access the service when the ISP provides no local number. But the 800 number is rarely truly toll-free. The ISP almost always charges a higher rate for using the service through the 800 number.

National ISPs

Many people use a national online service such as AOL to get their feet wet and to learn more about the Internet. When they feel comfortable, they move on to a local provider that gives more options and often better service.

National online services occasionally don't allow users with 28.8 Kbps modems to run at 28.8 Kbps. The modem banks they use may max out at 14.4 Kbps, leaving people with newer computers watching graphics download slowly as their wallets are being emptied. Be sure to check that the company offers at least 28.8 Kbps connections in your area.

If you like the idea of working with a national company but don't want to pay per-hour prices, a number of national companies now offer direct access to the Internet at a flat rate. Netcom, as shown in Figure 2.1, offers a $19.95 package that gives you unlimited Internet access and 24-hour support. Another national supplier is Earthlink, shown in Figure 2.2.

AT&T has started offering Internet access (through a service called AT&T Worldnet), as has Bell Atlantic and other Baby Bell companies, both locally and nationally.

Figure 2.1.

*Netcom advertises its
services and specials on its
Web site.*

Figure 2.2.

*Earthlink, another
affordable national ISP.*

Finding a Local ISP

Finding a local ISP is getting easier all the time. Phone books, friends, coworkers, as well as local computer newsletters, clubs, and stores are all good sources of information for finding your local ISP.

I know the following procedure is low-tech, but the classics live: Tear your fingers from the keyboard and pick up the phone book. Check the Yellow Pages for Internet service providers (look under *Internet* first, and then try *Computers—Internet Services*), and you should find a good starting point.

The next source for finding a local ISP is as close as your local computer store. Odds are that the staff of the store can recommend a few good services. The computer store might also have special deals with some local providers for trial subscriptions or discounted rates. It never hurts to ask.

If you happen to be lucky enough to be investigating ISPs at the same time a local computer club is having a computer show, you should know that providers flock to shows to have rate wars with the competition, and the winner is usually you. Here you have a collection of local ISPs in one area.

If you have access to the Internet (through a friend's computer, your local library, or your job), you can search online for an ISP. One good place to start is *the List* (http://thelist.iworld.com), a Web site dedicated to listing many of the ISPs in the U.S. and Canada. This site, shown in Figure 2.3, even boasts a global ISP list categorized by country or country code.

Figure 2.3.

Use the List to find a local ISP.

Eight Questions for Your ISP

If you're treading into an unknown area trying to find an ISP, arming yourself with some basic information is a good idea. The following questions should help you decide which ISP is going to get your business. If an ISP skirts the issue when you ask tough questions, strongly consider looking elsewhere. Just as in any other business, you can find good ISPs and bad ISPs.

1. What is the price structure?

   Some providers offer flat-rate fees for a certain number of hours online, for example, $18.00 for unlimited hours of connection time. Others structure their rates so that you pay, oh, $15.00 for the first 20 hours online and $1.50 an hour after that. Most ISPs charge your monthly subscription fee to a major credit card or even apply it to your local phone bill.

JUST A MINUTE

> Some ISPs require the payment of a setup fee of some sort when you first sign up, in addition to the regular charges. When comparing prices, be sure to take this fee into consideration. Sometimes the ISP that boasts the lowest monthly rate also hits new customers with a setup fee as high as $30.

2. What type of connection does the ISP have to the Internet?

   Either a T3 or T1 high-speed line is great; two lines (in case one of them fails) are better. A T1 can accommodate 100 to 150 users logged on at any one time. Some providers may brag that they have a T1 connection, when in fact they share the line with another company or provider. This "partial" T1 can still support a large number of users, but your provider has only half of them.

   Some of the larger providers must handle the load of hundreds of users dialed in simultaneously. These providers may have multiple T1s or even a T3. Only very large providers need a direct link using a T3 line.

3. What speed are the modems used for dial-up access?

   Actually, two modems are involved in connecting your computer to the Internet. One is the modem at your home and the other is at the ISP. The slower of these two modems determines your real connection speed to the Internet. The fastest modems now operate at 33.6 Kbps. Some providers have modems that run at only 14.4 or 28.8 Kbps.

   Another consideration if you want high-speed connections is whether the ISP offers ISDN connections. ISDN lines run at 64 Kbps but cost more than $500 to establish with all the hardware and software requirements. Consider this avenue only if you have serious Internet access needs.

4. How many dial-up modems are available, and how many customers use the service?

   Use this customers-to-modem ratio to determine the probability that you will have problems connecting to the ISP. Both the number of customers and number of modems are very important. Established ISPs (more than 150 customers) can run at about 10 customers to 1 modem with users facing a "reasonable" number of busy signals. If you don't ever want to receive a busy signal when you log on, look for an established ISP with a ratio of fewer than 10 customers per modem.

2

5. Is software included with the account?

   Some ISPs include a collection of basic software with your account. These basic programs might include a dial-up agent, a Web browser, an FTP client, a compression agent, a chat client, an e-mail application, or a newsreader. Although most of this software is shareware, having it initially makes working on the Internet a lot easier. For example, you can use this software to download a copy of Internet Explorer.

6. What kind of technical support is offered?

   Look for an ISP that provides support via e-mail and over the phone. Remember, e-mail support doesn't do much good if you can't log on in the first place. Ask your potential ISP what its telephone support number is (long-distance calls, of course, cost money) and what the hours are. Then call in—more than once, at different times—to see how long it takes to get a person on the line.

   Don't forget to ask how much tech support costs. Some ISPs (though not many locally) charge users for support. And make sure your ISP offers support for your type of computer and operating system.

7. Does the ISP have redundant equipment?

   Does the ISP have redundant equipment? That was worth repeating. Ask whether the company has backups for all critical equipment, including a spare router and spare servers. With all the hardware necessary to run an ISP, the service provider has to be able to handle sudden problems. While you're at it, check to see whether the equipment runs on an *uninterruptible power supply (UPS)*.

 Uninterruptible power supply (UPS): A UPS is a short-term battery supply that kicks in when a system's power is lost. The battery, serving as an auxiliary power supply, gives you enough time to close your applications and save your files.

8. How many newsgroups can I access?

   Newsgroups enable users with similar interests to share their thoughts with each other. Star Trek fans, for example, can congregate in a specific newsgroup to discuss characters, plots, and upcoming movies. Some ISPs offer limited newsgroup access; others have none.

Do You Want Your Own Web Page?

Internet Explorer 4 includes FrontPage Express and Web publishing software, so you can create and publish your own Web pages (as you learn to do in Part VI). If you think you might want to publish your own Web pages, you'll need space on a Web server to do so. One of the best places to get Web server space is on your ISP's server. Some ISPs offer a small amount of Web server space free to all customers; others charge a nominal additional fee.

In addition to the questions you should ask any ISP before you sign up—and those questions really are the most important—here are a few to consider if you plan to design a Web site:

☐ What are the charges for Web server space?

Many ISPs include free Web pages in some subscription packages. When there are charges, favor ISPs who charge by the amount of server space you use, not by the number of people who visit your page. When you pay for only the space, you always know what your bill will be.

☐ What would my URL (Web site address) be?

Addresses such as `http://www.isp.net/~yourname/` are common, and they're easy for other people to remember. More complicated URLs aren't as good.

Summary

When choosing an Internet service provider, you have to consider rates, support, and accessibility before you can make a good decision. Choosing a national or local ISP depends on the features you want. National ISPs offer more perks than just Internet access. But if you can do without a special user's newsgroup and just want to get online, start looking for a local service provider.

Be sure to question your national or local provider about Web sites. Chances are that putting up a small personal site won't cost you anything. If you plan to develop a business site, check rates and any hidden throughput charges that might be applicable.

Q&A

Q Is having an Internet service provider really necessary?

A Well, yes and no. You don't need an ISP to use your computer, but you do need one if you want to use the Internet. Unless you can afford the hefty $52,000 per year for a direct Internet connection, I suggest signing up with an ISP.

Q What are all the numbers associated with different types of modems?

A The numbers are the rates at which the modem can transfer data across the connection. A 14.4 modem, for example, can transmit and receive data at a rate of 14.4 kilobits per second (Kbps). The faster the transfer rate, the faster your connection to the Internet. Consider (for today, anyway) a 14.4 Kbps the bare minimum, 28.8 Kbps acceptably fast and widely supported, and 33.6 to 56.6 Kbps nice and speedy but requiring a more costly modem and not yet supported by all ISPs.

Q Can I find a local ISP in my area?

A Hard to tell. Local ISPs are popping up everywhere. You can turn to a number of sources. You can check with a local computer store or simply check your Yellow

2

Pages. If a computer show is nearby, you might want to look there, too. If you can't find a local ISP, look for a national ISP or online service that has a local access number in your area, so you can connect without making a toll call.

Q How much can I expect to spend?

A The rule of thumb these days is that you should be able to get unlimited Internet access and a little Web server space for no more than $19.95 per month (the price now offered by several online services and national ISPs). If you shop around, you can get an Internet account for as little as $15.00 per month (and maybe without Web server space), usually from a local ISP.

If you forego unlimited access for hourly changes, you can get deals that enable you to surf the net for up to 20 hours per month for under $10.00. But be warned—most beginners end up spending a lot more time online than they think they will. Unlimited access is affordable and highly recommended.

Quiz

Take the following quiz to see how much you've learned.

Questions

1. What is the difference between an online service (such as AOL or MSN) and a regular ISP?
2. Why is the customers-to-modems ratio important?
3. Which is the fastest connection?

   a. 14.4 modem

   b. 28.8 modem

   c. 33.6 modem

   d. ISDN line

Answers

1. Both online services and ISPs offer Internet access, which gets you the Web, e-mail, and Internet chats and discussion groups. But the online services offer special discussion groups, chats, news services, and other content available only to their own subscribers.
2. The smaller the ratio, the easier it is to dial in each time and not get a busy signal.
3. d. ISDN line. Among dial-up connections over ordinary phone lines, however, the highest number (33.6) wins. (This is the Internet, not golf.)

Activity

If you're currently using an ISP, re-evaluate your provider. Find out how your ISP compares to other, newer companies. Check out *the List* for any ISPs with Web sites in your area. Most ISPs advertise their rates and important information on their sites, so you might not have to do much more digging.

If you're looking for an ISP, check with your friends and neighbors for recommendations. Take a quick trip to the local bookstore or newsstand, and buy a computer magazine. Aim for one with a free access disk, and try it out.

Hour 3

Setting Up Internet Explorer 4

Three phases are involved in getting Internet Explorer 4 set up on your PC: Get the software, install the software, and configure the software to communicate with your ISP. In this hour, you learn how to do all three.

Before proceeding, make sure your PC meets (or exceeds) the minimum system requirements for Internet Explorer 4, which are a 486/DX2 66MHz or faster processor (Pentium recommended), 8 MB of RAM (16 MB or more highly recommended), and sufficient hard disk space for the installation option you choose. (You learn what the installation options mean during this hour.) The choices are 61 MB (Browser only), 66 MB (Standard), 90 MB (Full).

JUST A MINUTE

The disk space minimums just shown are required to *install* Internet Explorer 4. The amount of space occupied by Internet Explorer after installation, however, is 14 MB (Browser only), 15 MB (Standard), or 22 MB (Full).

At the end of the hour, you'll be able to answer the following questions:

☐ How can I get a copy of Internet Explorer 4 to install on my PC?

☐ What should I do before I begin to install Internet Explorer to make sure all goes smoothly?

☐ How do I install Internet Explorer 4 on my PC?

☐ After installing the Internet Explorer 4 software, how do I configure Internet Explorer 4 so that it knows about my ISP, my e-mail address, and so on?

☐ How can I update my Internet Explorer installation later, to add components or update programs?

TIME SAVER

> Do you have an Internet account yet? If not, Internet Explorer 4 can help you find one while you run the Connection wizard, described later in this chapter. As you learned in Hour 2, it's smarter to find your own ISP first. But in case you haven't had a chance, I wanted you to know that Internet Explorer can help you.

Getting the Software

Installing Internet Explorer 4 begins with getting your hands on the software itself.

If you already have an Internet account and just about any browser (a previous version of Internet Explorer, Netscape Navigator, or any other browser flavor), you can easily download and install Internet Explorer right over the Net, from Microsoft's Web site. If you're not yet online, you can pick up Internet Explorer in a variety of other ways.

In this section, you learn how to get your hands on Internet Explorer 4, no matter what you have—or don't have—now.

Downloading the Software

To use your current Web browser to download Internet Explorer 4, begin by connecting to the Internet and connecting to Microsoft's home page at

```
http://www.microsoft.com
```

I wish I could show you the exact URL and steps required to download Internet Explorer 4, but I'd be foolish to try. Microsoft changes this stuff every few months, so odds are I'd steer you wrong, and your friend Maxine would never do that. Instead, I recommend that you simply go straight to the home page.

3

On that page, you'll certainly see a button with the Internet Explorer 4 logo on it, usually accompanied by a slogan such as "Download it now!" or "Try it today!" or maybe "Do as you're told!" Click that link, and you'll jump to a page that tells you all about Internet Explorer 4 and provides a link for downloading it.

If you plan to download Internet Explorer 4, you should know a few things up front. First, downloading this particular software involves more than just clicking a link. When you work through the steps from Microsoft's home page, you'll need to make choices from drop-down lists and other items. You may be asked to choose

- A server location from which you will download Internet Explorer. Microsoft will display a list of servers from which you should try to select the one closest to you, geographically (although you can, technically, use any server in the list).

- An installation option. Downloading Internet Explorer can take a long time, from one to several hours. The installation options enable you to download only the parts of Internet Explorer 4 that you plan to use, to save downloading time. You can choose a Browser only installation that includes only the Internet Explorer 4 browser and a few options, a Standard setup that includes the parts most people use (the browser, e-mail, newsgroup software, and so on), or a Full setup that includes the works, even conferencing and chat software.

TIME SAVER

> If you choose the Browser only or Standard installation option, and later decide you want to use a part of Internet Explorer 4 that was not included in your choice, you can use the Product Updates option to add anything you left out. You learn about Product Updates later in this hour.

When you begin downloading, Microsoft first sends you a single, small program file (about half a megabyte) called IE4SETUP. Depending on your browser, that program may run automatically or you may have to run the program yourself (by double-clicking its file icon) while you remain connected to the Internet. The IE4SETUP program manages the rest of the download procedure, outside your browser. You probably should close your browser before continuing with the setup to prevent conflicts between the browser and the setup program. Be sure you remain connected to the Internet after you close your browser.

After IE4SETUP takes over, it offers you two options. It can download all Internet Explorer 4 files to your PC, so you can install the software later, offline, at any time. Or it can download and install the files simultaneously.

It's your life, but I recommend downloading first, and then installing for several reasons. First, getting all the downloading out of the way before running the installation gets you offline quicker, minimizing the chances that a momentary blip at your ISP will kick you offline and force you to start over. Technically, IE4SETUP has the capability to resume a download from the point where it left off, if the download is interrupted. But this feature is not 100% reliable—it's still best to download all in one shot.

Second, both the download and the installation will run more smoothly and reliably when they don't have to compete for your PC's resources. And third, if anything goes wrong during installation, it's easier to start over when you already have all the files.

JUST A MINUTE

> If you decide to download and install simultaneously, note that at some point during the download, the Setup wizard will open. At that point, you will perform all the steps described later in this chapter in the section titled "Installing the Software."

Getting the Software on CD-ROM

You can't download Internet software unless you already have some. It's like getting a loan; nobody wants to lend you money unless you don't need it.

Still, you can get Internet Explorer 4 without first having your Internet account. The easiest way to get Internet Explorer 4 on CD-ROM is to call up Microsoft and order it. The special telephone number for ordering Internet Explorer 4 on CD-ROM directly from Microsoft is

  800-485-2048

Microsoft charges $4.95 to send you the CD.

JUST A MINUTE

> The files required for installing Internet Explorer 4 come to over 20 MB, which makes shipping Internet Explorer 4 on disk impractical. Therefore, it's unlikely that Microsoft will make Internet Explorer 4 available on disk. If you do not have a CD-ROM drive, you must get Internet Explorer 4 by downloading it.

At this writing, you cannot yet buy Internet Explorer 4 in a box at a software store, but you inevitably will be able to. Although Internet Explorer is technically free when you download it, you pay a small price (about 15 bucks) for it in a software store, to cover the cost of the CD, box, and distribution.

With earlier Internet Explorer releases, Microsoft tended to throw the files in with almost every product you bought. Buy Microsoft Office 97 on CD-ROM, and you'll find Internet Explorer on the CD. Buy Word 97 or FrontPage 97, ditto. Sometimes, nothing on or in the software box tells you Internet Explorer 4 is there. If you browse around the folders on the CD, however, you'll probably find it.

3

For example, if you insert the Office 97 CD in your CD-ROM drive, open My Computer, and double-click the icon for your CD-ROM drive, you'll see a folder called ValuPack. In that folder, you'll find a folder called Iexplore. (See Figure 3.1, which shows all the files you need to set up Internet Explorer on your PC.)

Figure 3.1.

You can find Internet Explorer lurking on many Microsoft CD-ROMs, including this one for Office 97.

JUST A MINUTE

Because Internet Explorer 4 is new, when you buy Office 97 or another Microsoft software package, the CD may include Internet Explorer 3, not 4. If that happens, you can simply install version 3, and then use it to download and install version 4.

That sounds like a lot of extra work, but it's not. Most of the communications and configuration settings you make when setting up version 3 are re-used automatically when you install version 4.

If you haven't bought any Microsoft software lately, and don't plan to, here's a few final ways to get Internet Explorer 4:

☐ Some ISPs will mail you Internet Explorer 4 (or version 3) on diskettes or CD when you sign up with them (sometimes with a nominal charge, $5 or so, to cover the media and mailing).

☐ When an ISP doesn't offer Internet Explorer 4, it usually can supply another browser free or for a small fee. If your ISP sends you something other than Internet Explorer, install it and use it to download Internet Explorer 4.

☐ If your name and address have worked their way into the great computer direct-marketing database, your mailbox is regularly stuffed with free trial offers from ISPs and online services (50 hours free!) that include a browser on CD. You can use the CD and the free trial to download Internet Explorer 4, and then choose whether to stay with the ISP when your trial period is up.

☐   CD-ROMs with free trials or bonus software are frequently packaged with computer magazines. Browse magazine racks, paying special attention to any computer magazines wrapped in plastic bags. For the $5 or so a magazine costs, you may find a CD containing Internet Explorer 4 or another browser you can use to get Internet Explorer 4.

Preparing to Install the Software

Installing Internet Explorer 4 is amazingly simple. After you have the software, it takes only a few minutes; within the one hour allotted to a chapter in this book, you'll have time left over for a snack and a short nap. You perform the installation simply and step-by-step in a Windows wizard. Before beginning, though, it's best to make a few choices and to prepare your PC.

You'll be asked during installation whether you want "single-clicking." In other words, do you want to use the Active Desktop features you learned about in Hour 1 of this book? As the wizard will remind you, you can switch off the Active Desktop features later. So you may as well install them, if only to check them out.

The Setup wizard also asks whether you want to install the Browser only, Standard, or Full installation option. If you downloaded the software, you've already made this choice. If you're installing from a CD, you need to decide how much of Internet Explorer 4 you plan to use.

As a final step before beginning installation, you need to prepare your PC by closing all programs (except Windows 95). If you've used several programs since last starting Windows, it's a good idea to restart your PC just before beginning the installation, to clear out the odds and ends that a few evil, evil programs can leave in your PC's memory even after they're closed.

Oh...I promised you this lesson would leave time for a nap and a snack. Feel free to take one or the other (but not both) before moving ahead.

TIME SAVER

Before installing any big program (and Internet Explorer 4 qualifies), it's always a good idea to perform a little housekeeping on your hard disk first. Doing so will make Internet Explorer 4 (and everything else on your PC) run faster and more reliably, and will prevent problems down the road.

First uninstall any old, unused programs (except any old Internet programs, because Internet Explorer 4 can use their files to get configuration information), delete old files, and empty your Windows 95 Recycle Bin. Next, choose Programs | Accessories | System Tools to find ScanDisk and Disk Defragmenter. Run ScanDisk to find and repair any errors on your hard disk, and then run the Disk Defragmenter to reorganize your hard disk's contents for top performance.

Installing the Software

Ready to install? Be honest: Did you skip everything in this hour up to this point and jump straight to here? If so, go back and at least skim for anything useful (and no snack for you!).

When you're ready, locate the file icon for the program IE4SETUP.EXE, shown in Figure 3.2. (Depending upon how your copy of Windows 95 is configured, the file extension .EXE may or may not appear in the icon label.)

Figure 3.2.
Double-click this file icon to get the installation rolling.

TIME SAVER

The Internet Explorer 4 setup runs in a Windows wizard. To move from each step in the following procedure to the next, click the Next button that appears on every dialog. If during installation you change your mind about any choices you made in earlier steps, you can click the Back button to go back to any earlier step in the wizard and review or change your choices.

To Do: Install Internet Explorer 4

1. Double-click the Ie4setup.exe icon. A dialog opens, asking whether you want to install from the files on your hard disk or straight from the Internet.

2. I'm assuming you took my advice about not downloading and installing at the same time. If so, select Setup from the local folder and click OK. (If not, click Update installation from the Internet and do whatever the wizard tells you to do next.)

3. Read through the license agreement, select I Accept the Agreement, and click OK. The Installation Option dialog appears (see Figure 3.3).

4. If you already downloaded the Internet Explorer 4 file (as I recommended earlier), you've already selected whether you want the Browser only, Standard, or Full installation of Internet Explorer 4; just make the same choice again here.

    If you are installing from a CD or straight from the Web, choose the installation option you prefer.

5. When prompted about single-clicking or desktop update, click Yes.

6. In the dialog shown in Figure 3.4, the setup routine asks whether it's okay to store your Internet Explorer 4 files in the directory C:\Program Files\Microsoft Internet.

Figure 3.3.

Choosing an
installation option.

Unless you can think of a good reason why it's not okay, just click Next to accept
that location. If you want to be fussy about things and choose a different disk or
directory, type it (or click Browse to find it first), and then click Next.

Figure 3.4.

Choosing the disk
and directory
where the Internet
Explorer 4 files
will be stored.

After you choose the storage location, the setup routine begins setting up files on
your PC. As it does, it displays the progress report shown in Figure 3.5, to let you
know how things are going. If you're installing from a CD or a previously downloaded file, the process should take only a few minutes. If you're installing straight
from the Web, the process may take hours because the files must be downloaded
and then installed.

When the process is complete, a dialog like the one in Figure 3.6 appears.

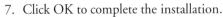

   7. Click OK to complete the installation.

3

Figure 3.5.

Setup keeps you informed of its progress as it sets up files on your PC.

Figure 3.6.

Setup tells you when it has finished setting up files.

Your PC restarts automatically; if after a minute or so it has not restarted, restart it yourself. Windows may take a few minutes longer than usual to stir back to life, but that's just because Setup is still finishing up. The next time you start Windows, it will come up about as quickly as it ever did, which I know wasn't fast but that's not my fault, is it?

Anyway, when Windows reappears, it looks dramatically, tragically different (see Figure 3.7). Actually, it looks awful, if you ask me. It looks like someone ingested all of Microsoft's advertising and then threw up on your screen. Don't worry—sanity is easily restored.

JUST A MINUTE

Some of the differences you see on your display—the link-like file icons and the channel bar—are a normal part of the Active Desktop. But the onscreen "Active Desktop" logo and other ugly stuff are just wallpaper, easily removed.

To get rid of it, locate the underlined phrase "Tell me about Active Desktop" in the lower right corner of your screen. Click that link to open a brief description of the Active Desktop. At the bottom of the description, another underlined phrase appears, "Restore my desktop wallpaper." Click that phrase, and then choose File | Exit to close the description.

If that doesn't work, right-click the desktop, and choose Properties. Then choose the Background tab and select a new wallpaper (or a wallpaper choice of "none").

Figure 3.7.

After the Internet Explorer 4 setup, Windows at first looks like this. Yikes.

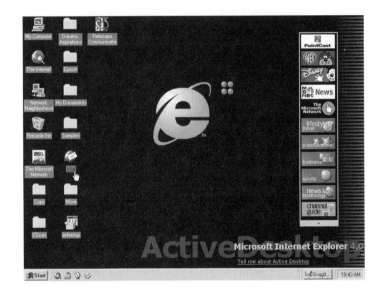

Configuring Communications

After installing the software, you have only one job left to get Internet Explorer 4 fully set up. You must tell Internet Explorer 4 how to communicate with your ISP or online service. You do this by running the Internet Connection wizard, which prompts you step-by-step for each piece of required information.

TIME SAVER

If you have an earlier version of Internet Explorer installed, the Connection wizard may be able to automatically configure its own communications using your previous setup.

The wizard may also be able to borrow certain communications information from other programs you have installed on your PC. For example, if you have an e-mail program already set up on your PC, the wizard may be able to copy your e-mail address and server address from that software.

Still, it's a good idea to have all of your communications information on hand, in case the wizard can't find or borrow something.

Preparing to Run the Connection Wizard

You'll find installation easiest if you approach it like cooking. You know that making a meal is easiest when you locate and lay out all the ingredients before you even light the stove. In

3

Internet Explorer 4's case, you need to gather some information, make a few choices, and prepare your PC before beginning.

Nothing terrible happens if you skip this preparation, but if you do, you may find yourself rummaging through the cupboard looking for paprika in the middle of the installation, and who needs that?

Before starting the Connection wizard, you'll need to have the following info jotted down. You can get all of this from your ISP or online service when you set up your Internet account.

TIME SAVER

> If you want, scribble the information you need between the items in the following list, unless you've borrowed this book from the library.

- [ ] The telephone number your modem dials to contact your ISP.
- [ ] The Internet address of your ISP's server. It will be made up of four sets of numbers separated by periods, for example, 205.240.155.2.

NEW TERM   **Server:** A server is a computer that serves files and programs to other computers that contact it through a network, like the Internet. Your PC communicates with an Internet server at your ISP, which is how it communicates with the Internet. Your PC also contacts mail servers (for e-mail), a news server (for newsgroups), and Web servers (to view Web pages).

- [ ] Your Internet username (sometimes called user ID) and password.
- [ ] Your full e-mail address.
- [ ] Your ISP's mail server addresses. Some ISPs use a single mail server address for both outgoing and incoming e-mail. Others have one server address for outgoing mail (called an SMTP server) and a different one for incoming mail (called a POP3 server).
- [ ] Your ISP's news server address, for accessing Internet newsgroups, sometimes also called discussion groups or Usenet. A few ISPs require a password for accessing newsgroups; if yours does, you'll need that, too.
- [ ] Your ISP's Internet Directory Service connection information, if your ISP provides one (few do). A directory service is an online "white pages" of people you can contact through e-mail; it helps you look folks up.

    If your ISP offers one, *and* if you want to use it, you'll need to supply the Connection wizard with something called LDAP account information. If your ISP doesn't offer, or you don't care, forget about it—it's optional.

TIME SAVER

If you have any previous Internet software set up on your PC, the Connection wizard automatically attempts to use the communications information from that software to set up Internet Explorer 4.

As you work through the wizard, it will from time to time show you a list of software on your PC where it finds information it can use. On those dialogs, you can choose to let Internet Explorer 4 use what it finds or to ignore the old software and set up from scratch.

Whenever you let Internet Explorer 4 use your old settings, the wizard immediately displays a summary of the settings it intends to use from the old software. You can then accept those settings or reject them and enter new settings.

Running the Connection Wizard

In most cases, the Connection wizard opens automatically the first time you open Internet Explorer. To try it out, point to the Internet Explorer icon on your desktop (see Figure 3.8) and single-click, or open the Start menu and choose Programs | Internet Explorer | Internet Explorer.

Figure 3.8.

The Internet Explorer desktop icon—one way to start Internet Explorer 4.

What you do next depends on what happens when you open Internet Explorer 4:

☐ If you see the screen shown in Figure 3.9, the Connection wizard has opened automatically. Proceed with the steps that begin under "To Do: Use the Wizard to Configure Communications."

☐ If the Connection wizard does not open, close Internet Explorer (choose File | Exit) and open the Connection wizard manually. To do that, open the Start menu and choose Programs | Internet Explorer | Connection Wizard.

TIME SAVER

To move from one step in the Connection wizard to the next, click the Next button that appears on every dialog that the wizard presents. If you change your mind about any choices you made in earlier steps, you can click the Back button to go back to any earlier step in the wizard and review or change your choices.

3

Figure 3.9.

This dialog is your starting point for the Connection wizard.

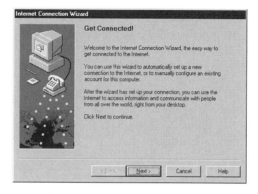

To Do: Use the Wizard to Configure Communications

1. In the dialog shown in Figure 3.9, click Next. The Setup Options dialog opens, as shown in Figure 3.10.

Figure 3.10.

Choosing among the setup options.

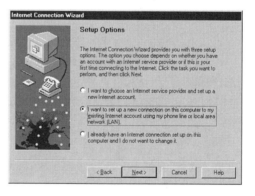

2. In the Setup Options dialog:

   If you want Microsoft's help choosing an Internet Provider, select the top option, I Want to Choose an Internet Provider. If you choose this option, you'll be connected through your modem to a special server at Microsoft that might be able to help you choose an Internet provider. To learn more about it, review Hour 2.

   If you have already established an account with an ISP and now want to configure Internet Explorer 4 for it, choose the second option, I Want to Set up a New Connection, and then move on to step 3.

JUST A MINUTE

The third option in the Setup Options dialog applies only if you have already set up your Internet account in Internet Explorer 4.

3. After you choose an option in step 2, the Dial-Up Connection dialog opens. If you already set up an Internet account on your PC, its name appears in the list on this dialog. You may choose it from the list, confirm the settings in the summary the wizard shows you, and then skip to step 8.

   If no previous account is set up on your PC, or if you want to set up a new account anyway, choose Create a New Dial Up Connection.

4. The Phone Number dialog opens. Complete the area code and phone number used to connect to your ISP.

JUST A MINUTE

> Although you include the area code in this dialog, your PC won't include the area code when dialing the Internet if it's the same as the area code on your own phone number—Internet Explorer 4 assumes it's a local call and therefore the area code is unnecessary. If your ISP's area code is the same as your own, but the area code still must be dialed, click the check box in the Phone Number dialog.

5. In the User Name and Password dialog, enter your Internet username and password. When you type the password, observe that asterisks appear on screen instead of the password; that's so no one can peer over your shoulder while you type to steal your password.

6. The Advanced Settings dialog gives you a chance to display some optional dialogs on which you can set up Internet accounts with unusual requirements. In particular, it displays a dialog on which you can choose to set up a type of Internet account called SLIP. Unless your ISP has told you that you have a SLIP account, assume that you can choose No in the Advanced Settings dialog.

NEW TERM **SLIP and PPP:** The two basic types of Internet connections through a modem are SLIP and PPP. These days, most ISPs offer only PPP accounts, so that's what the Connection wizard is designed to set up. But setting up a SLIP account takes just a few extra steps from the Advanced Settings dialog. After your Internet connection is up and running, you can forget all about PPP and SLIP; surfing the Web through either is the same.

7. In the Dial-Up Connection Name dialog, you can type a name to identify your Internet account. This is helpful if you have several different accounts to manage, or if you just like naming things. If you don't type anything, the wizard names the connection "Connection to" plus the telephone number.

8. In the Set Up Your Internet Mail Account dialog, you choose whether to set up your e-mail account now or leave it for another Connection wizard session. Choose Yes.

3

9. If you already set up Internet e-mail software on your PC, the software name appears in the list in the Internet Mail Account dialog. You may choose a program from the list and skip to step 15.

    If no previous e-mail program is set up on your PC, or if you want to set up a new e-mail account anyway, choose Create a New Internet Mail Account.

10. In the Your Name dialog, type your full name.

11. In the Internet E-mail address account box, type your complete e-mail address, as given to you by your ISP.

12. In the E-mail Server Names dialog (see Figure 3.11), type the names of your incoming (POP3) and outgoing (SMTP) mail servers. (The name might be the same for both.)

Figure 3.11.

Entering the names of your ISP's e-mail servers.

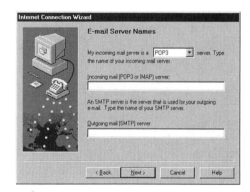

13. In the Internet Mail Logon dialog, type your e-mail username and password.

14. In the Friendly Name dialog, give your e-mail account a name to identify it. You can use any name you like.

15. In the Set Up Your Internet News Account dialog, you choose whether to set up your newsgroup information now or leave it for another Connection wizard session. Choose Yes.

16. If Internet newsgroup software is already set up on your PC, the software name appears in the list in the Internet News Account dialog. You may choose a program from the list and skip to step 21.

    If no previous newsgroup program is set up on your PC, or if you want to set up a new account anyway, choose Create a New Internet News Account.

17. In the Your Name dialog, type your full name.

18. In the Internet News E-mail address dialog, enter your complete e-mail address. Your e-mail address helps identify you on messages you send, and enables others on the newsgroup to respond to you privately, if they want to.

19. In the Internet News Server Name dialog (see Figure 3.12), type the name of your news server.

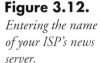

Figure 3.12.
Entering the name of your ISP's news server.

20. In the Friendly Name dialog, give your news account a name to identify it. You can use any name you like.

21. In the Set Up Your Internet Directory Service dialog, you may choose whether to set up an Internet Directory Service now or leave it for another Connection wizard session. To display some optional dialogs on which you can configure Internet Explorer 4 to contact an LDAP server, choose Yes. Otherwise, choose No and move ahead to step 22.

22. That's it! After you've dealt with the LDAP issue one way or another, a dialog appears, informing you that you've entered all the information Internet Explorer 4 requires. Click Finish to complete the setup.

COFFEE BREAK

Did you have a nap or a snack before starting setup, as I recommended? If you had a snack, you may now take a nap. If you had a nap, have a snack now. If you had a nap and a snack, take a walk or read the paper. Whatever you do, get away from your PC for a while. It gets spoiled if you pay too much attention to it.

Updating Your Installation

Eventually, you may want to change your Internet Explorer 4 installation. As mentioned earlier, if you change ISPs (or any communications settings), you can rerun the Connection wizard to choose new settings.

3

But suppose, for example, that when you downloaded Internet Explorer 4 from the Web, you chose the Standard installation option. Later, you decide you want NetMeeting for online conferences (see Hours 19 and 20), but NetMeeting would not have been downloaded or installed with the Standard installation. How can you upgrade?

The answer is Product Updates, a simple tool that connects to Microsoft online, compares the set of Internet Explorer 4 files on your PC with a list at Microsoft, and determines what you have and what you don't. If Product Updates finds any files you don't have, it gives you the option of downloading and installing them.

TIME SAVER

Product Updates does not simply add files you don't have. It also checks for, downloads, and installs new versions of files you do have. These new versions may contain enhancements, or fixes for flaws—*bugs*—in the older versions.

You can use Product Updates regularly to make sure you always have the latest, best Internet Explorer files on your PC.

3

You can use Product Updates no matter how you originally installed the software. If you installed from CD, you can still use Product Updates to get new files straight from the Web.

To use Product Update, you open Internet Explorer 4 and choose Help | Product Updates. After Internet Explorer connects to Microsoft, follow the prompts to select, download, and install new files.

Summary

Well, there's not a whole lot to sum up here. Either you installed Internet Explorer 4 successfully, in which case you can forget about almost everything you learned here, or you didn't, in which case you're not ready to read a summary. The one important thing to carry forward from this hour is that the Connection wizard not only helps you set up your account, but also lets you change your connection stuff if you switch ISPs down the road.

Q&A

Q Refresh my memory—why shouldn't I let the Internet Explorer 4 installation routine help me choose an ISP?

A Because, at this writing, Microsoft's directory contains a small proportion of the ISPs that are out there. Let Internet Explorer 4 help you choose, and you choose from a small pool. For example, I know I can use at least a dozen local and national ISPs in a local call from where I live. When I tested Microsoft's service, it showed me one.

Q My ISP gave me a news server address, and I entered it in the Connection wizard when I was asked to. But to be honest, I don't know what the heck newsgroups are.

A You'll learn all about them in Hour 16. Till then, chill.

Q I had enough free space on my hard disk (barely enough, but enough) to install Internet Explorer 4, so I did. My hard disk still has a little space on it (a few megabytes), but my PC is behaving very strangely. The pointer jumps around unpredictably, and sometimes my PC locks up.

A Windows 95 uses a technique called *disk caching* to run programs that require lots of memory. To cache efficiently, Windows needs lots of empty space on your hard disk (at least 50MB) to temporarily store data. If your hard disk is too full, Windows doesn't have enough cache space and big problems start.

You should look for stuff on your disk to delete, add a second hard disk, or replace your current disk with a new, bigger one. Adding more memory (RAM) to your system might also help, if you have less than 16MB now. But no matter how much RAM you have, your PC needs breathing room on its hard disk for the Windows cache.

Quiz

Take the following quiz to see how much you've learned.

Questions

1. Why is it smarter to download Internet Explorer 4 and then install it, instead of installing it and downloading it simultaneously?

2. What type of server would your PC connect to (through the Internet) to read Internet newsgroups?

    a. Overhand server

    b. Beverage server

    c. Body surfer

    d. News server

3. You can run the Connection wizard only once.

    a. True

    b. False

Answers

1. Three reasons: 1) Separating the two tasks gets you offline more quickly, reducing the likelihood of an Internet problem messing up your installation; 2) Making your PC manage an online session and an installation program simultaneously is a big load that may make the PC perform slowly or unreliably; and 3) Maxine told you not to.

2. d. News server.

3. b. False. You can run the Connection wizard any time you want to change or update your communications settings.

Activities

After installing Internet Explorer 4, you'll notice a globe icon on your desktop labeled Welcome to Internet Explorer. If you want a brief introduction to Internet Explorer 4, and to be led through registering your copy of Internet Explorer 4 with Microsoft, click that icon, and then follow the prompts that appear. Any time you're not sure what to do, point to something—words or a picture—and click. See what happens.

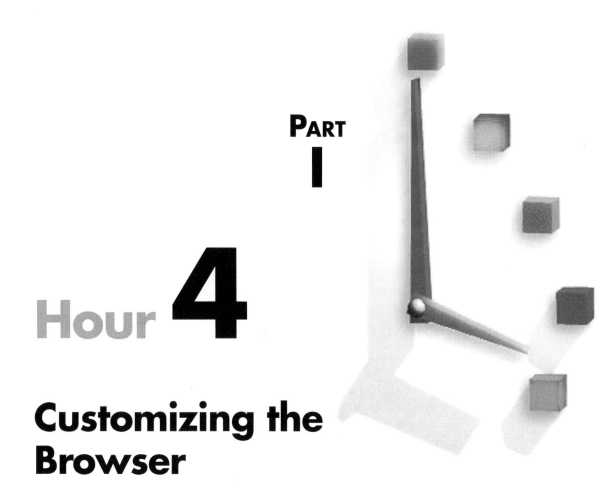

Hour **4**

Customizing the Browser

In this hour, we have a logical problem to address, something along the lines of *chicken v. egg.*

On the one hand, the various ways you can customize Internet Explorer 4's Web browsing component (or just "the browser") to change its behavior or protect your PC from unwanted intrusion (and, if you want, to protect yourself from Web content you'd find offensive) will make the most sense to you after you've spent some time browsing. So it makes some sense to learn browsing before you learn about customization and security. On the other hand, if you're concerned about this stuff, you may not want to do much browsing before setting up—or at least knowing how to set up—your security system.

So which comes first: browsing or customization? In this book, customization comes first; browsing comes in Part III. I figure it's just as easy to learn up front how to protect yourself and how to adjust Internet Explorer 4's behavior in other useful ways. You don't need to do any customizing right away—in fact, most people never fiddle with these settings at all. But after you've been introduced to customization here, you'll be prepared to manage security at any point along the way that you feel it becomes important.

At the end of the hour, you'll be able to answer the following questions:

- [ ] Where is the dialog I use to customize Internet Explorer 4?
- [ ] How does Internet Explorer protect my PC's security online, and how can I customize my security settings to meet my needs?
- [ ] How can I ask Internet Explorer 4 to censor Web pages containing material I find objectionable?
- [ ] How can I change my communications settings without running the Connection wizard?
- [ ] How can I decide which program is used automatically for each type of Internet activity—e-mail, news, and so on?

Finding the Browser's Customization Options

The nice thing about the browser is that all of its customization settings are in the same place, the Internet Options dialog (see Figure 4.1). The Internet Options dialog contains six tabs, each of which you use to customize a different aspect of Internet Explorer 4.

You can open the dialog in several ways, and it doesn't matter which way you choose. You can

- [ ] Open Internet Explorer 4, and then choose View | Internet Options.
- [ ] Right-click the e icon on your desktop, and then choose Properties from the context menu that appears.
- [ ] Right-click the Launch Internet Explorer Browser button on the taskbar, and then choose Properties from the context menu that appears.
- [ ] From the Start menu, choose Settings | Control Panel to open Control Panel, and then click the Internet icon.

JUST A MINUTE

The Internet Options dialog's name changes, depending on how you open it. When you open it from within Internet Explorer 4, its title bar says "Internet Options." When you open it any other way, its title bar says "Internet Properties." But otherwise, it's the same dialog. You use it the same either way, and the effects of what you do in the dialog are the same, no matter what it's called.

4

Figure 4.1.

You customize Internet Explorer 4 using its Internet Options dialog.

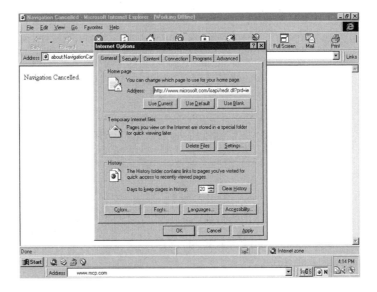

When you open the Internet Options dialog, its General tab is always open first. On the General tab, you can change the Internet Explorer home page to any page you like. You learn about changing your home page and using other settings on the General tab in Part III.

 Home page: Your home page is a Web page designated as the one to which Internet Explorer 4 goes to automatically when you open it and any time you click the Home button on the toolbar (see Part III).

In the remainder of this hour, you meet each of the five remaining tabs in the Internet Options dialog: Security, Content, Connection, Programs, and Advanced.

Understanding and Managing Security

On the Security tab, you customize the settings for Internet Explorer's security system.

To help protect you and your PC, the security system considers all the places you could visit with Internet Explorer, and divides them into four different zones:

☐ Local intranet zone: Includes all pages on your local intranet, if you have one.

New Term **Intranet:** An intranet is an internal, private network, usually a company network, that looks and acts like the Internet but isn't open to the outside world.

☐ Trusted sites zone: Includes Web sites you have selected as trusted sites, those for which you may want less strict security than others.

☐ Internet zone: All Internet Web sites that you have not included in your trusted sites zone or your restricted sites zone.

☐ Restricted sites zone: Sites you don't particularly trust, generally ones for which you'll want higher security than for other zones.

Using the Security tab of the Internet Options dialog (see Figure 4.2), you can add sites to your trusted sites and restricted sites zones, and choose security settings for each of the four zones.

Figure 4.2.

The Internet Options dialog's Security tab, where you customize your security settings.

Adding Sites to Zones

You add sites to only your trusted sites zone and restricted sites zone.

To Do: Add a Site to a Zone

1. Open the Security tab.
2. In the Zone list, select the zone to which you want to add sites.
3. Click the Add Sites button. The dialog shown in Figure 4.3 appears. The list in the top of the dialog shows sites already in the selected zone.
4. In the text box at the bottom of the dialog, type the Internet address (URL) of a site you want to add, and then click Add to add it to the list.

JUST A MINUTE

If you don't know what a URL is yet, you will soon. It's the address of a Web site or page, for example, http://www.microsoft.com.

4

Figure 4.3.

Click Add Sites to add sites to your trusted sites or restricted sites zone.

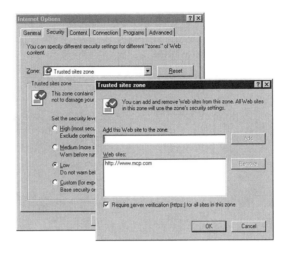

Choosing Security Settings for Each Zone

The security settings determine how aggressive the security system in Internet Explorer will be when communicating with Web sites.

For example, you can view pages on any site, regardless of your security settings. (To prevent access to a site, you use the Content Advisor as described later in this chapter.) But if a site in a zone for which high security is in place tries to send a script or other program code that could give your PC a virus or other problem, Internet Explorer will prevent the code from reaching your PC.

NEW TERM **Script:** A script is a program (often written in a language called Java) that a Web site sends to your PC to be run by your browser. A script isn't really part of a Web page, but it may make some special features of a Web page work, such as advanced multimedia or data collection. In general, you can reject scripts and still browse most Web pages, although you may not be able to take advantage of advanced features the scripts enable.

Following are descriptions of the three predefined security levels:

☐ High: All potentially damaging content (such as scripts) is automatically refused.

☐ Medium: Internet Explorer prompts you before accepting any potentially damaging content, giving you the opportunity to accept or reject it.

☐ Low: Open the gates, sweetie. Internet Explorer will accept anything.

By default, each of the four zones has a reasonable security setting: high for restricted sites, medium for the Intranet and Internet zones, and low for trusted sites.

But if you tire of being prompted every time an Internet page sends some JavaScript to your PC, you might want to change the security level for the Internet zone to low. Conversely, if you've experienced lots of problems with downloaded scripts, you might want to apply high security to the whole Internet zone. And if you trust your coworkers, you might want to change your Intranet zone to low security.

To Do: Change the Security Level for a Zone

1. Open the Security tab.
2. In the Zone list, select the zone for which you want to change security.
3. Select the security level you want.
4. Click OK.

Restricting Pages by Content and Author

On the Content tab (see Figure 4.4), you can control what gets on your PC, and what doesn't, in two more ways:

- ☐ Content Advisor enables you to screen out certain sites if those sites may contain content—language, violence, and so on—that you consider offensive or from which you want to shield another user of your PC (your kids, your parents, your puppy,...).
- ☐ Certificates let you verify the identity of sites as an extra precaution before sending sensitive information to them, such as sending your credit card information when making an online purchase.

Figure 4.4.

Use the Content tab to restrict the pages you interact with by their content or author.

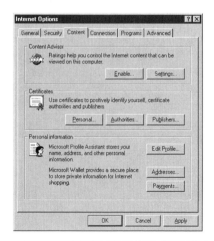

Restricting Sites by Content

You might think that Content Advisor scans the content of sites, hunting for dirty words and lingerie photos, and then screens that content out. But it doesn't do that.

4

Content Advisor relies on a rating system from the Recreational Software Advisory Council (RSAC), which also rates entertainment software and video games. The ratings assign a score (0 to 4) to a Web site for each of four criteria: language, nudity, sex, and violence. The higher the score in each category, the more intense the content. For example, if a site has a score of 0 in the language category, it contains nothing worse than "inoffensive slang." A language score of 4, however, indicates "explicit or crude language" on the site. When a Web site has been rated, the rating is built into the site, so that Content Advisor can read the page's score before displaying anything.

Using the Content tab, you choose your own limit in each RSAC category. For example, suppose you are okay about violence up to level 3 but want to screen out all sexual content above a 2. After you set your limits and enable Content Advisor, Internet Explorer refuses to show you any page whose RSAC rating exceeds your limits in any category.

There's one problem: Only a tiny portion of sites online have been rated. Enabling Content Advisor therefore blocks not only rated pages you might find offensive but also *all* pages—offensive or not—that have not been rated, which means most of the Web. (You can choose an optional setting to allow unrated pages, but doing so defeats the purpose of Content Advisor because those pages will be permitted regardless of their content.)

Just a Minute

> Content Advisor handles the Web only; it provides no protection against offensive material or contact in chat, e-mail, newsgroups, or other Internet services.

Given this, Maxine recommends you use the Content Advisor only to safeguard very small children, limiting them to the small number of rated sites. Older children using the Web for schoolwork and such will probably need access to unrated sites. If that concerns you, supervise your kids while they're online. *You* be the content advisor. That said, here's how to set up Content Advisor and choose your settings.

To Do: Set Up Content Advisor

1. On the Content tab of the Internet Options dialog, click the Enable button. A dialog opens, prompting for your Supervisor password. The Supervisor password prevents others from disabling Content Advisor or changing the settings.

2. Type a password, and then press Tab to jump down to the Confirm Password box. Type your password again, and then press Enter. The Ratings tab of the Content Advisor dialog opens, as shown in Figure 4.5.

Figure 4.5.

*Content Advisor
tells Internet
Explorer to block
pages that exceed
your personal
limits for the
intensity of
language, sex,
nudity, and
violence.*

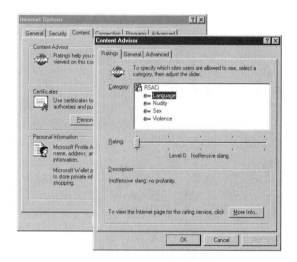

3. Click the Language category. The Rating scale shows the current setting for Language.

4. Point to the slider (the rectangle) on the Rating scale, click and hold, and drag the slider along the scale. As the slider reaches each marker on the scale, a description appears below the scale, telling what type of language that setting permits. The farther to the right you pull the slider, the more lenient the setting. (Think of 0 as a G rating, 1 as PG, 2 as PG-13, 3 as R, and 4 as X.)

5. Release the slider at your preferred setting for Language.

6. Repeat steps 3, 4, and 5 for each of the other three categories: Nudity, Sex, and Violence.

7. When you have finished choosing ratings, click the General tab (see Figure 4.6). On the General tab, you can selectively check or uncheck the check box for two important options:

☐ Users can see sites that have no rating. Check this check box to allow the display of unrated pages. Content Advisor will continue to block rated pages that exceed your settings but will permit unrated pages, regardless of their content.

☐ Supervisor can type a password to allow users to see restricted content. When this check box is checked and someone tries to open a page Content Advisor would block, a dialog pops up, prompting for the Supervisor password. If the password is typed, the page appears. This useful option gives your kids the opportunity to appeal to you for a temporary censorship waiver for a particular Web site.

4

Figure 4.6.

On the Content Advisor's General tab, you choose options for Content Advisor.

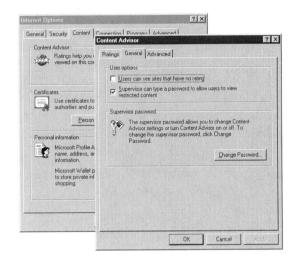

8. After selecting your options on the General tab, click OK. Content Advisor is enabled, and the Content tab of the Internet Options dialog reappears.

By the way, you'll notice that the check boxes on the Content Advisor portion of the Content tab have changed:

☐ Use the Disable button to open a dialog on which you can disable the Content Advisor.

☐ Click Settings to change your rating choices and options.

Note that the supervisor password is required to use either of these buttons.

If you're already surfing the Web, enable Content Advisor just for fun, choose fairly strict settings, and then surf awhile to see what Content Advisor blocks. When you're finished, disable Content Advisor.

Understanding Certificates

Certificates are the photo IDs of the online world. Put simply, a certificate positively identifies the company you're communicating with, so you can decide whether to accept program code, send your credit card or other info, or do anything else that might expose you to risk. When you visit a site that uses certificates, the certificate appears on the screen.

On most certificates, buttons appear, giving you a few options: You can accept the certificate (to interact with the site) or reject it.

Again, if you're not comfortable fiddling with this stuff, you can ignore it. The default settings work great.

From the Content tab, you can deal with certificates in three ways, using the three buttons described in the following list. Each button opens a simple dialog in which you select certificates or certificate providers:

☐ Personal: The Personal button displays a dialog in which you can list your personal certificate, which is used to identify you to a server. Personal certificates are rare animals, used only by pros who have authorization to change the information on a server.

☐ Authorities: The Authorities button displays a list of companies that issue certificates (see Figure 4.7). In the dialog, you can clear the check box of a company, if you have reason to suspect that the company is not issuing valid certificates or that someone is issuing fraudulent certificates in that company's name.

☐ Publishers: The Publishers button displays a list that works a lot like the trusted sites list, described earlier in this hour. If a software publisher or certificate issuer is on the list, any software sent by the publisher or from a company using a certificate from the issuer is automatically accepted by Internet Explorer 4. In general, a company gets on this list when you click a button on the company's certificate, indicating that you will always accept code from this source. You can use the Publishers list to see whom you've accepted and delete anyone you've changed your mind about.

Figure 4.7.

Click the Authorities button to choose which certificate publishers you will accept certificates from.

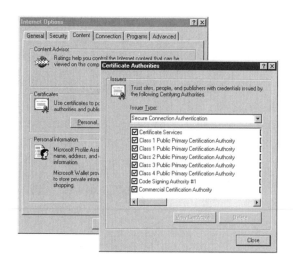

4

Updating Your Connection Settings

On the Connection tab of the Internet Options dialog (see Figure 4.8), you can customize or update the communications settings you set up in Hour 3 with the Connection wizard.

Figure 4.8.

Use the Connection tab to customize your Internet connection.

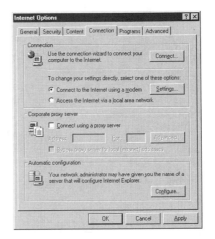

Running the Connection Wizard from Internet Options

Right from the Connection tab, you can click the Connect button to start the Connection wizard. Then you can change any settings you want for your ISP connection, mail servers, news server, and directory server (see Hour 3).

The Connection wizard displays your current settings as you go along, so you needn't reenter all your settings. Just click the Next button until you arrive at the settings you want to change. Make your changes, and then continue clicking Next until you see the Finish button. Click Finish to finish changing your settings.

Updating Your ISP Settings

If you want to make changes to just your ISP connection (and not to your mail, news, or directory settings), you can do so without opening the Connection wizard. Instead, click Settings on the Connection tab. The Dial-Up Settings tab appears (see Figure 4.9).

JUST A MINUTE

Besides changing a connection set up with the Connection wizard, the Connection tab provides two advanced connection options (see Figure 4.8) for those using Internet Explorer 4 from a company's local area network. From the tab, you can configure a proxy server for connecting to the Internet through your company network, and you can connect to a special server in your company that will configure Internet Explorer for you. Your network administrator can tell you whether you need either of these options, and how to use them.

From the list at the top of the Dial-Up Settings dialog, you can select a different ISP connection to use Internet Explorer through, if another one is already set up on your PC. You can click Properties to modify the settings (such as phone number or modem setup) of the connection selected in the list, or click Add to create a new connection.

Figure 4.9.

Click Settings in the Connection tab to modify your ISP connection.

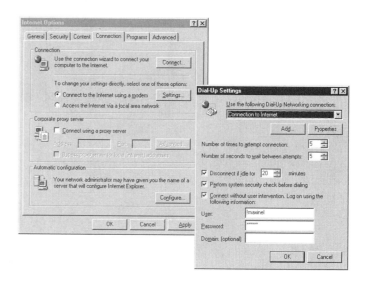

Beyond enabling you to edit your connection, the Dial-Up Settings dialog lets you customize a few aspects of your connection that you cannot change in the Connection wizard:

☐ Number of times to attempt connection: If the connect dialog can't establish a connection on the first try (because of a busy signal at your ISP, for example), it will automatically redial a set number of times. Choose that number here.

☐ Number of seconds to wait between attempts: The number here determines the number of seconds Internet Explorer waits between the failure of an attempt and trying again.

4

☐ Disconnect if idle for: A check mark here tells Internet Explorer to disconnect you automatically from the Internet if you're idle (not actively accessing new information) for the specified number of minutes. This feature is designed to save you connect-time fees (if you do not have an unlimited access account) if, for example, your neighbor comes to the door while you're online and babbles for an hour about the neighborhood crime watch committee.

TIME SAVER

> Most ISPs disconnect you after a set number of minutes of inactivity. If your ISP automatically disconnects you after, say, 15 inactive minutes, raising the number of minutes in the Dial-Up Settings dialog above 15 accomplishes nothing; your ISP will kick you off before Internet Explorer gets the chance.

☐ Perform system security check before dialing: A check mark here instructs Internet Explorer to request your system username and password before connecting to the Internet, as an extra security precaution. Note that this check box pertains to a *system* password—the one you use to log onto Windows or your network—not your Internet username and password. If you don't use a username and password to get into Windows, this check box is irrelevant.

☐ Connect without user intervention: A check mark here instructs the connect dialog to automatically supply your username and password to connect to the Internet, so that you don't have to type or confirm these. This is a great timesaving option, but it also makes your Internet connection vulnerable to unauthorized access by others in your home or office.

Choosing Programs for Internet Activities

A browser such as Internet Explorer 4 is designed to open other programs to perform certain tasks it cannot perform itself. For example, on the Web you'll see e-mail addresses presented as links you can click. When you click one, Internet Explorer opens an e-mail program so you can compose a message to the e-mail address you clicked. On the Programs tab of the Internet Options dialog (see Figure 4.10), you can choose or change which programs Internet Explorer opens.

Under Messaging, you choose the programs to use for e-mail (Mail), newsgroups (News), and Internet phone calls (Internet call). The defaults for these are Internet Explorer's own messaging program, Outlook Express, for mail and news, and NetMeeting for phone calls. If you'd like to use different programs for these activities, select them from the drop-down list.

Figure 4.10.

Use the Programs tab to choose which programs Internet Explorer uses for e-mail, newsgroups, and Internet phone calls.

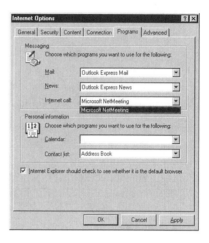

TIME SAVER

The programs you choose in the Programs tab must already have been installed on your PC to appear in the drop-down lists.

Understanding the Advanced Options

The Advanced tab of the Internet Options dialog (see Figure 4.11) enables you to customize the behavior of Internet Explorer to an exacting degree. The default settings in this tab will work just great for most users, so you should leave the Advanced options alone unless you really need to change something about the way Internet Explorer behaves.

Figure 4.11.

Use the Advanced tab (when absolutely necessary) to fine-tune Internet Explorer's behavior.

4

For example, as you learn in Part III, while you're typing the address of a Web page you want to visit, Internet Explorer can guess the address before you finish typing it and instantly fill in the rest of the address for you. This feature, known as AutoComplete, is handy, but suppose AutoComplete gets on your nerves. To disable AutoComplete (and make Internet Explorer stop guessing addresses), you could open the Advanced tab and clear the check mark from the Use AutoComplete option, which appears near the top of the list.

As you learn in Part III, all the cool multimedia stuff you see on the Web—pictures, video, animation, sound, and more—makes Web surfing slower. If you want to speed up your browsing, and don't care about experiencing multimedia, you can clear one or more of the check boxes in the Multimedia section of the list to prevent Internet Explorer from accessing that type of multimedia.

TIME SAVER

> At any time, you can restore all Advanced options to their original, default settings by clicking the tab's Restore Defaults button. That's a great way to set things right if you change something, don't like the results, and can't remember what you changed.

Summary

A few options in the Internet Options dialog are terrifically useful, such as those that enable you to control the behavior of your Internet connection. But most of the stuff in the Internet Options dialog is best left alone, at least until you've gained enough experience with Internet Explorer to make informed choices.

Even at this early stage, however, it's useful to know about this dialog and get a good feel for what you can do there. If you have a problem down the road, there's a good chance you'll solve it using the Internet Options dialog.

Q&A

Q You say a lot about making security and certificate settings accordingly. But how am I supposed to know who to trust and who not to?

A Ultimately, you can't. But you can make some good choices, using as your guides experience and self-knowledge.

Experience is the most important. Suppose you like to visit a certain Web site, but you've noticed that your PC or Internet Explorer 4 has problems every time you visit there, or soon thereafter. You may determine that the site is sending poorly written plug-ins, JavaScript, or other code to your PC, especially if you see error messages that mention JavaScript or Java. You could just keep away from that site, but you can also configure security or certificates to prevent the site from sending you code. That way, you can still enjoy parts of the site that don't rely on the code, while keeping your PC safe.

Self-knowledge is determining how much risk you feel like taking. If you like to live on the edge, and figure you can correct anything some bad code might do to you, you may want to leave security wide open so you can sample all that the Web has to offer. If you keep very sensitive data on your PC, or pull your hair out when your PC acts up, you ought to keep your security tight to save yourself the hassle of dealing with the effects of sloppy code.

Quiz

Take the following quiz to see how much you've learned.

Questions

1. It's a good idea to change your customization settings at random, just to see their effects.
   a. True
   b. False
2. You perform most Internet Explorer 4 customizations using the Internet Options dialog, which you open by
   a. Choosing Options from the Internet Explorer menu bar
   b. Choosing View | Internet Options from the Internet Explorer menu bar
   c. Choosing View | Options | Customize from the Start menu
   d. Clicking the Change button from the Internet Explorer toolbar
3. On the Web, a certificate is
   a. A form of positive ID for a Web site or software publisher
   b. A form of currency
   c. An academic degree
   d. The husband of ladytificate
4. Content Advisor can protect you from potentially offensive content found on
   a. The Web, chat, and newsgroups
   b. The Web and chat
   c. The Web
   d. A small portion of the Web

4

Answers

1. b. False. Leave your customization settings alone until you have a reason to change them.
2. b. None of the other choices works. (Try 'em!)
3. a. Didn't understand d? "Lady Tificate," "*Sir* Tificate." Get it? Sorry.
4. b. Content Advisor can't control what you see anywhere but on the Web and in chats, and really doesn't do much that's useful in those places, either.

Activity

Open the Options dialog, and then click the Advanced tab. Don't change anything, but scroll through the list and study what you can change. This is useful preparation for understanding all the different things that happen while you're online.

4

PART

II

The Active Desktop

Hour

Hour 5

Meet the Active Desktop

People react to Internet Explorer's Active Desktop modifications to the Windows shell (introduced in Hour 1) in two common ways. Some folks want to learn just enough about the changes to do what they used to do in Windows and stay out of trouble. Others want to exploit what the Active Desktop offers.

This hour is for folks in the first group; those who want to know the basics of how Windows tasks—such as opening folders and programs—are accomplished under the Active Desktop. This hour gets you over the hump, so to speak, when getting over the hump is all you really want. And in case you decide the hump is too high, this hour also covers disabling a part of the Active Desktop to return Windows 95 to its old self, which has no effect on your ability to use the Internet Explorer browser.

Hour 6, by the way, is for folks in the second group. Building on what you learn in this hour, Hour 6 shows you how to make the most of the Active Desktop.

At the end of the hour, you'll be able to answer the following questions:

☐ How do I get that Active Desktop wallpaper off my screen?

☐ How must I change the way I open and select file icons with my mouse?

☐ How do I use new stuff that the Active Desktop puts in my Start menu and taskbar?

☐ How can I disable some of the Active Desktop, if I've already had enough of it?

Killing the Active Desktop Wallpaper

First things first: I mentioned this in Hour 3, but in case you skipped it, I have to point out that the eye-pain wallpaper that appears on your desktop after installation (see Figure 5.1) is easily removed. It's just wallpaper—it's not part of the Active Desktop, and it has no effect on your ability to use the Active Desktop.

Of course, you may like the Active Desktop wallpaper. Different strokes; to each his own; you can leave it alone. Maxine loves you no matter what.

Figure 5.1.

You can easily remove the Active Desktop wallpaper, and it leaves no sticky residue.

5

To Do: Remove the Active Desktop Wallpaper

1. Locate the underlined phrase "Tell me about Active Desktop" in the lower-right corner of your desktop.

2. Point to that icon, and click just once. A brief description of the Active Desktop opens.

3. At the bottom of the description, another underlined phrase appears, "Restore my desktop wallpaper." Click that phrase, then choose File | Exit to close the description.

TIME SAVER

> If for any reason the preceding "To Do" doesn't strip off the wallpaper, try this instead. Right-click the desktop, choose Properties from the menu that appears, and choose the Background tab. In that tab, select a new wallpaper from the list, or choose (none).

Changing Your Mouse-Moves

Repeat after me:

"If it's underlined, single-click it. If it's not underlined, double-click it."

As a Windows user, you're accustomed to doing a lot of double-clicking. In regular, "classic" Windows 95, you double-click the icons on your desktop to start a program or open a folder. In folders you do the same, and you also double-click files to open them in their associated programs. For example, you can double-click the icon for a Word document to open that document in Word.

In the Active Desktop, files, folders, and program icons are links, just like the links you'll encounter on the Web. You can tell they're links in two ways (see Figure 5.2) when you point to them:

☐ Their labels are underlined, just the way text links on the Web are underlined.

☐ The Windows pointer turns into a pointing finger, which always indicates a link.

NEW TERM   **Link:** A link is text, an icon, or a picture you can click to make something happen. On the Web, clicking links takes you to different Web destinations, plays multimedia, and downloads files. In the Active Desktop, clicking links opens programs, folders, and files.

5

Depending on your configuration, the underlining on icon labels may appear at all times or only when you point to an icon. You learn how to choose between these modes in Hour 8.

Figure 5.2.

When an icon or folder is configured as a link, its label is underlined, and when you point to it the pointer becomes a pointing finger.

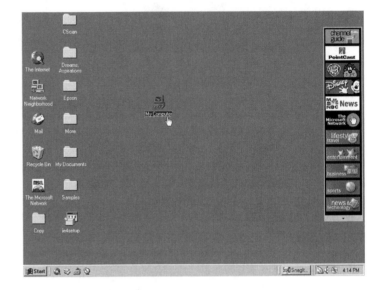

Whenever an icon on your Windows desktop or in a folder appears as a link, a single-click does the job. Single-click a program icon to start the program. Single-click a folder to open the folder. Single-click a file icon to open that file in its associated program.

CAUTION

Single-clicking does not work everywhere. You'll learn about that in the following steps and after.

To Do: Practice Opening Icons

1. On your Windows desktop, point to the My Computer icon. The pointer changes to a pointing finger, and My Computer is highlighted.

2. Click the left mouse button once. The My Computer folder opens. Note that it looks a little different than you're used to, with a new toolbar and a colorful panel along its left side. You'll learn more about that new look in Hour 6.

3. In the My Computer folder, point to Control Panel. The pointer changes to a pointing finger, and Control Panel is highlighted.

5

4. Click once. The Control Panel opens.

5. Point to Fonts. The pointer changes to a pointing finger, and Fonts is highlighted.

6. Click once. The Fonts dialog opens (see Figure 5.3).

7. Now look closely at the icons in the Fonts dialog. Their labels are not underlined.

8. Point to an icon in the Fonts dialog. The pointer does not change, and the icon is not highlighted.

9. Click once. The icon is highlighted, but nothing opens.

10. Double-click the icon. A sample of the font opens.

11. Click the X in the upper-right corner of the Font dialog to close it.

Figure 5.3.

You will come across folders and file lists where icons are not links, and you must revert to double-clicking.

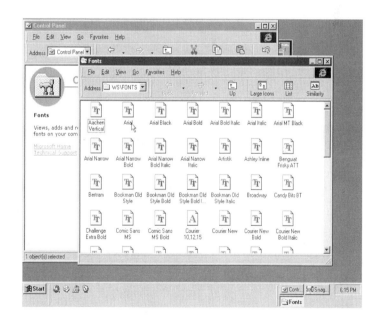

The moral? The Active Desktop turns into links most but not all icons. In particular, within a program (which Fonts actually is), icons generally require old-fashioned double-clicking. And within file and folder lists shown by a program—such as those you use to open and save files in many programs—double-clicking still reigns supreme.

To use the Active Desktop conveniently, you must recondition yourself: When you see underlining and the pointing finger, click. When you don't, double-click. With a little practice, you'll find that you make this switch without even thinking about it.

Dealing with a New Start Menu and Taskbar

Like most programs you install in Windows, Internet Explorer adds a few items to your Windows Start menu. But Internet Explorer adds more than most programs do. Now is a good time to learn what you'll find there.

Favorites

Your Internet Explorer Favorites list is a list of Web sites, Web pages, or other files and programs. The list—which you create and maintain yourself—can be displayed a few ways in Internet Explorer, as you learn in Part III. But the very same list can be displayed right from the Start menu, even with Internet Explorer closed.

To Do: Look at Your Favorites List

1. Click the Start button on the Windows taskbar.

2. Choose Favorites. The Favorites list opens as the menu shown in Figure 5.4.

Figure 5.4.

You can display your Internet Explorer Favorites list from the Start menu.

I said you create the Favorites list, and that's true—but your list will still have some entries, even if you haven't yet created any. Microsoft includes some Favorites with Internet Explorer to get you started. And if you had a previous release of Internet Explorer installed on your PC, any Favorites created in that release have been carried over to Internet Explorer 4.

5

The principal use of the Favorites list is to quickly get to Web pages you like to visit often. But you can also use it to conveniently get to almost anywhere in Windows. You learn about using Favorites for local, Windows purposes in Hour 6. In Part III, you learn about using Favorites for Web purposes.

For now, though, all you need to understand about Favorites is that they're there and you'll be seeing them. Also understand that if you click anything you see now in your Favorites list, Internet Explorer will open, connect you to the Internet, and go straight to the Web site whose name you clicked. So unless you really want that to happen (and maybe you do), don't click anything in Favorites just yet.

New Items You Should Know About

Also on your Start menu, you'll find an Internet Explorer menu.

To Do: Opening the Internet Explorer Menu

1. Click the Start button on the Windows taskbar.
2. Choose Programs | Internet Explorer.

The Internet Explorer menu (see Figure 5.5) offers separate items for opening Internet Explorer (to surf the Web), Outlook Express (to exchange e-mail or newsgroup messages), and Connection Wizard (to update your connection settings). If you've installed Chat and NetMeeting (see Part V), you'll see each of those as a menu item, too, plus other Internet Explorer 4 odds and ends.

Figure 5.5.

Internet Explorer adds some handy items to your Start menu.

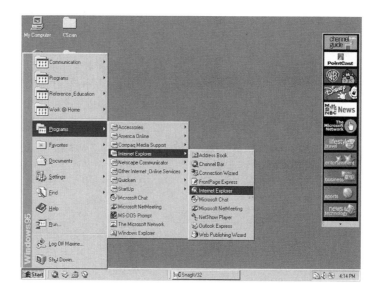

The beauty of the separate menu items is that you can go straight to the part of Internet Explorer you need. If your first order of business is e-mail, you can open Outlook Express without first opening the Internet Explorer browser.

Finally, you'll notice a new row of buttons on the Windows taskbar (see Figure 5.6). These buttons are called quick launch buttons, and they offer you an alternative way to open Internet Explorer and its components. You can ignore them, learn to use them (in Hour 6), or remove them from your taskbar (see Hour 8).

Figure 5.6.

The quick launch buttons offer an alternative way to open Internet Explorer and its components.

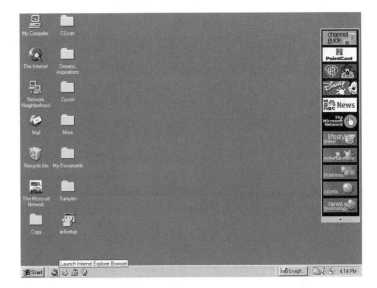

Switching Web View On and Off

Well, now that you've toured the basics of the Active Desktop, what do you think? I hope you're starting to get adjusted. In the long run, I think you'll find it an easier way to work.

If you've already decided the Active Desktop is not your cup of tea, or if you want to put off learning it until another time, you can disable it. Actually, you can customize the Active Desktop to enable some of the features you want to use and disable the ones you don't. You learn how to do that in Hour 8.

For now, though, I'll show you how to switch off the part of the Active Desktop that's most likely throwing you: the single-clicking part. Note that disabling single-clicking has no effect on other aspects of the Active Desktop (the channel bar, the Internet Explorer toolbars on folders, and so on), and it has no effect on your ability to browse the Web with Internet Explorer. It just reverts clicking techniques to the pre-Active Desktop, classic Windows style.

5

CAUTION

All upcoming procedures in this book assume that you have not disabled the Active Desktop in any way. For example, in an upcoming hour, you may be instructed to open My Computer by single-clicking it. If you disable single-clicking now, it's up to you to remember to double-click stuff in Windows as you move through this tutorial.

To Do: Disable Single-Clicking

1. Click My Computer to open it.
2. On the My Computer menu bar, choose View | Folder Options. The Folder Options dialog box appears (see Figure 5.7).

TIME SAVER

You can display a Folder Options dialog box like the one in Figure 5.7 from any folder in Windows by choosing View | Folder Options. Note that the changes you make in the Folder Options dialog affect all of Windows, including the desktop, all folders, and Windows Explorer, no matter which folder you were in when you opened the Folder Options dialog. It doesn't matter which folder you use to make this change.

Figure 5.7.

In any folder, choose View | Folder Options to open a dialog box in which you can choose between single-click Web style Windows and double-click Classic style.

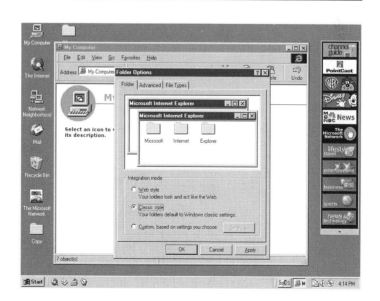

3. On the General tab of the Folder Options dialog, choose Classic style.
4. Click OK. The link formatting is removed from the icons on your desktop, and double-clicking comes back into fashion.

If you decide to give single-clicking another chance, you can return to the Folder Options dialog box, and choose Web style.

Summary

"If it's underlined, single-click it. If it's not underlined, double-click it."

"If it's underlined, single-click it. If it's not underlined, double-click it."

"If it's underlined, single-click it. If it's not underlined, double-click it."

Or, if you can't quite get the hang of it, just disable single-clicking. I won't tell.

Q&A

Q In my old Windows, each time I opened a folder, the folder before it stayed open on the desktop. Now, with the Active Desktop, every time I open a folder, the old one closes behind it. I'm not really complaining, mind you. It's just weird and, well, I guess I have a little trouble coping with change. My therapist said my toilet training must have...

A Let Maxine clear things up. First, in Windows you've always had a choice between single-window mode and multiple-window mode. In single-window mode, each time you open a new window, the previous one closes behind it. In multiple-window mode, all windows stay open until you close each one individually.

In the Active Desktop, you still have that choice; in Hour 8, you learn how to switch. But Active Desktop's default setting is single-window mode, because the new Internet Explorer toolbar on every folder makes getting around in single-window mode much easier than it used to be and easier probably than multiple-window mode.

Q Does drag and drop still work in the Active Desktop?

A Yes, you drag and drop files into folders, and files on programs, like you always did. The only difference is that you have to be a little more careful when clicking and holding.

Under classic Windows, if you accidentally released the mouse button after clicking to drag, nothing happened (except that the file icon was selected). Under the Active Desktop, if you click and then accidentally release, Windows thinks you've single-clicked, and opens the file, program, or folder you clicked.

If you find drag and drop too tricky now, try clicking and holding the right mouse button, dragging, and then releasing. When you release, a menu opens, offering you the option of moving the icon where you released, putting a copy there, or putting a shortcut there.

5

Q **If you don't tell me that something works differently under the Active Desktop, can I assume that I can just apply the old classic Windows technique?**

A Pretty much. Most stuff works the same way. You can still click the X button in the upper-right corner to close a program or a file, drag windows around on the screen, drag window borders to resize program windows, and minimize, maximize, and restore like always. Choosing stuff from the menu bar, clicking buttons, and scrolling haven't changed a bit.

The one tricky spot may be selecting one or more files when performing a multifile operation, such as dragging a group of files to a folder. The Active Desktop makes such operations a little easier, but again, you have to be precise in your mouse work. You learn how in Hour 6.

Quiz

Take the following quiz to see how much you've learned.

Questions

1. You can tell that a file, a folder, or a program icon is a link when
   a. Its label is underlined
   b. You point to it and the pointer becomes a pointing finger
   c. You click it only once and it opens
   d. All of the above

2. The Active Desktop enables you to operate anything with a single click.
   a. True
   b. False

3. To disable single-clicking
   a. Restart your PC
   b. Open My Computer and choose Mouse | Clicking | Double
   c. Open My Computer and choose View | Options, then choose Classic style
   d. Switch to the Mac

4. Removing the Active Desktop wallpaper that appears right after you install Internet Explorer will
   a. Disable Active Desktop and Internet Explorer
   b. Hurt Microsoft's feelings
   c. Leave a sticky paste residue
   d. Make your desktop more attractive

5

Answers

1. d. All are true of icons in the Active Desktop.
2. b. False. When you're inside most applications, the Active Desktop affects nothing, so double-clicking is still required. Some Windows folders may still require double-clicking.
3. c. All the other choices do *nada*.
4. b. is a possibility, but d is the best answer.

Activity

Explore your Windows desktop, using only the techniques you learned in this hour. Open and close all programs and files on your desktop, and open and close your Favorites menu.

After practicing this way for awhile, open Windows Explorer (the file manager) by choosing Start | Programs | Windows Explorer. It looks different under the Active Desktop. Using what you learned in this Hour about recognizing links and single-clicking, can you find your way around in Windows Explorer?

Hour **6**

Getting Around in Windows

Windows 95 debuted a few years ago, so the following is a sorry observation: Most day-to-day Windows users don't know much about getting around in Windows. They know the minimum necessary to open their programs and accomplish their work, but that's about it.

So here you have an opportunity. If you already know your way around Windows pretty well, in this hour you can learn how to get around the Active Desktop way. If you really don't know much about getting around, here's your chance to finally learn.

At the end of the hour, you'll be able to answer the following questions:

☐ How do I take advantage of the new look to every Windows folder window?

☐ How do I use the Internet Explorer toolbars that now appear on folder windows?

☐ How can I rearrange and otherwise customize those toolbars?

☐ How do I use (and create) the buttons on my links toolbar?

☐ How can I take advantage of the taskbar's new capabilities?

Using the New Web View Folders

As you learned in earlier hours, all your folder windows have a new look under the Active Desktop; the new look is sometimes described as "Web page styling." Your folders (and Windows Explorer) now have an attractive title and graphic within them.

Other than applying the clicking techniques you learned about in Hour 5 and using the new toolbars as described next in this hour, you needn't do anything differently in these folders.

However, the folders do include enhancements you may want to take advantage of. For example, when you point to an icon in a folder, a description of that icon—including its size and type—now appears in the panel along the left side of the folder window; peek ahead to Figure 6.1. (Try it out in any of your folders.) Some folders include special enhancements. For example, if you open Control Panel (choose Settings | Control Panel from the Start menu), you'll see two links you can click to connect to Microsoft customer service.

Keep in mind that under the Active Desktop, a folder can do anything a Web page can. That means that in the future, you'll see even more elaborate enhancements, such as animations or data collection, right in a folder window.

Using the New Folder Window Toolbars

By now, no doubt you've noticed that the toolbar area of your Windows folder has changed. The tools you've always used in Windows 95 have been replaced with a new set of toolbars (see Figure 6.1).

JUST A MINUTE

If your toolbars look sort of, but not exactly, like those in Figure 6.1, don't worry. The toolbars can be customized, as you learn later in this hour, so everyone's toolbars don't look the same.

Although you may not realize it yet, the new toolbars are Internet Explorer's toolbars, the very same ones you see while browsing the Web. Internet Explorer uses three separate toolbars:

- ☐ The standard buttons toolbar includes buttons you use for moving from folder to folder on your PC, or from page to page on the Web.

- ☐ The address bar is a text box in which you type or choose a path and filename to jump directly to a file, a folder, or a Web page.

- ☐ The links toolbar is populated with quick links, buttons that take you quickly to pages you choose as important.

Figure 6.1.

In the Active Desktop, all folders borrow Internet Explorer's toolbars. Isn't that nice?

You can choose which of these toolbars appear, and the order they appear in, top to bottom. You can make two toolbars share one line in the toolbar area, and switch easily among them. This flexibility enables you to keep the tools you use most often at hand while hiding the rest. Hiding the tools you don't use clears more space in the window for the folder's contents or the Web page you're viewing.

Turning Toolbars On and Off

You turn toolbars on or off from the Toolbar menu (see Figure 6.2), which you display by choosing View | Toolbars. In the Toolbar menu, check marks appear next to any menus that are already on. Clicking the name of a toolbar turns it on (if it's off) or off (if it's on).

Note that changes you make in the Toolbar menu affect all toolbars in Windows, no matter which folder you made the change in. For example, if you choose to display the address bar in one folder, all other folders show it, too.

JUST A MINUTE

> Don't worry if your Toolbar menu says two toolbars are on but you see only one. Two toolbars are sharing one line, to save space. You learn how to deal with that in the next section, "Arranging Toolbars."

Figure 6.2.

*Choose View | Toolbars
to turn each toolbar on
or off.*

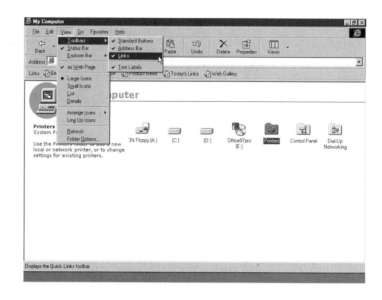

Arranging Toolbars

The three toolbars can be arranged in any order, and can overlap one another.

If you look closely at Figure 6.3, you'll notice that a small vertical bar appears at the left end of each toolbar. To move a toolbar to a new spot in the toolbar area, point to its vertical bar, click and hold, drag up or down to the new position, and release.

Figure 6.3.

*Drag the vertical bar to
move a toolbar.*

If you drop a toolbar on top of another toolbar, the two will share the same line in the toolbar area. When two toolbars share a line, one appears in full and the other is mostly hidden, except for its name and its vertical bar, which is to the left of its name.

JUST A MINUTE

> The standard buttons toolbar doesn't display its name; instead, the Back button appears with the vertical bar when the standard buttons toolbar is hidden.

You can reveal a hidden toolbar (and hide the other) in a few ways:

- ☐ Double-click the vertical bar on either toolbar.
- ☐ Drag over the other toolbar.
- ☐ For a hidden links toolbar or address bar, double-click the toolbar's name.

To Do: Display and Arrange Toolbars

1. Open any Windows folder (My Computer, for example).

2. Choose View | Toolbars, and make sure all three toolbars are currently on. If a toolbar is off, turn it on.

3. Observe the toolbar area. Do you see three separate toolbars, or are two sharing a line? If any two are sharing a line, point to the vertical bar of one, click and hold, and drag to the bottom of the toolbar area to move the toolbar there.

4. In the top toolbar, point to the vertical bar. Click and hold, drag to the bottom, and release. The top toolbar jumps to the bottom position in the toolbar area.

5. In the address bar, point to the vertical bar. Click and hold, drag the address bar on top of the standard buttons toolbar, and release. The address bar and the standard buttons toolbar now share a line, and the standard buttons toolbar (except for the Back button) is hidden.

6. Point to the word *Address* in the address bar, and double-click. The standard buttons toolbar appears in full, and the address bar (except for the word *Address*) is hidden.

7. Double-click the word *Address* again. Now the standard buttons toolbar is hidden, and the address bar appears in full.

8. Close the folder you've been using, and open any other folder. Observe that the toolbars are just the way they appeared in the previous folder before you closed it.

JUST A MINUTE

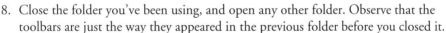

In this hour, you learn how to use each toolbar when working in a Windows folder. In Part III, you learn how to apply the same tools on the Web.

6

Using the Address Bar

On the Web, you use the address bar as a place to type the URL of a Web site to visit. In a Windows folder, you use the address bar like a drop-down directory. In fact, you use it exactly like you use the drop-down directory lists in Windows programs when choosing a location to save or open a file.

When you click the down arrow at the right end of the address bar, a complete directory of your PC's contents appears. From that list, you can click an entry to open a disk, a folder, a file, or a program.

TIME SAVER

> Instead of clicking the arrow, you can drop down the address bar list by double-clicking inside the list box.

To Do: Navigate Your PC with the Address Bar

To Do

1. Open My Computer.
2. If you don't see the address bar, display it.
3. Click the down arrow at the right end of the address bar. A directory list drops down (see Figure 6.4), showing all your disks and top-level directories.

Figure 6.4.

Drop down the address bar list to navigate disks, folders, and files on your PC.

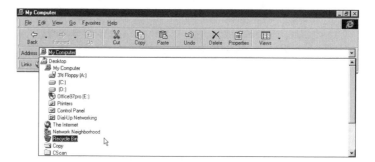

4. Click any folder in the list. The folder opens, and My Computer disappears. Observe that the address bar now shows the name of the folder you opened.

5. Drop down the address bar again. The full list appears again, but now the current folder is highlighted in the list.

Using the Standard Buttons

The standard buttons toolbar is "smart," says Microsoft. In effect, the buttons on this toolbar change depending on what you're doing.

When you're in a folder, the buttons include those that are useful there, such as Up, Cut, and Delete. When you're on the Web in Internet Explorer, other buttons useful only online, such as Stop and Refresh, appear. Two buttons are useful everywhere, so they always appear on the standard buttons toolbar: Back and Forward.

6

Back and Forward

The Back and Forward buttons move you back and forth within the trail of folders you've visited in the current Windows session.

For example, suppose you open a folder called Tinkers, then one called Evers, then one called Chance. From the Chance folder:

☐ Click Back once to go back to Evers.

☐ Click Back twice to go back to Tinker.

Forward reverses the action of Back, taking your forward again after you've used Back. After using Back to go back to Tinker, you can

☐ Click Forward once to go to Evers.

☐ Click Forward twice to go to Chance.

JUST A MINUTE

It's important to understand two basic facts about Back and Forward. First, there is no "back" until you've gone somewhere. When you first open a folder from the desktop or Windows Explorer, the Back button is unavailable because there's nowhere to go back to. As soon as you move to another folder (by opening it from an icon or from the address bar), Back is available to go back.

Second, Forward is available only after you've used Back. If you click Back three times, you can click Forward three times to return to the folder you were in before you used Back.

TIME SAVER

When you intend to jump multiple steps Back or Forward, you needn't click the buttons multiple times. When the Back and Forward buttons are available, you'll see a tiny arrow on the right side of each button. Click that arrow, and a list drops down (see Figure 6.5), showing all the folders to which you can go back (or forward). Click an item in the list to go straight to that folder.

Figure 6.5.

Click the little down arrow on the Back or Forward button to display a list of folders you've been to, from which you may select one.

Up, Cut, Copy, Paste, Undo, and Delete

The Up, Cut, Copy, Past, Undo, and Delete buttons perform basic Windows tasks—all tasks you're familiar with from classic Windows and its applications. Just to refresh your memory:

- ☐ Up moves up one level in the directory hierarchy. For example, if you're looking at the folder c:\WINDOWS\SYSTEM, clicking Up once opens the c:\WINDOWS folder; clicking Up twice opens c:\.

- ☐ Cut, Copy, and Paste are used for cut and paste and copy and paste functions. You begin such operations by selecting the files or folders you want to copy or cut and paste (see "Selecting Files and Folders" later in this hour). To move the selected files or folders, click Cut, move to the folder where you want the files and folders moved, and then click Paste in that folder. To copy the selected files or folders, click Copy, go to the new folder, and then click Paste.

- ☐ Undo undoes your very last action in the folder. Right after you delete a file or folder, clicking Undo brings it back.

- ☐ Delete deletes selected files or folders, and sends them to the Recycle Bin.

Views

The Views button switches you among the various Windows folder views, which control the way files and folders are represented in the folder window. The available views follow:

- ☐ Large icons: All files and folders appear in the folder in rows and columns of large icons (see Figure 6.6), with text labels.

- ☐ Small icons: Same as Large icons view, only with smaller icons so more icons can appear at once in the window (useful in folders that contain many files).

- ☐ List: Files and folders appear in a list (see Figure 6.7) showing just the small icons and filenames.

- ☐ Details: Just like List view, except the list includes detailed file information, such as file size and date modified.

JUST A MINUTE

Don't see the View button on your standard buttons toolbar? It's at the extreme right end of the toolbar, and so usually doesn't appear unless you display the folder maximized (filling the screen). To maximize a folder, double-click its title bar.

6

Figure 6.6.

Large icons view.

Figure 6.7.

List view.

You can use the View button two ways to change views:

☐ Click the View button. Each time you click, the view changes to the next option. Keep clicking until you see the view you want.

☐ Click the tiny down arrow on the right side of the View button, and a list drops down, showing the four View options (see Figure 6.8). Click the one you want.

Figure 6.8.

Click the tiny right arrow on the View button to display a list of View options.

Using the Links Buttons

The buttons on the links toolbar are really just favorites. If you open your Favorites list and then choose the Links folder in it, you'll see the same items you see as buttons on your links toolbar. The links you start out with are provided by Microsoft. But you can delete Microsoft's links and add links of your own.

☐ To learn how to add a new favorite to the Links folder, see "Creating Favorites," later in this hour.

☐ To learn how to delete Microsoft's links, and to add Web sites to your links toolbar, see Part III.

Selecting Files and Folders

Other than single-clicking, it's selecting files (highlighting them when you want to move, copy, or do something else to them) that can make adjusting to the Active Desktop the most confusing. After all, you used to select a file in Windows by single-clicking it. Now single-clicking a file opens it.

To select a file in Active Desktop, you point to it and wait a second. That's it. After a second, the file appears highlighted.

JUST A MINUTE

The point-to-select method works only where you see the file or folder formatted as a link, which in general is only in Windows folders, in Windows Explorer, and on the desktop. In file selection dialogs in applications, you still must click a file to select it.

To select multiple files, as you might in a folder or in Windows Explorer to move or copy a group of files at once, you may apply a variety of techniques:

☐ Select one file by pointing to it. Then press and hold Ctrl, and point one by one to the other files. As you select each file, earlier selections remain highlighted. When you have finished selecting files, release Ctrl, and proceed with your operation.

☐ When the files you want to select are arranged contiguously in their folder or in Windows Explorer, point to the first file to select it. Then press and hold Shift, and press an arrow key to continuously select files in the direction of the arrow key.

TIME SAVER

Because of the way selections and clicking function in the Active Desktop, right-clicking becomes a more valuable technique than ever.

In case you didn't know, pointing to almost anything in Windows and then clicking the right mouse button (not the usual left) displays a pop-up menu of items for dealing with that item. Because you can't accidentally open something by right-clicking it, right-clicking is a convenient and reliable way to perform many activities in the Active Desktop. Try it.

Creating Favorites

In Part II, you learn a lot more about the Favorites list, whose main gig is getting you quickly to Web sites you visit often. Still, it's worth knowing that you can also add your favorite Windows folders to your Favorites list, so you can open them easily from anywhere in Windows.

This capability is especially valuable for folders you keep deep within your folder hierarchy. For example, from the desktop, it would take a good deal of clicking to open the hypothetical folder C:\Windows\System\Tools\Diagnostics\Repair Tools. If you create a favorite for that folder, you can open it in a few clicks by choosing it from the Favorites menu, which you can display from the Start menu or the menu bar on any folder (see Hour 5).

To Do: Add a Windows Folder to Your Favorites List

1. In a folder window or in Windows Explorer, open the folder you want to add to your Favorites list.

2. From the Folder's menu bar (or from Windows Explorer's menu bar), choose Favorites. The Favorites menu opens.

3. From the menu, choose Add to Favorites. The Add to Favorites dialog appears (see Figure 6.9), and the folder's name appears in the Name box.

4. Click OK to add the folder to your Favorites list. If you want to keep this folder in a particular folder in your Favorites list, click the Create in button in the dialog to show the Favorites folder, click a folder to select it, and then click OK to create the favorite.

Figure 6.9.

To add a folder to your Favorites list, open the folder and choose Favorites |

Add to Favorites.

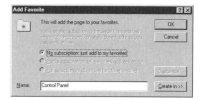

JUST A MINUTE

Saving a new favorite in the Links folder of the Favorites list not only adds it to the list, but also adds it as a new button in your links toolbar.

TIME SAVER

You can organize your favorites, moving them into and out of folders, deleting them, and so on. You learn how in Part III.

Using the New Taskbar

Some things about the Active Desktop force you to deal with them, such as single-clicking. Other changes affect the way things look, but don't force you to do anything different, unless you want to.

Take the taskbar (please!). If you want to, you can easily ignore all Active Desktop enhancements to the Windows taskbar, and use the taskbar as you always have. If you want to take advantage of the taskbar's new capabilities, read on.

Using Quick Launch Buttons

The first thing you'll notice about the taskbar are the quick launch buttons, the row of buttons to the right of the Start button (see Figure 6.10). With one exception (the View Desktop button), they all do things you can do in other ways already. They just make doing these things more convenient.

Figure 6.10.

The quick launch buttons.

For example, to open Internet Explorer from its desktop shortcut, you must clear your desktop and then click. Opening Internet Explorer from the Start menu also requires a few clicks and mouse moves. Opening Internet Explorer with a quick launch button requires one click, no matter what else is open.

| If you forget what each button does, remember that they all have tooltips. Point to a quick launch button and wait a second, and its name appears. |

TIME SAVER

Here's what each quick launch button does:

- Launch Internet Explorer Browser: Opens Internet Explorer (see Hour 9), exactly the same as if you clicked the Internet icon on your desktop or chose Start | Programs | Internet Explorer | Internet Explorer.

- Launch Mail: Opens Outlook Express for using e-mail or newsgroups (see Hour 13), exactly the same as if you clicked the Mail button in Internet Explorer or chose Start | Programs | Internet Explorer | Outlook Express.

- Show Desktop: A neat convenience, the Show Desktop button instantly minimizes all open programs and folders to your taskbar, so you can see and use the stuff on your desktop.

- View Channels: Opens the Channel viewer (see Hour 8).

Putting Folders on the Taskbar

You've always been able to minimize programs to the Windows 95 taskbar, and switch among running programs by clicking their buttons in the taskbar. Well, now you can put other stuff—folders and files—right on the taskbar (see Figure 6.11). Putting a folder or a file on the taskbar makes its contents quickly accessible while your display is occupied by another program or open folder.

Figure 6.11.

A folder on the taskbar.

To put a file or a folder on the taskbar, show its icon on the desktop, in another folder, or in Windows Explorer. Point to the icon, click and hold, and then drag it to the taskbar and release. Note that the folder or file does not actually move to the taskbar. It just becomes accessible from the taskbar.

To remove a file or a folder from the taskbar, right-click its name in the taskbar, and choose Close from the pop-up menu that appears.

Observe that when you put a folder on the taskbar, its contents are spread out across the taskbar. When all the contents do not fit, an arrow appears at the right end of the contents; click the arrow to scroll more contents into view. Click on a subfolder to open it in a window; click on a file to open the file.

6

TIME SAVER

> If you drop two or more folders or files on your taskbar, your taskbar gets pretty crowded, and the contents of the taskbar become overlapped in the same way toolbars are overlapped. Some folders display in full; others are hidden, and only their names and vertical bars appear. To display the contents of a hidden folder on the taskbar, double-click its name.

Putting Toolbars on the Taskbar

You can display two of the Internet Explorer/Active Desktop toolbars—address bar and the links toolbar—in the taskbar. From the taskbar, you use the links toolbar exactly as you would in Internet Explorer.

Take special note, though, that in the taskbar the address bar does not show the file directory, as it does in a folder. Instead, on the taskbar, the address bar is a place where you can type the URL of a Web page you want to go to; it works just like the address bar you use in Internet Explorer, which you learn all about in Hour 9.

To open a toolbar in the taskbar, you point to an empty area of the taskbar (a spot not occupied by buttons or in between buttons) and click the right mouse button (not the usual left button). On the pop-up menu that appears, choose Toolbars. A submenu like the one in Figure 6.12 opens. Then choose the toolbar you want to display.

Figure 6.12.

Right-click an empty spot on the taskbar to choose a toolbar.

TIME SAVER

> As Figure 6.12 shows, you can choose two other "toolbars" from the pop-up menu in addition to the links toolbar and the address bar. Desktop puts all the icons on your desktop—My Computer, Network Neighborhood, the works—on your taskbar, so you can access them without clearing the desktop. And Quick Launch enables you to display (or remove) the quick launch buttons.

To Do: Put the Address Bar in the Taskbar

1. Right-click an empty area of the taskbar. A pop-up menu appears.

2. Choose Toolbars. A submenu appears, listing toolbars.

3. Choose Address Bar. The pop-up menu closes, and the address bar appears in the taskbar (see Figure 6.13).

4. Right-click an empty area of the taskbar (or right-click the word *Address* in the taskbar). A pop-up menu appears.

5. Choose Toolbars | Address Bar. The address bar closes.

Figure 6.13.

The address bar in the taskbar.

Organizing the Taskbar

With all the stuff you can put on your taskbar, it can get pretty crowded. The obvious solution to that problem is not to put too much stuff on your taskbar. Remember, putting stuff on the taskbar is supposed to make things more convenient, and a cluttered taskbar defeats that purpose.

Still, if you wind up with lots of overlapping stuff in your taskbar and want to keep it there, here are some tips for handling it:

☐ Lots of people don't know this, but you can size your taskbar (see Figure 6.14). If you point very carefully to the top edge of the taskbar, you'll see the pointer change to a two-pointed arrow. Click and drag upward to make the taskbar two or three rows high. When you do, you give the taskbar more real estate on which to spread out all the stuff you put there, so you can see more of it at once. You can also drag the top edge downward to crunch the taskbar back to one row, no matter how much stuff it has on it.

☐ When the taskbar doesn't have enough room for all the minimized programs on it, it hides some of the buttons for open programs and displays a pair of up and down arrows next to the program buttons (see Figure 6.15). Click the up or down arrow to scroll through the button of open programs, to see those that are hidden.

☐ When the taskbar doesn't have enough room for all the files, folders, and toolbars on it, it overlaps them. Bring hidden folders or toolbars into view by double-clicking their names or dragging their vertical bars.

☐ When a folder's contents are too long to fit in the taskbar, a small arrow appears at the right end. Click it to scroll the rest of the folder's contents into view.

6

Figure 6.14.

You can stretch your taskbar to show more of the stuff you put on it.

Figure 6.15.

When all the program buttons won't fit, scroll arrows appear so you can scroll to display the buttons.

Summary

With the exception of selecting files and folders by pointing to them, all of the stuff you discovered in this hour is optional.

If you're the type who opens Windows, and then jumps right into an application and works mainly there, you'll have little use for all this Active Desktop hoo-hah. But if you tend to multitask (run several programs at once), move files among folders, and do a lot of other fiddling-around-in-Windows stuff, you'll find the Active Desktop gives you handy new ways to accomplish those tasks.

6

Q&A

Q **You showed in an earlier hour how to shut off single-clicking. Can I shut off any of this other Active Desktop stuff without uninstalling Internet Explorer 4?**

A Yep. In fact, you can remove the whole thing, as you'll learn to do in Hour 8. Still, you do have an incentive to learn to do things the Active Desktop way anyhow: In the next major release of Windows (the successor to Windows 95), all Active Desktop stuff will come standard.

In the meantime, remember that with the exception of clicking, selecting, and toolbars, most of the Active Desktop stuff doesn't have to change your life. If you don't want to put toolbars on your taskbar, don't do it. You're the boss.

Q **How come I can put the address bar and links toolbar in my taskbar, but not the standard buttons toolbar?**

A If you think about the role of the taskbar and that of the standard buttons, you'll recognize that the two have incompatible purposes. The taskbar is for dealing with things *externally*, jumping among open programs, files, and folders, and opening and closing same. The standard buttons deal with *internal* activities, those you're performing within a window or a program. Where should the Back button lead from the taskbar? Where could Up lead? There's just no job for the standard buttons on the taskbar, so Microsoft—in a rare moment of recognizing that it shouldn't create purposeless features—didn't give you the option to put it there.

Quiz

Take the following quiz to see how much you've learned.

Questions

1. To choose which toolbars to display in folders:
    a. Uninstall Internet Explorer
    b. Choose View | Toolbars
    c. Click the Toolbar button
    d. Click the taskbar

2. To display a toolbar that's hidden because it's sharing a toolbar line or the taskbar with another toolbar:
    a. Double-click the hidden toolbar's vertical bar
    b. Double-click the hidden toolbar's name
    c. Click and drag the hidden toolbar's vertical bar
    d. Any of the above

3. You select a file or folder by
   a. Considering it carefully
   b. Pointing to it and waiting a second
   c. Pressing the Shift key
   d. Clicking the taskbar
4. If you need to get to something that's on your desktop, but the desktop is cluttered with open folders and programs:
   a. Click the Show Desktop quick launch button on the taskbar to clear the desktop
   b. Click the Start button
   c. Click a Bic
   d. Click and Clack

Answers

1. b. is the only choice that works.
2. d. You can use a, b, or c to display an overlapped toolbar.
3. b. On the Active Desktop, you point to select. No clicking!
4. a. Show Desktop clears the decks for you.

Activity

Experiment with your toolbars. Drag them into different positions, turn them on and off, and see whether you can come up with a configuration that works best for you.

Hour 7

Discovering Channels

Aside from all the single-clicking stuff you discovered in Hours 5 and 6, channels are the most significant way Internet Explorer 4 changes the way you work—on the Web and in general.

Traditionally, the way you get information from the Internet is that you go out and get it. And each time you want to catch up with the latest information, you go out and get it again. The idea behind channels is this: When you want to stay abreast of a particular kind of information, the information should be delivered to you, automatically, whenever there's news. (Channels achieve this through a technology called *server push*, which is something techies like to bring up. But you don't need to know about server push; you just need to learn how to use channels.)

Channels are a part of the Active Desktop, and as such, it's appropriate that you meet them here and now. In this hour, you get a quick and simple tour of what channels can do for you.

At the end of this hour, you'll be able to answer the following questions:

- ☐ What is a channel, and what does it do?
- ☐ How do I find channels?
- ☐ When I find a channel I like, how do I sign up for it?

☐ How do I update my channels with the latest information?

☐ How do I work with channels in Internet Explorer's full-screen view?

After you've learned how to browse the Web (in Part III), you'll be prepared to do much more with channels. In Hour 12, you can apply your newfound Internet Explorer 4 expertise to make channels do more for you.

What's a Channel?

Suppose you get your news by going out and buying a newspaper every morning. That's a great way to go. Papers cover the news better than TV or radio, except for National Public Radio, if you ask Maxine. But buying a daily paper cannot immediately inform you of events that happen between editions, such as global crises or stock price fluctuations. And if you get your paper at the newsstand, you don't get the news at all unless you *actively* pursue it. Walk past the stand, and you'll be as ignorant as a talk-radio caller.

JUST A MINUTE

> In case you were wondering, channels are free of charge, at least today.

A lot of people keep a TV or a radio news channel playing all day while they work, clean, or do other stuff. When they do, the news is automatically delivered to them as it happens (or as reporters find out about it). These people get their information *passively*—they don't have to go get it because it comes to them. This system has the advantage of automatically delivering the latest available information to the listener or viewer.

A Web-based channel is an attempt to bring something of that TV and radio information delivery style to the Web. Through a channel, an ICP can deliver content automatically to you, without your having to go look for it. You remain passive—the *content* becomes active (hence, *Active Desktop*).

NEW TERM

ICP: An ICP (Internet Content Provider) is a company that publishes stuff on the Web. The term is just coming into vogue, and is used most often to describe companies supplying channels to market their products or services.

Other than updating themselves automatically, channels are just glorified Web pages. Still, they do a few things that regular Web pages don't do. You view ordinary Web pages in the Internet Explorer window. But you can view channels in five ways:

☐ In the Internet Explorer 4 browser (see Figure 7.1). A channel is still a Web page. Most are designed to be best viewed in full-screen view (described next), but any channel can be viewed in Internet Explorer's regular browser view, too.

☐ In full-screen view (see Figure 7.2). Full-screen view is a special Internet Explorer 4 window that is the main view through which you'll view channels. It's basically a full-screen Internet Explorer window with the menu bar and some toolbars stripped away to make more room for full-screen channel content. When you view most channels, Internet Explorer switches to full-screen view automatically.

☐ As a screen saver. Channels not delivered as desktop items can be presented as your Windows screen saver. You'll learn how to make this happen in Hour 12.

☐ As a desktop item (see Figure 7.3). Some channels are not presented in the Internet Explorer window, in regular or full-screen view. Instead, they appear on your desktop as regularly updated items you can see any time, without opening Internet Explorer. For example, an item might supply stock price updates right on your desktop.

☐ Via e-mail. Some channels can optionally be delivered as e-mail messages, so you can review the latest content in Outlook Express (see Hour 13).

TIME SAVER

While viewing a channel in the Internet Explorer browser, you can view the same channel in full-screen view by clicking the Full Screen button on Internet Explorer's toolbar. To switch back to the regular Internet Explorer window, click the Full Screen button again.

Figure 7.1.

You can view a channel in the Internet Explorer browser, like any other Web page.

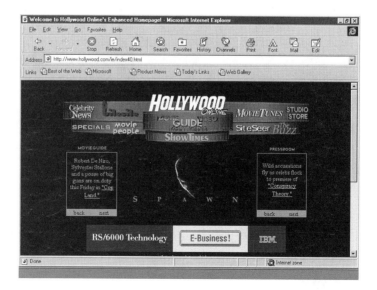

Figure 7.2.

You view most channels in Internet Explorer's full-screen view.

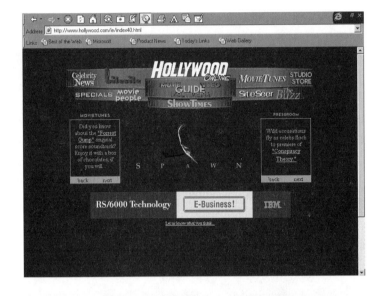

Figure 7.3.

Desktop items are special channels that deliver information to your desktop.

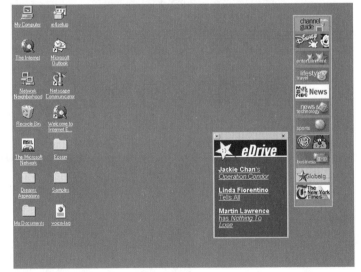

7

Finding Channels

As channels become more popular, you'll come across them all over the Web. When visiting a site related to a particular topic or, more likely, company, you'll see a link for subscribing to a channel that delivers information on the same topic or company.

NEW TERM **Channel subscription:** To use a channel, you must first subscribe to it. Subscribing to a channel instructs the channel's server to send you regular updates of the channel content, and configures the channel so that it knows when and how you want to be updated with new information. You learn how to subscribe in the next section.

Right now, though, channels are new. So Microsoft is trying to help you find channels by supplying the Channel Guide, a channel for finding other channels. The Channel Guide contains links for subscribing to all the channels currently available online (as far as Microsoft knows).

To open the Channel Guide, click the Channel Guide button that appears in the channel bar on your desktop. The Channel Guide opens, offering links to channels and general information about channels (see Figure 7.4).

Figure 7.4.

Microsoft's Channel Guide helps you find channels that may interest you.

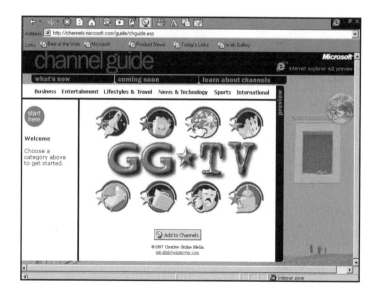

7

Although the Channel Guide is a good place to find full-screen channels, Microsoft's Active Desktop Gallery is a great place to find new desktop items (see Figure 7.5). You learn how to open and use the Active Desktop Gallery in Hour 12.

Figure 7.5.

Microsoft's Active Desktop Gallery leads you to desktop items you may enjoy.

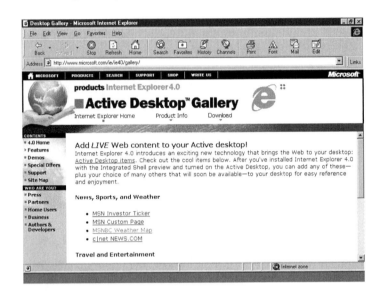

Subscribing to Channels

You subscribe to a channel by first navigating to a channel or a Web page that contains a link for subscribing to the channel, such as Microsoft's Channel Guide.

The link or button you click to subscribe usually features the channel icon, and the words Add to Channels or Add Active Channel. Clicking the link or button opens the Add Channel dialog, in which you set up your subscription.

JUST A MINUTE

To make the subscription process a little easier, Microsoft has given you a set of buttons on your channel bar, each leading to a channel page. Clicking one of these buttons opens the channel, where you can find a button for formally subscribing to the channel.

After the Add Channel dialog opens, all you have to do is follow its prompts. Give it a try. You can begin online or offline.

7

Different channels may allow different subscription options, so the following dialogs and steps may not apply exactly for every channel you subscribe to. But the general idea is always the same.

To practice, I'll show you how to use the channel bar to subscribe to *The New York Times* channel.

To Do: Subscribe to a Channel

1. On the channel bar, click the button labeled News & Technology. Internet Explorer opens in full-screen view, (and your Internet connection opens, if necessary) and a channel showing links to News & Technology channels appears.

2. In the channel, click the button labeled *The New York Times*. *The New York Times* channel opens.

Some channels, such as *The New York Times* channel, do not require you to click a button to add a channel. Instead, the Add Channel dialog opens automatically when you open the channel.

3. The Add Channel dialog opens, as shown in Figure 7.6.

   The dialog tells you which channel you're about to subscribe to, and offers three subscription options:

   No, just add it to my channel bar: A button for this channel is added to your channel bar so you can easily visit the channel online at any time. However, you are not subscribed to it.

   Yes, but only tell me when updates occur: When you update channels (as described later in this hour), you'll be notified when this channel has new content, but the new content will not be downloaded automatically.

   Yes, notify me of updates and download the channel for offline viewing: When you update channels, you'll be notified when this channel has new content and that content will be downloaded automatically to your PC so you can view it anytime, even offline.

Updating channels: Updating channels means checking for new content, notifying you of new content, and optionally downloading all new content (if you chose a Full subscription).

7

4. Choose a subscription option, and click OK to finish subscribing.

Alternatively, you can customize the subscription by clicking the Customize button. The Customize button opens the Subscription wizard, which leads you through a few simple dialogs on which you can choose when new content should be downloaded and whether you should be notified by e-mail when new content is available. On the wizard's final dialog, you can even select the schedule by which updates will be made automatically (see Figure 7.7, later in this hour).

Figure 7.6.

Subscribing to a channel.

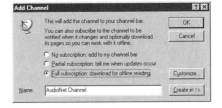

JUST A MINUTE

> Besides subscribing to channels, Internet Explorer supports another kind of subscribing: subscribing to a Web page. Although the basic idea of subscribing to a Web page resembles using channels, it's not quite the same thing. You learn about subscribing to Web pages in Hour 12.

After you subscribe to a channel, a button for it appears in the channel bar, and an item for it appears in the Channels folder of your Favorites menu. You can use either to navigate to that channel at any time. Note that the channel's button in the channel bar will "gleam" (appear to have a bright highlight around it) anytime Internet Explorer detects new content on that channel. The gleam goes away after you update the channel, as described next.

JUST A MINUTE

> Your channel bar does not automatically lengthen to accommodate new buttons. Instead, a small arrow appears at the top or bottom of the bar, so you can scroll more channels into view. If you don't like scrolling, you can resize your channel bar manually, as explained in Hour 12.

Updating Channel Content

When and how channel content is updated depends on the choice you make for the Schedule option when subscribing. By default, most channels are updated automatically according to a schedule set by the channel's publisher. You can use the Subscription wizard to choose a different schedule.

On the final dialog of the Subscription wizard, which opens if you click Customize on the Add Channel dialog (see Figure 7.7), you'll see a drop-down list from which you can choose one of several predefined scheduling options. Alternatively, you can select the Manually option at the bottom of the dialog to prevent all automatic updates and update only when you choose to.

TIME SAVER

Observe that Figure 7.7 includes a check box, Dial as Needed if Connected Through a Modem. If a check appears in this check box, whenever the scheduled update time comes, your PC will dial the Internet, update your channels, and then disconnect, all with no assistance from you (other than leaving your PC switched on).

Figure 7.7.

If you click the Customize button while subscribing, a wizard opens and leads to this dialog, in which you can set the schedule for updates.

TIME SAVER

After subscribing, you can change the schedule and other options for a subscription from the Subscriptions list. Open the list from within Internet Explorer by choosing Favorites | Manage Subscriptions. Point to the channel whose subscription options you want to change, and wait until the icon is selected. Then click the Properties button to open a dialog in which you can change any of the options for that subscription.

7

If you choose Manually, you can update channels manually in a variety of ways:

- [ ] From the Internet Explorer menu bar, you can update all channels at once by choosing Favorites | Update All Subscriptions.

- [ ] From the Windows desktop, you can update all channels at once by choosing Settings from the Start menu, and then choosing Active Desktop | Update Now from the menu that appears.

TIME SAVER

After a channel has been updated—regardless of how or when it was updated—you may disconnect from the Internet and read the channel at your leisure, offline.

Using Full-Screen View

When you open a channel from the channel bar, or click Internet Explorer's Channels button, or click the Full Screen button while viewing a channel, you see the channel in full-screen view (see Figure 7.8).

Full-screen view is really just Internet Explorer with a few cosmetic changes. Observe in Figure 7.8 that full-screen view strips away Internet Explorer's menu bar, leaving maximum onscreen space available for information delivery.

JUST A MINUTE

In full-screen view, Internet Explorer's standard buttons toolbar is available but rarely necessary. (You learn more about using Internet Explorer's toolbars in Part III.) Most channels that run in full-screen view are designed for easy navigation, and include their own onscreen buttons and links for getting around.

Another interesting difference about full-screen view is that when you display the Channel list in the Explorer bar (by clicking the Channels button in Internet Explorer's toolbar; see Figure 7.9) in full-screen view, you can easily display and hide the Explorer bar at any time. When you move the pointer to the far left edge of the screen, the Explorer bar slides into view. When you move the pointer back to the right, the Explorer bar disappears, and you can see the whole channel you're viewing.

Figure 7.8.

Full-screen view is your channel viewport.

NEW TERM **Explorer bar:** The Explorer bar is a panel along the left side of the Internet Explorer 4 window. It contains handy lists of links. In upcoming hours, you learn how to display in the Explorer bar a list of search tools, your Favorites list, or a list of pages you've previously visited.

Figure 7.9.

Use full-screen view and the Channel list (which you display by clicking the Channels button) to move among your channels.

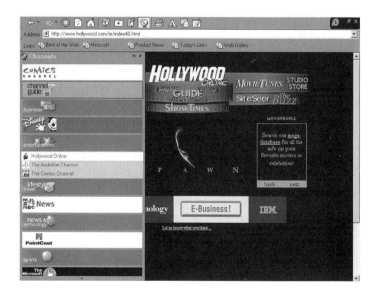

In full-screen view, the Explorer bar lists your subscribed channels. You can jump conveniently among your channels by displaying the Explorer bar and then clicking the name of a channel in the Explorer bar.

To close full-screen view (and return to the regular Internet Explorer window), click the Full Screen button.

To close the Channel list in the Explorer bar, click the X button in the Explorer bar's upper-right corner.

Summary

If you've been on the Web before, you know that channels are a big change. If you're new to Web browsing, channels may appear to be not that different from the rest of the Internet —but after you explore Part III, you'll understand how different channels really are.

Q&A

Q How do I delete a channel button from my channel bar? I don't want all those dopey ones Microsoft put there.

A Each button on the channel bar is a file, a *channel shortcut*. You can delete it like any other desktop file. The best way is to right-click the button to display a pop-up menu, and then choose Delete from the menu. The shortcut is sent to the Recycle Bin, like any other file you delete.

Q Looking at the available channels, I see a few interesting ones. But mostly, they look like glorified commercials. Is that the way it's gonna be with channels?

A Yep. At least for now, channels look more like a terrific new medium for advertising than a great new way to get information. No doubt companies will try to entice you to subscribe to their channels, for which you will be rewarded with regular junk promotions. But as with TV, the effort involved in supplying any useful content must be paid for somehow, and the advertising prevents ICPs from charging fees—at least for now.

Quiz

Take the following quiz to see how much you've learned.

Questions

1. A desktop item is

    a. Any icon or folder on your Windows desktop

    b. A channel that displays regularly updated information on your Windows desktop

    c. A news item relating to desktop technology

    d. A special pointer for opening channels

2. Which of the following is the most likely text to appear on the proper link or button for subscribing to a channel you're viewing?

    a. Channel

    b. Add to Favorites

    c. Submit

    d. Add Active Channel

3. When a button on the channel bar gleams

    a. The channel has been subscribed to.

    b. There's new content for that channel you've not yet seen.

    c. The channel is outdated and will soon be canceled.

    d. The channel is very happy.

4. An ICP is an

    a. International Carrier Pigeon

    b. Internal Combustion Program

    c. Internet-Capable Person

    d. Internet Content Provider

Answers

1. b. The others look likely, but only b describes the real desktop item.

2. d. The other choices will all accomplish something, but that something won't be subscribing to a channel.

3. b. The gleam is your signal that there's something new to see on a channel.

4. d. When we're talking about the Web, ICP means d. In other contexts, it may have other meanings, but that's not my fault.

7

Activity

If you're new to the Internet, hold off exploring channels until you've read Part III and learned your way around the Web. But if you feel comfortable exploring the Web now, check out each button Microsoft put on your channel bar to see what the button has to offer.

Hour 8

Customizing the Active Desktop

Want to change something about the way the Active Desktop looks or acts? You're in good company—that's what everybody asks Maxine these days. I tell 'em, "Give the ol' AD a chance, she'll grow on you." But no sale.

So here's a rundown of how you can customize the desktop after installing Internet Explorer 4. And at the end of this hour, if you find that you just plain want to remove all of the Active Desktop—the channel bar, taskbar enhancements, the works—you'll learn how to do that while still keeping the rest of Internet Explorer around for Internet tasks.

At the end of the hour, you'll be able to answer the following questions:

☐ How can I switch back to the old, classic Windows ways of opening icons (double-click) and selecting icons (single-click)?

☐ How do I switch off the Web page look and feel in folders?

☐ Is there an easy way to disable Active Desktop items (such as the channel bar)?

☐ How can I add an attractive background picture to a folder window?

☐ How can I remove the Active Desktop altogether?

CAUTION

All the procedures and discussions in Hours 9 through 24 assume, by and large, that the Active Desktop default settings are in place. If you customize the desktop as described in this hour, it's up to you to adjust your actions. For example, if you disable single-clicking, when a procedure in an upcoming Hour tells you to click, you may have to double-click.

Turning Single-Clicking On or Off

I explained the following in Hour 5, but it bears repeating. If you don't like opening stuff by single-clicking or selecting stuff by pointing at it, you can disable these techniques so that Windows works the old way (double-click to open, single-click to select).

Note that you cannot turn off single-clicking for only some folders. No matter which folder you open in step 1 of the following To Do, the settings you choose will apply to all of Windows: all folder windows, the desktop, and Windows Explorer.

JUST A MINUTE

Note that disabling single-clicking has no effect on other aspects of the Active Desktop (the channel bar, the Internet Explorer toolbars on folders, and so on), and it has no effect on your ability to browse the Web with Internet Explorer. It just reverts clicking techniques to the classic Windows style.

To Do: Disable Single-Clicking

1. Open any folder (it doesn't matter which).
2. From the folder's menu bar, choose View | Folder Options. The Folder Options dialog appears (see Figure 8.1).
3. In the General tab of the Folder Options dialog, choose the Classic style option.
4. Click OK. The link formatting is removed from the icons on your desktop, and double-clicking comes back into fashion on the desktop and in all folders.

To give single-clicking another chance, return to the Folder Options dialog, and choose Web style.

8

Figure 8.1.

In any folder, choose View | Folder Options to open a dialog in which you can choose between single-clicking and double-clicking.

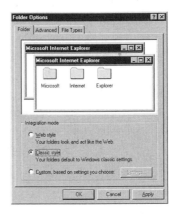

Choosing Custom Folder Options

From the dialog shown in Figure 8.1, you have the option to choose Custom folder options, which differ from the standard settings applied if you choose Web style.

JUST A MINUTE

The custom settings you choose affect all folders in Windows, regardless of which folder you make them in.

To Do: Apply Custom Settings

1. Open any folder, and choose View | Folder Options. The dialog shown earlier in Figure 8.1 appears.

2. Choose the Custom option.

3. Click the Settings button. A dialog like the one in Figure 8.2 appears.

Figure 8.2.

You can customize the folder options settings.

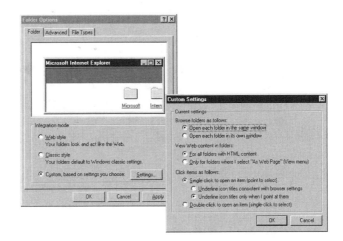

4. Under Browse folders, choose whether you want each new folder to open in the same window, closing the previous one behind it (single-window mode), or for each new folder to open in a new, separate window, leaving previous windows open, too.

TIME SAVER

> Because of the Back button and other features of the Active Desktop, single-window mode is convenient. But if you do a lot of dragging and dropping between folders, you may prefer to switch to separate windows.

5. Under View Web Content in Folders, choose whether you want to show Web page styling on all folders, or only on folders for which you choose the "as Web page" option. You learn more about Web page styling in the next section.

6. Under Click Items as Follows, choose how you want to perform clicking and selections:

Choose the top option, Single-Click to Open an Item (Point to Select), to enable the default Active Desktop settings: Click to open; point (and wait a second) to select. Choose the bottom option to revert to classic Windows clicking techniques: Single-click to select; double-click to open.

If you choose the top Click Items as Follows option (Single-click), you can also choose one of the options beneath it. The first choice leaves link formatting (the underlined icon labels) visible at all times. The second option shows the underlining only when you point to an icon.

JUST A MINUTE

> When choosing custom settings, it's generally best to leave the link underlining on at all times. Because there still will be situations in which you must double-click, leaving the link formatting on gives you a visual cue, telling you at a glance where you may single-click.

Turning Web Page Styling On or Off

As you know from Hour 6, folders on the Active Desktop can look and act a lot like Web pages (see Figure 8.3), and even include pictures. You can selectively switch off this Web page styling for any folder, if you don't care to look at it. Figure 8.4 shows My Computer with its Web page styling turned off.

8

JUST A MINUTE

You can easily apply one kind of Web page styling—a background—to a folder yourself. Later in this hour, you learn how.

Figure 8.3.

My Computer demonstrates how folders can be formatted as Web pages on the Active Desktop.

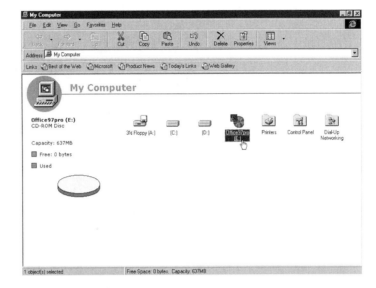

Figure 8.4.

This is how My Computer looks with its Web page styling switched off.

If you choose to switch off Web page styling, keep a few things in mind:

☐ Switching off Web page styling affects only the folder window in which you do it. If you remove Web page styling from a folder, and then open a different folder in the same window, it too shows no Web page formatting. If you close the window and open a different folder window, the different window will still show its Web page styling. You'll see how this works in the To Do that's coming up.

☐ Switching off Web page styling removes from the folder window any pictures and background. (You learn to add a background to a folder later in this hour.) But it has no effect on the other ways the Active Desktop enhances a folder. After you switch off Web page styling, the Internet Explorer 4 toolbars remain on the folder, and icons are still formatted as links (unless you've also disabled single-clicking, as described at the beginning of this hour).

☐ After switching Web page styling off, you can switch it back on again, at any time, by repeating the steps you used to switch it off.

To Do: Switch Off Web Styling on Folder Windows

1. Open My Computer, and observe the Web page styling.

2. From within My Computer, click the Control Panel icon, so that Control Panel opens in the same window that was occupied by My Computer. Observe Control Panel's Web styling.

3. From Control Panel's menu bar, choose View | as Web Page. The Web styling vanishes from Control Panel.

4. Click the Back button to reopen My Computer in the same window. The Web styling is gone there, too.

5. From My Computer's menu bar, choose View | as Web Page. The Web styling returns to My Computer (and to Control Panel, by the way).

Disabling Active Parts of the Active Desktop

In one operation, you can shut off (and hide) all special Active Desktop elements on the desktop, including the channel bar and any desktop items you have added (see Hours 7 and 12). Note that doing so has no effect on the Active Desktop's Windows navigation features, such as single-clicking or Web styling on folders. It simply removes from your desktop the active stuff that communicates automatically with the Web.

8

JUST A MINUTE

The following steps conveniently disable all active elements in one pop. See Hour 12 to learn how to selectively disable one or more items while leaving others enabled.

To Do: Disable Active Desktop Items

1. Right-click on an empty area of your desktop (but not on an icon, a window, or the taskbar) to display the desktop's pop-up menu.

2. Click Active Desktop at the top of the menu to display the Active Desktop submenu (see Figure 8.5).

3. Choose View as Web Page.

JUST A MINUTE

Disabling the Active Desktop elements does not delete them from your PC; it just shuts them off and hides them. You can repeat the preceding procedure to restore them.

Figure 8.5.

You can disable or enable active desktop stuff from the desktop's pop-up menu.

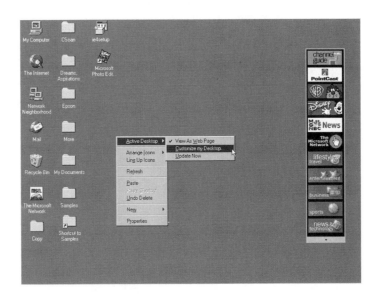

Giving a Folder a Background

Adding Web page formatting to folders is not the exclusive province of software developers. You can add Web page formatting to a folder yourself. For example, you can add a special background to a folder.

The Web page formatting described in this section affects only the folder within which you start the procedure, and no other folder. This enables you to apply a different look to different folders.

To Do: Add a Background to a Folder

To Do

1. Open the folder to which you want to add a background.

2. Choose View | Customize this Folder. A wizard like the one in Figure 8.6 appears. You have three options:

   ☐ Create or Edit an HTML Document. This option opens the folder as a Web page document in your Web authoring software (see Part VI), where you can apply any kind of formatting you can apply in a Web page, including pictures and fonts.

   ☐ Choose a Background Picture. This option lets you choose a graphic file to use as the folder background.

   ☐ Remove Customization. This option removes all Web page formatting you have previously created with either of the first two options, reverting the folder to normal.

Figure 8.6.

*Choose View |
Customize this
Folder to customize
the current folder.*

3. Select Choose a Background Picture, and click Next. A list of picture files opens, as shown in Figure 8.7.

   The list shows your Windows wallpaper pictures, which are stored in your Windows folder. You can choose any of these, or click Browse to browse your PC for another image file to use. You can use just about any type of graphics file, including .JPG, .BMP, or .GIF.

Figure 8.7.

Choose your background picture, or Browse for one.

TIME SAVER

Observe in Figure 8.7 that you can also choose a new color for the text labels on icons in the folder, and the color of the background of those labels. Change one or both of these settings if your new background picture makes icon labels difficult to see or read.

4. After selecting a picture, click Next. A final dialog appears, congratulating you for adding a background to the folder.

5. Click Finish. The dialog closes, and the folder reappears, showing its new background (see Figure 8.8).

Figure 8.8.

The finished folder, with its own background.

JUST A MINUTE

When you add a background to a folder, you're adding Web page formatting. If you disable Web page formatting as described earlier in this hour, you won't see any folder backgrounds you've added.

Removing the Active Desktop Completely

By now, you should be pretty comfortable with the Active Desktop. But if you just plain hate it, you can remove it. I've shown you how to modify selected aspects of the Active Desktop, so you could change just the part you don't like and leave the rest in place. But if you don't like *any* of it, you can simply wipe out the Active Desktop.

Note that if you remove the Active Desktop, you retain the Internet Explorer 4 browser and its components: Outlook Express for e-mail, FrontPage Express for Web Page authoring, and so on. But you remove all the enhancements Internet Explorer has made to Windows, including:

- ☐ Single-clicking on icons
- ☐ All folder window enhancements, including Internet Explorer toolbars and Web page styling
- ☐ All taskbar enhancements, including quick launch buttons, toolbars in the taskbar, and folders in the taskbar
- ☐ All desktop items, including the channel bar
- ☐ The Favorites menu in the Programs menu and in folder windows

To Do: Remove the Active Desktop

1. Close all programs (except Windows).
2. From the Start menu, choose Settings | Control Panel to open Control Panel.
3. Choose Add/Remove Programs to open the Add/Remove Programs dialog (see Figure 8.9).
4. From the list, choose Microsoft Internet Explorer, and then click the Add/Remove button. A dialog like the one in Figure 8.10 appears.
5. Choose Remove the Windows Desktop Update component, but keep the Internet Explorer Web browser.
6. Click OK.

7. Windows spends a few moments removing the Active Desktop; follow any prompts you see.

8. When the procedure finishes, you may be prompted to restart your PC. Even if you're not so prompted, restart your PC anyway.

If in the future you decide you want the Active Desktop back (fickle you!), the best way to restore it is to reinstall Internet Explorer 4 (see Hour 3).

Figure 8.9.

Open Add/Remove Programs in Control Panel to remove the Active Desktop.

Figure 8.10.

To remove the Active Desktop but retain Internet Explorer, choose Remove the Windows Desktop Update Component.

Summary

After you become accustomed to the Active Desktop, and gain a little confidence with it, you'll see that it really is flexible and easy to use. Soon you'll enjoy putting your own, personal touch on the desktop and on your folders. Have fun.

What? You don't like the Active Desktop. Then get rid of it. It's your PC.

Q&A

Q Can I still use and choose my Windows wallpaper in the Active Desktop?

A Sure. In general, the Active Desktop does not take away any of the ways you've always been able to customize Windows. It only adds. If you open your Display Properties dialog, you'll see that the Web tab has been added, but nothing has been taken away. You can still use the Appearance tab to choose your Windows colors, use the Background tab to choose wallpaper and a screen saver, and so on.

Q Web page styling of folder windows seems, well, pointless. Any reason to keep it enabled?

A It's new, so nobody has taken much advantage of it yet. But in coming months, you'll see more. For example, when you install new programs, the folders created by those programs may include cool-looking, dynamic formatting. And like Maxine always says, "If it ain't broke, don't disable it."

Quiz

Questions

1. To disable single-clicking throughout Windows:

    a. In any folder, choose View | Folder Options, and then choose Classic style from the dialog.

    b. In My Computer (and *only* My Computer), choose View | Folder Options, and then choose Classic style from the dialog.

    c. Right-click the desktop and choose Single-clicking mode.

    d. Get a new mouse that supports the G-628 no-click protocol.

2. For a folder background, you can use only

    a. A GIF image

    b. A JPEG image

    c. An attractive image

    d. An image in just about any popular format

3. When the current custom Folder Options setting is single-window mode

    a. You must close a window before Windows lets you open a new one.

    b. When you open a folder from within a folder, the new folder window replaces the previous one in the window.

    c. All folders open full-screen.

    d. All of the above.

8

4. When you remove the Active Desktop, you remove
   a. All enhancements to Windows, but not the Internet Explorer 4 browser program or its components (such as Outlook Express)
   b. All enhancements to Windows, including the Internet Explorer 4 browser program and its components (such as Outlook Express)
   c. Single-clicking, but no other enhancements to Windows
   d. The Active Desktop wallpaper, but no other enhancements to Windows

Answers

1. a. Disabling single-clicking in any folder disables it throughout Windows.
2. d. Folders can use as a background just about any type of image file.
3. b. You move among folders within one window in single-window mode (the default in the Active Desktop).
4. a. You can delete the Active Desktop enhancements to Windows and leave the rest intact.

Activity

Get together picture files containing stuff that's meaningful to you: Scans of family photos, your kids' computer drawings, and so on. As you organize your files in folders, look for opportunities to add a background to a folder that relates to the folder's contents. For example, if you have a folder of programs for the family, put a family background on it. Or use your company's logo as the background for work-related folders.

PART

III

Browsing the Web with Internet Explorer

Hour

Hour 9

Navigating the Web with Internet Explorer

The World Wide Web is the fastest growing part of the Internet, as well as the most exciting. Using Internet Explorer, you can go places you've never imagined and have access to information and resources that might otherwise be unattainable.

In this lesson, you find the answers to the following questions:

- [ ] How can I deal with so much information on the Web?
- [ ] How do I navigate the Web?
- [ ] What are all those buttons for on my browser?
- [ ] How do I keep a permanent record of my favorite sites?
- [ ] Is there any way to keep track of where I've been?

Navigation Basics

To start exploring the Web, you must be familiar with several basic things. You must understand how individual pages on the Web can be viewed and explored, you need to know how hyperlinks work, and you need to be familiar with browser toolbar buttons. When you're familiar with these important parts of the Web, you're halfway there.

Navigating Web Pages

If how to navigate an individual Web page seems simple and obvious to you, you might want to skip to the next section. However, you'd be surprised at the number of beginners who fail to realize how to get around on a Web page.

The key is to realize that any particular Web page can be as long or as short as the Webmaster programs it to be. Many people, when they get on the Web for the first time, think that what appears on their screen is all there is.

The page in Figure 9.1, for example, contains lots of text, links, and action, but there's one thing you should notice right away. Both the horizontal and vertical scroll bars are active, which tells you that this page is wider and longer than will fit in the screen.

Figure 9.1.

You can probably tell that there's more than meets the eye on this Web page.

Time Saver

It's always a good idea to maximize your browser window to take up your entire monitor. This will ensure that you can view the most information possible. The only time this may not be true is if you have a large (17"or bigger) monitor, in which case adjusting your browser to take up half the screen should be fine.

9

Unless the specific piece of information you want is at the very top, you'll want to make a habit of scrolling down a Web page when you first encounter it. This enables you to know the amount and type of information on the page. A well-designed Web page should at least point you toward important information without requiring you to scroll a lot.

Follow That Link

The simplest and most useful tool on the Web is the hyperlink. This little underlined colored word can take you to a page next door or halfway around the world. The hyperlink is the key to the nonlinear nature of the Web.

It's also why the Web is so easy to use. With a glance, you know immediately where you can go from any page. For instance, the page shown in Figure 9.2 (http://www.shareware.com) has text links to New Arrivals, Browsers, and more. Because these words look different than other words on the page, you know you can click them to go to another page.

Figure 9.2.

Text hyperlinks are easy to see and follow on the Web.

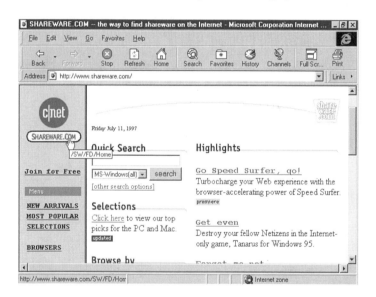

However, not all hyperlinks are so obvious. Often, webmasters will create graphics that are hyperlinks. If you look again at the page in Figure 9.2, you will see the clnet logo. It may not be obvious, but this is a link, too.

TIME SAVER

> When trying to find links on a page with a lot of graphics, pay special attention to your cursor. When the cursor passes over a link, the cursor turns into a hand.

You should know about one last type of graphical hyperlink: the image map. An image map is a special type of graphic that takes you to different pages depending on where on the graphic you click. For instance, if you saw a graphic with a row of books, you might go to a different page depending on which book your cursor was on when you clicked.

Toolbar Buttons

You need to do more than simply click on links to go from one place to another. Internet Explorer has a number of toolbar buttons to help you navigate the Web. The following is a list of the most common toolbar buttons. Don't worry if a few seem to be missing; they will all be covered before you're through with this book.

Button	Function
⇦ ▾	Takes you back to the previous page visited
⇨ ▾	After using the Back button, takes you forward one page
⊗	Stops the process of loading the currently requested page into your browser
🗎	Requests that the current page be loaded again (refreshed) for display
🏠	Takes you to the user-defined home page
📁	Brings up a frame in your browser window that displays your favorite Web sites; Favorites are covered more fully in the next section
🕘	Brings up a frame in your browser window that displays recently visited pages
🖨	Prints the displayed page

JUST A MINUTE

When you first install Internet Explorer, your Home page is defined as Microsoft's Web site. If you would rather have another Web site as your home page, choose View | Internet Options | General. In the Address field, type the URL of your desired home page, and then press Enter.

These buttons, along with hyperlinks, will enable you to do the majority of your Web browsing. However, Internet Explorer offers an additional set of buttons that enable you to accomplish even more. These Links buttons, pictured in Figure 9.3, are pretty much self-explanatory. Perhaps you'd like to take a few minutes to explore them now.

Figure 9.3.

These buttons take you to special places on Microsoft's Web site.

Your History

If you were to walk around a large library long enough without any clues as to where you were going, it wouldn't take long before you were lost. Fortunately, most libraries have colored lines on the floor that show you where you're going and where you've been.

Laying Tracks

Fortunately, Internet Explorer keeps track of where you've been during each visit to the cyberlibrary that is the Internet. As you visit each page on the Web, Internet Explorer makes a note of it and stores this information in a History file.

JUST A MINUTE

> You can adjust how far back your History goes with Internet Explorer by choosing View | Options | General. Simply select the number of days you want Internet Explorer to keep track of your travels. (Too high a number could affect Explorer's performance.)

Going Back

After you have browsed some Web pages, Internet Explorer has some "history" to go on. You now have two ways to "go back in time" to return to pages you've already visited. You might have noticed the small down arrow next to your Back and Forward buttons.

If you click the little arrow next to the Back button, a pop-up menu appears, listing the Web sites you have visited during the current session (see Figure 9.4). This short history is a way to quickly move backward and forward through links that you are interested in during a particular session. This same list of items is available also from the File menu.

For a more complete view of your history, click the History button that you were shown earlier in the hour. Clicking this toolbar button gives you many more history options to choose from.

Figure 9.4.

Quickly access recently visited sites.

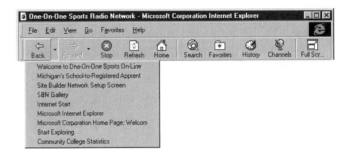

While your History button is selected, Internet Explorer displays your history options in a separate browser frame (see Figure 9.5). To go to any link displayed in this window, simply click the link.

Figure 9.5.

Go anywhere you've been lately with a click.

Notice that you can display a list of visited sites from a past week, a past day, or the current session. This gives you great flexibility when browsing. Because the History frame stays open until you close it, you can jump from site to site quickly. You can also resize the History frame by clicking and dragging on the frame's border.

JUST A MINUTE

If you right-click on a History item, you'll see even more flexibility in Internet Explorer's History capabilities. You can choose to easily delete a certain history item or copy it to another location.

9

Choosing Your Favorites

One of the biggest disadvantages of Internet Explorer's History is that it's never really permanent. History links come and go due to your computer's memory limitations and other factors, and you'll never be quite sure exactly where they are all the time.

Wouldn't it be nice if there were a way to instantly go to an often visited or favorite site without having to find it every time? With Internet Explorer, you can define your favorites—those places on the Internet that you find yourself visiting all the time. Using favorites involves two basic steps, which are described next.

Adding Favorites

Adding a favorite in Internet Explorer is easy. Simply go to a site for which you want a permanent record and choose Favorites | Add To Favorites and then press Enter. That's it—really. From now on, simply clicking either the Favorites menu or the Favorites toolbar button will show you all the sites you've saved for easy access (see Figure 9.6).

Figure 9.6.

Internet Explorer displays favorites much like your History.

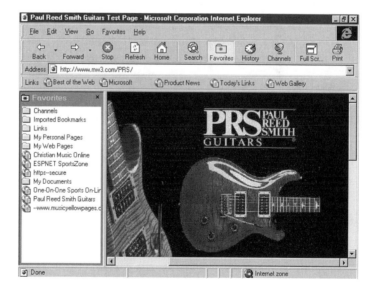

When you first start to surf the Internet, this process of simply adding sites as you come to them will be sufficient. As you become more experienced and need to keep track of more sites, you'll need to be able to do more. Internet Explorer makes organizing your Favorites easy.

Editing Favorites in Explorer

Choosing Favorites | Organize Favorites takes you to a window that looks almost identical to any other Windows 95 browser window (see Figure 9.7)

Figure 9.7.

*The Organizing Favor-
ites window should look
familiar.*

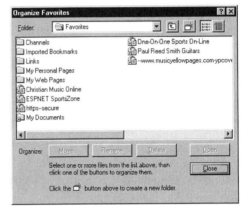

Practice doing a few common tasks when editing favorites: creating a new folder and moving favorites. Before you can follow along, you must have saved some favorites first.

To Do: Organize Favorites

1. Open the Organizing Favorites window, and right-click anywhere in the window.

2. Choose New | Folder from the resulting pop-up menu.

3. Type the name of your new folder. I have several sports-related links I'd like to put in this folder, so I'll name mine **Sports**.

4. Click and drag any links in the Organize Favorites window to your newly created folder.

5. Click the Close button.

If you chunk your links into categories, you will see that what might have been a hodgepodge of links is now nicely organized. Although organizing favorites has some limitations, such as your inability to change the order of favorites by simply dragging and dropping them, the basic Windows 95 functions are still available:

☐ Folder button. Click the Folder button at the top of the window to create a new folder into which you can move related bookmarks.

☐ Delete button. This button removes a selected favorite from your list.

☐ Move button. Click this button to display a dialog that enables you to move your bookmark to any location.

JUST A MINUTE

In case you were wondering, you can edit your favorites directly from Windows 95. Simply go to the `C:\Windows\Favorites` directory and have at it.

Getting Files with Internet Explorer

File Transfer Protocol. Although it sounds scary, FTP is nothing more than a protocol (or set of rules) for transferring files. Among the many machines on the Internet, some (called FTP sites) act as dedicated electronic libraries of files. Each library contains files of text, graphics, and software tools that you can read, view, and use on your own computer at home.

JUST A MINUTE

Unlike a library, some of the files available through FTP cost a little. Files for which you pay some small fee for are usually called shareware programs. The authors share these programs for a small fee to help them write even more. Some of the best software in the world started out as shareware.

FTP is a fast, efficient, and reliable way to transfer information. It was one of the first Internet services developed to enable users to transfer files from one place to another. Internet Explorer makes it easy to use this powerful Internet service.

The FTP Primer

Although it's not necessary to know a great detail about FTP to use it, a few pieces of information should help you:

☐ Anonymous or not? Many FTP sites are referred to as anonymous FTP sites because just about anybody can get on them and download files. For most private FTP sites, you need a user ID and password to gain access.

Just because an FTP site is an anonymous site does not necessarily mean it has unlimited access. A site may limit the number of anonymous users during business hours, restrict anonymous users to particular areas, or not allow the downloading of certain files.

☐ FTP structure. FTP sites are structured very much like your hard drive. They have a root directory (just like your hard drive) and subdirectories under the root directory. FTP, however, uses forward slashes instead of backward slashes.

☐ File types. Many types of files are available through FTP. The file type determines what Internet Explorer does with the file when you try to download it. Table 9.1 outlines some common file types.

Table 9.1. File extensions explained.

Extension	Compressed File Type?	Type of File
.txt	No	Plain text file
.ps	No	PostScript printer file
.exe	Yes/No	Executable or self-extracting file
.zip	Yes	Standard Windows compressed file
.jpg, .gif	No	Standard graphics file
.avi, .mov	No	Multimedia file
.wav, .au	No	Audio file

You might see other extensions, such as .gz, .tar, and .z, which are UNIX files you most likely won't be able to use.

But how do you get these files using Internet Explorer? In the next section, you find out.

Downloading Files

Now that you know a little bit about FTP, it's time to download something useful. Because you might need something to decompress all those compressed files, download a wonderful product called WinZip.

To Do: Download a File

1. In the Internet Explorer Address field, type http://www.winzip.com.
2. Scroll down the page until you see a link that tells you to download the latest evaluation or demonstration version of WinZip. At the time this was written, this link was Download 6.2 Evaluation Version.

To Do

9

3. Scroll down the screen until you see the Download link. At the time this was written, this link was Download WinZip 6.2 for Windows 95 and NT. A dialog appears asking you what you want to do with the file (see Figure 9.8).

4. Choose Save This Program to Disk, and then click OK.

Figure 9.8.

If Internet Explorer can't display a file, it asks you what to do with it.

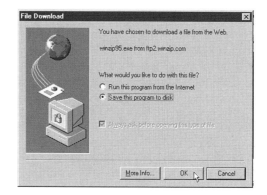

5. When the Save As dialog appears, select the location where you'd like the file saved (and make sure the Save as Type setting is Application), and click the Save button.

6. When the download is complete, choose Start | Run. Select the file you just downloaded, and press Enter.

7. Choose the WinZip Setup option and follow the directions to set up Winzip.

Whether you download a file from an FTP site or a Web site, this process will be similar for most non-text files. If Internet Explorer tries to display a non-text file in the browser window, just click the Back button, right-click the file's link, and choose the Save Target As option from the resulting pop-up menu. You can then proceed to save the file as you normally would.

Summary

This lesson explained the basics of navigating the Web. You learned how to make use of hyperlinks and toolbar buttons to get around on the Internet. You were also told how to use some of the tools that are available to help you organize the Internet, such as History and Favorites. Finally, you were taught how to use Internet Explorer to download files from the Internet with ease.

Q&A

Q I'm accessing the Web via modem, and to be honest, I'm really frustrated with how long it takes some Web pages to load because of all the graphics. Is there anything I can do?

A Yes. Many people choose to not display graphics in Internet Explorer because they want to get to the relevant information faster. To do this, chose View | Options | Advanced. In the Multimedia section of the resulting dialog, clear the check mark next to Show Pictures, and then click OK. Images will now appear as placeholders instead of the images themselves. If you find you do want to display an image, simply right-click it and choose the Show Picture option from the pop-up menu.

Q I have access to a private FTP site. Can I use Internet Explorer to access this type of site as well?

A Yes again. You have to type the URL of a private site a little differently. To access a private FTP site, type the URL into the Address field using the following format: `ftp://userid:password@ftp.site.domain`. If I had private access to `ftp.private.com` with a User ID of `bunny` and a password of `rabbit`, I'd type `ftp://bunny:rabbit@ftp.private.com`.

Quiz

Take the following quiz to see how much you've learned.

Questions

1. Which of the following isn't a hyperlink on a Web page?

    a. Text

    b. Graphic

    c. The browser window scroll bar

2. What are your options for setting a home page?

3. Internet Explorer is unable to download text files from FTP sites.

    a. True

    b. False

Answers

1. c.

2. Limitless. You can even define a file on your hard drive as your home page if you'd like.

3. b. False. You use the right-click method to do it.

Activity

Your biggest task, both now and in the future, will be to have a large and easily accessible list of bookmarks. Well, you might as well start now. Spend an hour or so cruising the Net, making at least 10 bookmarks as you go. Then edit them into at least two different categories. If you don't want to keep them all, feel free to delete some after you've organized them.

Hour 10

Searching the Web with Internet Explorer

You now know enough to realize there is no way in the world that you can locate everything you want and need by simply surfing the Web. You need some sophisticated tools to help sift through the billions of Web pages and other resources out there.

Fortunately, many of these tools are available for free, and they're right at your fingertips. This hour shows you how to search for virtually anything using Internet Explorer 4.0. When you're finished with this hour, you'll know the answers to the following questions:

☐ Which basic search concepts do I need to know?

☐ How do I conduct searches using Internet Explorer, Yahoo!, and Infoseek?

☐ Which other search engines can I use?

☐ How do I search newsgroups?

Searching Basics

When using a search engine on the Web, several concepts and techniques are almost universal and don't vary a great deal from site to site. Before you look at some searching specifics, perhaps it would be helpful to know some of these basic elements first.

Searching Options

No matter what search engine you use, you always follow the same basic steps: Point your browser to the search site, find the field to enter your search term, and then click the search button. There are some variations, of course, but you usually follow the same basic pattern. Figure 10.1 shows what a typical search site looks like.

Figure 10.1.

The Infoseek search site offers a typical search interface.

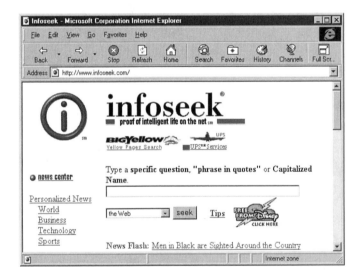

Most search engines now offer you a number of choices on how to conduct your search. The most common, as you can see in Figure 10.1, is a choice of *where* to search. Infoseek, located at http://www.infoseek.com, enables you to search the World Wide Web, Usenet newsgroups, news wires, e-mail addresses, and more.

Most search engines now give you a choice of many different sources to search. This hour focuses mainly on searching the Web, but feel free to try out some of the other options as well. Keep in mind that this keyword type of search is best when you are looking for a specific word, phrase, or other element.

10

You can also browse many search engines by category. Browsing by category is effective when you're looking for general information in a specific area but aren't looking for a specific result. You look at this type of searching in the "Using Yahoo! to Find Things" section later in the hour.

Framing Your Search

No matter where you go, the terms and *operators* you use to help you in your search determine your success.

NEW TERM **Operator:** An operator is usually anything that modifies a term or an equation. In $2 + 2 = 4$, the plus sign is an operator. When searching on the Web, you can often use special symbols or words to build a search equation, which is often more effective than searching for a single word or phrase.

As with other elements in search engines, you'll find a fair amount of variability from one search site to another. Most search engines can make use of Boolean operators, which are designed to put conditions on a search. These types of operators, as well as a few other common operators and techniques, are listed next:

JUST A MINUTE

> Most search engines require that you use all capital letters for Boolean operators so that they can be distinguished from the search terms themselves.

- □ AND (or +): A Boolean operator requiring that both terms be present to produce a hit. For example, cars AND mustangs (or cars +mustangs) would likely rule out all results (or hits) on Mustang horses and produce results only on Ford Mustang cars.

- □ OR: A Boolean operator that accepts hits from either term. For instance, mustangs OR cars would produce hits when either term was present.

- □ AND NOT (or -): With this Boolean operator, you can specifically exclude a term. As an example, mustangs AND NOT cars (or mustangs -cars) would produce hits on documents containing the word *mustangs* without being accompanied by *cars*. In a sense, the AND NOT operator is the opposite of the AND operator.

- □ Case: Many search engines are also case sensitive. If you are searching for a proper name, such as Queen Victoria, go ahead and capitalize the proper names—it might make for a better search.

- □ Quoted Phrases: Many search engines enable you to search for an exact phrase. For instance, if you were searching for dealers of classic cars, you'd probably find fewer, and more relevant, hits if you searched for "classic car dealers" instead of classic AND car AND dealers.

10

TIME SAVER

Almost every search site out there has a Help or Search Tips link on its search page. In addition to general search advice, this link will take you to a page that outlines specific techniques that work particularly well for that site. It's highly recommended that you check out these tips when going to a search site for the first time.

Search Results

The last (and easiest) part of any search are the results. In general, most search engines display the results similarly. The search results, also called *hits*, are generally displayed as a URL or a Web page title followed by a description of the page or a snippet of actual text from the page.

Many search engines also put a percentage or other number next to each hit to indicate how strongly it matched your search term. At these search sites, the results are usually listed in order from strongest to weakest hits. In addition, most search engines display only between 10 and 25 hits per page, but give you the option of viewing more pages of hits if you want. Figure 10.2 shows a typical search results page with all these elements.

Figure 10.2.

This page of search results is representative of what you will find throughout the Web.

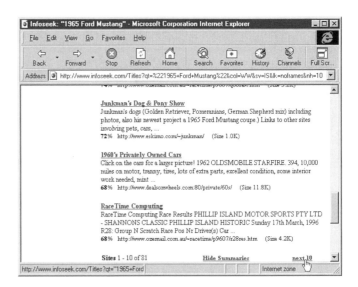

Using Internet Explorer's Built-In Search

Sooner or later, you will no doubt discover that many of your searches will be for easy-to-find information. In these cases, going directly to a high-powered search engine to use all its bells and whistles is kind of like driving a Lincoln Mark V across the street to pick up some milk.

10

Fortunately, Internet Explorer gives you quick access and a simple interface to many of these powerful search engines so you can get to information fast. Using this built-in feature is easy.

To Do: Check Out Internet Explorer's Built-In Search

1. Click the toolbar's Search button. Explorer splits your window into two halves, with one half displaying the search options and the other showing the page you were on before clicking the Search button.

2. Type a simple one- or two-word search phrase in the search text field.

3. Click the radio button next to the search engine you would like to use.

4. Finally, click the Search button to see the results (see Figure 10.3).

Figure 10.3.

The results are conveniently displayed in a separate window pane.

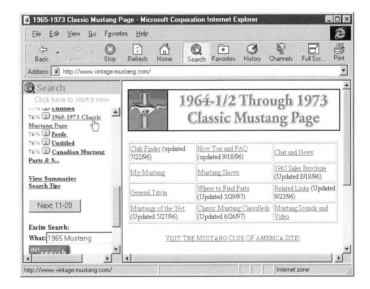

As you can see in Figure 10.3, the results are displayed in the right window pane to enable you to keep searching if you like. To view the site you located in the entire window, simply click on the toolbar's Search button to turn the search pane off. One last feature: If you click on the Search button in the toolbar again, you'll see that Internet Explorer saved your place so that you can continue searching from where you left off!

JUST A MINUTE

You'll notice that there weren't a whole lot of extras offered for your search. This type of search is pretty much a basic search option to help you get to easily located material very quickly. For more high-powered and effective searches, go on to the next section.

Infoseeking on the Web

One of the better search sites is Infoseek. Infoseek claims to be the fastest, largest, most feature-rich and accurate search engine on the Internet. Part of this is due to its Ultraseek Technology, which allows it to not only have one of the biggest Web databases on the Net, but also one of the best organized and easiest to search.

One of Infoseek's best features is its ease of use. Simply enter your search phrase, click Seek, and you're off. If you point your browser to Infoseek at http://www.infoseek.com and conduct a standard search for Star Trek, for example, Infoseek offers you over 96,000 pages to choose from (see Figure 10.4).

Figure 10.4.

Infoseek produces lots of hits quickly from its large searchable database.

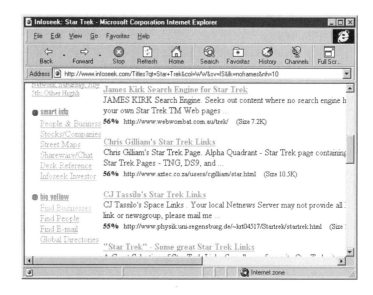

TIME SAVER

Remember when you were told to read the Help links on a search engine's home page? Well, Infoseek has a Tips link on its home page that you really should read. Quote marks, hyphens, plus signs, and capitalized words all have special meanings to Infoseek. Check it out!

In addition to the standard search, Infoseek also enables you to search for other information such as street maps and shareware—through its Smart Info service (http://www.infoseek.com/Facts)—directory browsing, and Internet Yellow Pages information (click on the Big Yellow link from Infoseek's home page). This is truly a must-see search site.

Using Yahoo! to Find Things

Yahoo!, the original Web search engine, is still going strong. Started by David Filo and Jerry Yang when they were graduate students at Stanford University, Yahoo! contains hundreds of thousands of pages in its database. Like many other sites, it allows you to search by term and browse by category.

Searching for a Term

Although many people use Yahoo! to browse by category, it is an effective search engine by itself. Try a search now.

To Do: Search with Yahoo!

1. Go to the Yahoo! search site at `http://www.yahoo.com` and click the Options link. You can also go directly to this page by pointing your browser to `http://www.yahoo.com/search.html`.

2. In the Search field, type **Star Trek**.

3. Under Select a Search Method, choose an exact phrase match.

4. Under Select a Search Area, choose Web Sites.

5. Choose to find only new listings added during the past 1 month.

6. Finally, tell Yahoo! to display 10 matches per page. Your screen should look like Figure 10.5.

7. Click the Search button.

Figure 10.5.

Yahoo! can help you find new pages in a hurry.

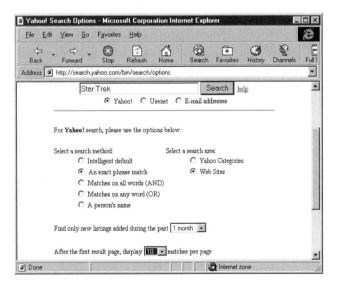

At the time this book was written, Yahoo! found 57 matches for Star Trek sites added in the last month. Just for fun, you might want to repeat the search, but this time ask Yahoo! to return all sites entered in the last 3 years.

TIME SAVER

Yahoo! has a nice feature you should know about. If you scroll down to the bottom of a Yahoo! search results page, you'll see an Other Search Engines option, followed by links to several other search engines. If you click on one of those links, Yahoo! automatically submits your latest search request to the search site you clicked on. This is an excellent way to search several sites at once.

Searching by Category

Yahoo! is probably even better known for its browsable categories. Yahoo! is divided into 14 categories, which are then divided into subcategories. Obviously, if you are going to perform a browse by category, you need to know which category your search belongs to. To compare a standard search with a category browse, you'll look for Star Trek again.

To Do: Search Yahoo! Categories

1. Start at the Yahoo! search site by returning to http://www.yahoo.com.

2. Scroll down to Yahoo!'s listing of categories.

3. Because Star Trek is likely to be found under Entertainment, click that link. You see a listing of each Entertainment-related category Yahoo! has in its database.

4. At this point, you have two choices: the Movies and Films category or the Television category. Look for information on the television series by clicking Television. (Notice that you can conduct a standard search at any point during this process).

5. Scroll down until you see the Shows link and click it.

6. Star Trek was a science fiction show, so click the Science Fiction/Fantasy/Horror link.

7. Scroll down until you see a Star Trek link. Click it to see all the listings under Star Trek (see Figure 10.6).

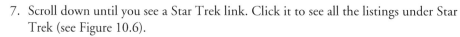

JUST A MINUTE

You can search Yahoo! categories also by simply clicking Yahoo Categories under Select a search area (on the standard search page). With this method, however, you'll get categories that may not contain information you want (for instance, a category on Star Trek action figures).

10

Figure 10.6.

The Yahoo! Star Trek category has lots of links.

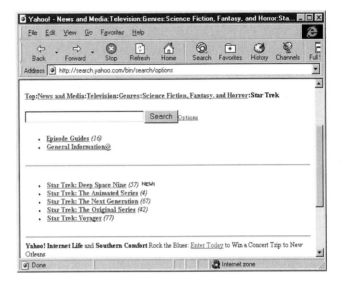

Although it may appear that a category search requires more steps to get somewhere than a standard search, it really doesn't. After you have found Star Trek, you now have a listing of only those pages you want to see. If you remember, with a standard search you have to view hits a few at a time and wade through dozens of sites before possibly finding the one you want.

Another major advantage in using Yahoo's category search database is that while you are searching for your subject, you can do some surfing at the same time. For instance, in looking for Star Trek, you might notice that there are also some Dr. Who Web pages.

TIME SAVER

When searching for a complicated category, such as *computer training manuals*, which category would you start with? Generally, try using the biggest category first. In this instance, more information probably exists on computers than on training (Education) or manuals (Reference). It would be best to try searching under the Computer category first.

The Best of the Rest

You can choose from dozens of search engines. Several of these, which you look at briefly in this section, offer unique advantages. Although all search engines try to be comprehensive, you'll almost always find sites with one index that you wouldn't find with another. So if you search one index and don't find quite what you're looking for, try another—and another.

Although some people view the multiple "competing" indexes of the Internet as a waste of resources, experienced searchers are grateful for the multiple coverage. As the Web continues to grow exponentially, it seems ever more unlikely that any one procedure or program would be able to index it all.

Deja News

Deja News is the official Usenet newsgroups search site. You can search newsgroups with other search engines such as Infoseek, but for a quick, comprehensive search of Usenet, Deja News is excellent. You'll realize the true usefulness of this site after reading Hour 16.

Deja News offers a Quick Search when you're looking for articles on a particular topic. You can also conduct a Power Search, which helps you further refine your search to make it more effective. You can even enter a topic you're interested in, and Deja News will provide a list of related newsgroups you might want to go to!

Continuing with the Star Trek theme, do a search for Spock on Deja News.

To Do: Deja News Search for Spock

1. Point your browser to Deja News at `http://www.dejanews.com`.
2. In the Quick Search field, type **Spock**.
3. Click the Search button. You see results similar to those pictured in Figure 10.7.

Figure 10.7.

That pointy-eared Vulcan is still alive and well on Usenet.

10

Inktomi's Hot Bot

Another search site that bears looking at is Inktomi's Hot Bot site, at `http://www.hotbot.com`. Like Infoseek, they have an impressive index to search from.

They have a unique search interface as well. A click to their Expert search page reveals a powerful and flexible search engine. With Hot Bot, you can restrict your search by Time, Location, and Domain. You can even search for a particular type of media.

Search Site Grab Bag

It's impossible to cover all search engines available on the Internet. As of this writing, over 250 search sites are available. Table 10.1 shows a listing of some of the better search engines not covered in this hour.

Table 10.1. Other search sites.

Search Site	URL
Excite	`http://www.excite.com/`
AltaVista	`http://www.altavista.digital.com/`
Magellan	`http://www.mckinley.com/`
Lycos	`http://www.lycos.com/`
Open Text	`http://www.opentext.com/`
WebCrawler	`http://www.webcrawler.com/`

Finally, take a look at Table 10.2 for a listing of some other unique search sites.

Table 10.2. Unique search sites.

Search Site	Purpose	URL
shareware.com	Searches for shareware	`http://www.shareware.com/`
Four11	Searches for e-mail addresses	`http://www.four11.com/`
MetaCrawler	Searches by geographic region	`http://metacrawler.cs.washington.edu/`

Summary

In this hour, you learned a lot about how to search on the Web. In addition to seeing examples of excellent search sites such as Infoseek, Yahoo!, Deja News, Hot Bot, and Internet Explorer's own search interface, you also learned a great deal about *how* to search.

You were told how to use Boolean and other operators to help you in your search. You discovered how to interpret search results and learned how to conduct a standard search as well as how to browse a category directory.

Q&A

Q I'm always being told that thousands of documents match my search query. How many of them do I really have to look at to find what I want?

A Certainly not thousands. If you have defined your search effectively, you can usually find what you're looking for in the first 20 to 30 hits. Rarely will a useful hit show up after the 50th hit or so.

Q A lot of search sites are out there. Are there two or three that you would recommend I stick with?

A This is one of those questions that will get 10 different answers from 10 different people. I primarily use Excite and Infoseek and almost always find what I'm looking for. They are fast, I don't have to wait a long time for results, and the hits are relevant. My advice is to try one of four or five different sites for a few days each, and then choose one or two that you are most comfortable with.

Quiz

Take the following quiz to see how much you've learned.

Questions

1. Name one advantage and one disadvantage of using Internet Explorer's built-in search capability.

2. Web-based search sites are effective for searching much more than just the World Wide Web.

    a. True

    b. False

3. If you were searching for information on the Detroit Pistons basketball team, which search would probably be the most effective?

    a. "Detroit Pistons"

    b. basketball

    c. detroit pistons

10

Answers

1. One advantage is that it is easily accessible and fast. One disadvantage is that it is not as feature-rich as the full search engines.

2. a. True. You can search newsgroups, look for people, and much more.

3. a. "Detroit Pistons"

Activity

Here's a way to find the best search site for you. Choose something you'd like to look for. For the best results, don't choose a one-word category such as *cars* but something more specific such as *surfboard sales*. From all the search sites in this hour, choose five and conduct an identical search on each one. Make note of how many hits each site produced, how relevant those hits were, and how comfortable you were using them.

10

Hour 11

Extending Your Browser Power

Out of the box, Internet Explorer 4 does plenty, but not absolutely everything that can be—or will be—accomplished. You see, clever people are forever inventing new things to do on the Web: new kinds of multimedia, new games, new kinds of interactivity. Often when they do this, they create something no browser supports.

Rather than force everybody to go out and get a new browser every month, developers have designed the better browsers (such as Internet Explorer 4) to be *extensible.* That means new capabilities can be programmed into the browser, or added to it, without a wholesale upgrade of the browser itself.

In this hour, you discover the ways you can soup up Internet Explorer to endow it with new capabilities. You discover also the ways some sites soup up Internet Explorer for you.

At the end of the hour, you'll be able to answer the following questions:

☐ How do I upgrade my copy of Internet Explorer with the latest components and files?

☐ What are *plug-ins* and *scripts*, and how do I use them?

☐ How can I give Internet Explorer the power to play or display a new file type simply by giving Windows that power?

New Internet Explorer Components

The most important way Internet Explorer can be upgraded is by Microsoft itself. You already know that Internet Explorer is surrounded by a family of component programs, such as Outlook Express and NetMeeting, that are part of Internet Explorer but also separate applications.

Over time, even when no new version of the Internet Explorer browser has debuted, Microsoft will probably upgrade one or more of its components, and may even add new components. You can ensure that your copy of Internet Explorer is fully equipped by regularly checking for and installing upgraded and new components.

The best way to learn about new components is to check out the Internet Explorer Web site, where you'll find announcements of any new Internet Explorer-related software (see Figure 11.1). When new or upgraded components are available, their descriptions are always accompanied by a link for downloading the new software and instructions for installing it.

Figure 11.1.

Visit Internet Explorer's home page regularly to check for new or updated Internet Explorer components.

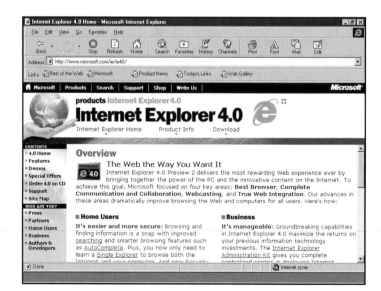

11

Another way to keep Internet Explorer up-to-date is to use Product Updates. Internet Explorer's Product Updates function contacts Microsoft on the Web, checks for any new or upgraded components or other enhancements and fixes to Internet Explorer, and offers you a list from which you may choose to install any of the upgrades or new components. This function is so smart that it automatically downloads only files that are not already on your PC, so you don't have to redownload all 20+ MB of Internet Explorer just to get the upgrades.

JUST A MINUTE

The Product Updates function not only gets you any new or updated files, but also can be used to get components you did not originally install. For example, if you chose Standard installation (instead of Full) when you first installed Internet Explorer 4, you can use Product Updates to get components left out of the Standard installation, such as Chat and NetMeeting.

To Do: Try Out Product Updates

1. Begin with all programs closed, including Internet Explorer. (You can be online or offline.)

2. Open Internet Explorer, and choose Help | Product Updates from the menu bar.

   Internet Explorer connects to the Internet (if necessary) and opens the Components Download page at Microsoft (see Figure 11.2). A dialog appears, asking for your permission to compare the Internet Explorer 4 files on your PC with the most up-to-date list at Microsoft, to determine what you have and don't have.

3. Click Yes.

   After a few moments, a list of all Internet Explorer files and components appears (see Figure 11.2). In the Status column at the far right, the list tells whether each item is already installed on your PC or due for an upgrade.

4. To automatically download and install all files and components that are not already installed on your PC, click the Upgrade All link that appears in the upper-right corner of the page. To selectively download and install components, click the check box next to each item you want to install, and then click the NEXT button.

5. Follow the prompts. Completing the installation is very much like installing Internet Explorer 4 the first time (see Hour 3).

Figure 11.2.

*Use Product
Updates to check
for and install any
upgrades, enhance-
ments, or new
components for
Internet Explorer.*

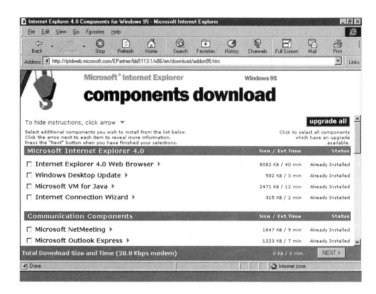

Understanding Plug-Ins, ActiveX, and JavaScript

As part of being extensible, Internet Explorer can, in effect, be reprogrammed through the Web to acquire new capabilities. This happens chiefly through three types of program files:

☐ Plug-ins: Invented by Netscape for its Navigator browser (but also fully supported by Internet Explorer), plug-ins allow third-party applications to be transparently melded with Internet Explorer. After a plug-in has enhanced Internet Explorer, its new capabilities are fully integrated. New activities take place in the browser window, and new menu items—if any are necessary—appear in Internet Explorer's menus.

☐ Scripts (Java, JavaScript): Internet Explorer supports programs, called *scripts,* written in the Java and JavaScript languages (and sometimes other languages, such as one called VBScript), which are used increasingly to enable advanced multimedia, forms, and other cool stuff on leading-edge Web pages.

☐ ActiveX files: An ActiveX-enabled file includes program code that teaches Internet Explorer how to display it. For example, Internet Explorer doesn't know how to display a Microsoft Word file all by itself. But in recent versions of Word, Microsoft has designed the Word file format as an ActiveX-enabled file type. When you open a Word file in Internet Explorer, the ActiveX code built into the file teaches Internet Explorer how to display the file. ActiveX gives programmers the ability to put almost any type of file on the Web and have Internet Explorer users use that file without special plug-ins or helper applications.

11

JUST A MINUTE

> Often, before a script or a plug-in is installed on your PC by a Web site, a dialog appears giving you the chance to prevent the installation, in case you don't want the code or are concerned that it might have ill effects on your PC. To some extent, you can control when and how these dialogs appear. You can even prevent sites from sending code at all, or allow sites to send all the code they want without prompting you. For more information, see Hour 8.

In general, you don't have to do anything special to take advantage of scripts or ActiveX; they're delivered to Internet Explorer automatically by Web sites. Although plug-ins are occasionally delivered automatically, more often than not you must deliberately download and install a particular plug-in to enjoy whatever it does.

Finding Plug-Ins

Usually, when you come across a Web site or a file that requires a particular plug-in, it's accompanied by a link for downloading the plug-in. Occasionally, though, you may have to go plug-in hunting.

Fortunately, two excellent indexes are devoted to plug-ins. The first is the Plug-In Plaza at `http://browserwatch.internet.com/plug-in.html`. This page has an extensive list of all available plug-ins, as well as the companies creating the plug-ins.

On the page's top level, you can view the plug-ins by type (multimedia, graphics, sounds, and so on) or by platform (Windows, Macintosh, UNIX, and OS/2). See Figure 11.3. Just select the listing type you want and scroll through the list and see what's available. You can download the plug-in directly from this page or visit the developer and read the latest news about the plug-in.

Another excellent plug-in resource is the Plug-in Gallery & Demo Links page at `http://www2.gol.com/users/oyamada/`. Here, you can view the list of plug-ins for certain types of applications, such as video players and image viewers. Or, if you're looking for a particular plug-in, just click on the list for that type, and select the name of the plug-in you're looking for (see Figure 11.4).

The list of plug-ins available from the Plug-in Gallery isn't nearly as complete as that in the Plug-In Plaza. You'll find the Plug-in Gallery useful, however, because it has tons of links to demo pages, pages that rely on one or more particular plug-ins. Sometimes, it's difficult to know whether you've successfully installed the plug-in. Having a link to a site where you can test the plug-in is a great convenience.

11

Figure 11.3.

The Plug-In Plaza offers lists of plug-ins of a particular type or for a particular platform.

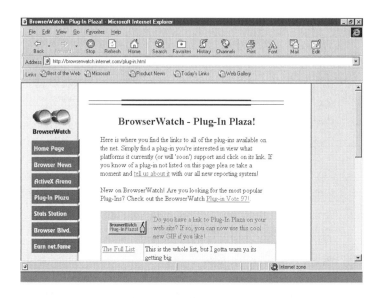

Figure 11.4.

The Plug-in Gallery & Demo Links page offers easy-to-manage lists of plug-ins for specific types of data.

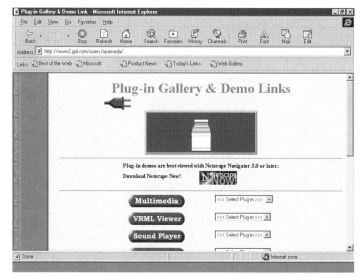

Installing and Using Plug-Ins

Because plug-ins can come from any software publisher, no single method exists for installing them. Typically, though, you have to run some sort of installation program, and then specify the directory in which your Web browser is installed. Some sophisticated plug-ins can even be installed into multiple Web browsers, so that you have access to the tool no matter which browser you use.

11

So when you come across a link to a plug-in, carefully read any instructions you see, click the link, and follow any prompts that appear. You'll do fine.

Although there's no standard method of installing plug-ins, using them is pretty much the same. Because they work with the browser, you never really see the plug-in. Typically, you access the plug-in only when you access a file type that Internet Explorer doesn't recognize. Then, the plug-in that can handle that file type kicks into action. Even then, the impact on Internet Explorer's user interface is minimal. Typically, the plug-in displays a toolbar with a small set of icons to let you work with the selected file.

Important Plug-Ins to Have

In general, you should begin exploring with Internet Explorer as-is and install plug-ins only as they become necessary. However, you should consider getting two plug-ins right away because they're so broadly supported on the Web.

The first is the RealAudio player, which you'll find at `http://www.realaudio.com` (see Figure 11.5), among other places. The RealAudio player enables Internet Explorer to play streaming audio feeds, from radio broadcasts to news updates to live music. The RealAudio home page also provides links to fun places where you can try out RealAudio.

New Term **Streaming audio and video:** This term refers to audio and video that begins to play on your PC before it has been completely downloaded. The main use of streaming audio and video is to present live Web broadcasts of audio or video content, or to reduce your wait when playing a very large audio or video file.

Figure 11.5.

Download RealAudio to play streaming audio through Internet Explorer.

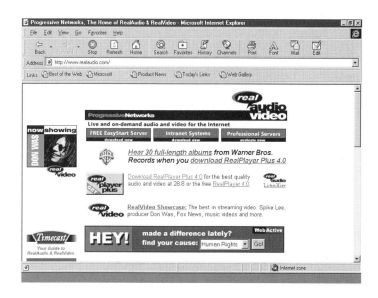

The other enhancement you'll soon need is ShockWave, from MacroMedia, at `http://www.macromedia.com`. A set of plug-ins that install and work together, ShockWave enables Internet Explorer to play what are called "shocked sites," pages featuring highly interactive multimedia. The MacroMedia site also features fun links to cool shocked sites.

Figure 11.6.

Download ShockWave to enjoy "shocked" Web sites.

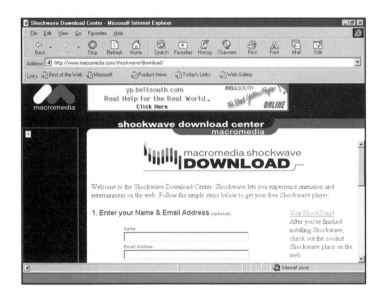

Helper Applications

Unlike plug-ins, helper applications do not work in Internet Explorer's window. Rather, helper applications are simply any program that has been configured to handle a particular type of file or program that Internet Explorer can't handle itself. For example, Outlook Express is a helper application for e-mail files. Click an e-mail link online, and Outlook Express opens automatically.

Internet Explorer doesn't need to be configured to use helper applications; it simply makes use of the Windows file types registry. If Windows has a program registered to automatically handle a given file type, that's the file Internet Explorer opens, when necessary.

In particular, the Windows file-types registry keeps tally of the program to use for each MIME file type. MIME (*multipurpose Internet mail extensions*) is a standard that determines the file types for various objects that travel through the Internet, particularly such things as file attachments on e-mail messages. Because the file types registry has entries in it for each common MIME file type, Internet Explorer always knows what to do with any file you receive that falls under the MIME specification.

11

To Do: Examine Your File-Types Registry

1. Open any folder and choose View | Options | File Types to open the File types tab. (See Figure 11.7.)

2. Scroll through the list and see which applications have been configured.

3. To see which extensions are associated with a particular application, just highlight the application.

Figure 11.7.

From any folder, choose View | Options | File Types to configure which helper applications work on which files.

Summary

Internet Explorer is equipped to do so much, you may never come across a situation in which it needs enhancement. But that goes against history. No matter how fast developers enhance their browsers, the new file types and programs stay one step ahead. Knowing how to deal with scripts, plug-ins, and helper applications ensures that you don't get left behind when something new and wonderful hits the Web.

Q&A

Q **You say I can prevent script code from reaching my PC if I think the code will hurt anything. How could code hurt anything?**

A Realistically speaking, nothing terrible is likely to happen to your PC or Internet Explorer if it picks up some script code that's badly written. The worst thing that's likely to happen is that the code fails to do whatever it was supposed to do, while you just browse ahead and forget about it.

Still to be considered, though, are broad ethical questions having to do with privacy and security. Should a developer have the power to reprogram something on your PC? Do you feel comfortable with that? Perhaps more importantly, any program code that reaches your PC might carry a virus. The risk is small, however, and you're just as likely to pick up a virus from a file or a program you download deliberately as from a script.

Q Should I go out and get as many plug-ins as I can find, so I'm ready for anything?

A Nah. For the most part, plug-ins are rarely necessary. Smart Web developers want to reach as many people as possible, and they know that forcing people to get a plug-in may scare some folks off (and eliminate those with browsers that don't support plug-ins). When you come across something you really want to see or do, and it requires a plug-in, make your move. Otherwise, don't worry about it.

Quiz

Take the following quiz to see how much you've learned.

Questions

1. Which of the following is a type of program code that a Web site might send to your PC?
     a. PC*jr* BASIC
     b. JavaScript
     c. DOS
     d. All of the above

2. The Windows file-types registry
     a. Lists the file types Windows wants most for wedding presents
     b. Lists all the files installed on your PC
     c. Assigns a program to automatically handle each of many different file types
     d. Assigns Internet Explorer to handle all files in Windows

3. Plug-ins are installed automatically, whenever necessary.
     a. True
     b. False

4. To get the latest Internet Explorer files and components
   a. Write a letter to Microsoft, and use the code XB1CCDhhT%$*&^-XX1
   b. Send $35 to Macmillan Publishing (make checks payable to *Maxine London*)
   c. Do nothing: Internet Explorer is self-nurturing, and will develop naturally
   d. Choose Start | Programs | Internet Explorer | Product Updates

Answers

1. b. Of the choices, only JavaScript is a likely contender. Of course, anything's possible.

2. c. The file-types registry tells Windows (and Internet Explorer) which program to open to handle each type of file.

3. b. False. Often, you must deliberately install a plug-in.

4. d. Only d accomplishes the job. Choice b is optional and completely ineffective, but recommended nonetheless.

Activity

Even if you think you have all the latest Internet Explorer files and components, try the Product Updates routine described in this hour. If you're right, it will take only a minute to find out and you can tell Maxine, "I told you so." If you're wrong, you can quickly pick up the latest and greatest before moving ahead.

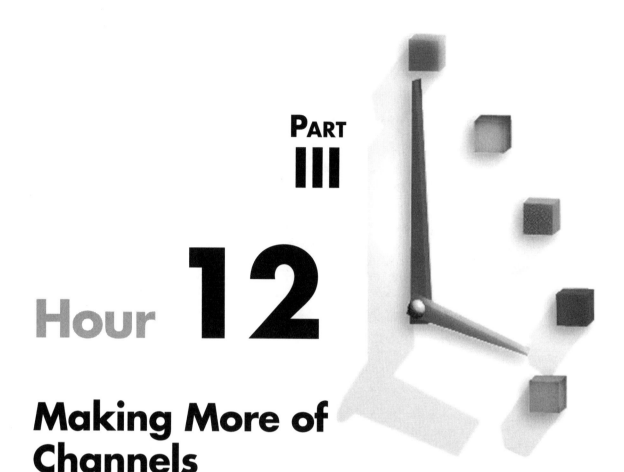

Hour 12

Making More of Channels

Way back in Hour 7, Maxine introduced you to channels. But at that point in the tutorial, you hadn't even browsed the Web yet. So a lot of the more advanced aspects of channel surfing (hee hee!) had to wait until you gained some more experience.

Now you're a Net pro, and it's time to learn to do much more with channels. In this hour, you learn how to perform a number of advanced channel tasks and use a near-cousin to channels: Web page subscriptions.

At the end of the hour, you'll be able to answer the following questions:

☐ How can I use my subscribed channels as screen savers?

☐ What are desktop items, and how do I subscribe to them?

☐ How can I change the size, position and organization of the channel bar?

☐ How can I subscribe to a regular Web page as if it were a channel?

☐ How can I remove subscriptions to channels, desktop items, and Web pages?

Using Channels as Screen Savers

After you've subscribed to a few channels, you can configure Windows to use one or more channels as screen savers, which display automatically when your PC has been inactive for a time. You can configure a single channel to appear as a screen saver, or you can configure multiple channels to cycle as screen savers, switching from one to the other every so often.

"Maxine, why would I want channels for screen savers?" you ask. "I'm not sure I want channels at all. I'm not sure I want a screen saver. All I want is a decent wage for a full day's work." Fair enough. But here's the deal: Using channels as screen savers enables you to treat your PC like C-SPAN or CNN while you're not working at it. When you haven't touched the mouse or the keyboard for a while, the screen saver automatically takes over your display.

If you use one or more channels, information you want to keep posted about (news, stock prices, and so on) appears on your display, and that information is updated regularly (according to the scheduling options you chose when subscribing; see Hour 7). In effect, the screen saver option lets you treat any channel like a desktop item, keeping it on your screen to update you at any time.

You cannot use desktop items as channel screen savers. They're always on the desktop anyway, so what would be the point?

To Do: Use Channels as Screen Savers

1. Subscribe to the channel(s) you want to use as screen saver(s).
2. Right-click the desktop and choose Properties from the context menu. This opens the Windows Display Properties dialog.
3. Choose the Screen Saver tab (see Figure 12.1).
4. Drop down the list under Screen Saver, and select Channel Screen Saver.
5. Click the Settings button. The General tab of the Screen Saver Properties dialog opens (see Figure 12.2).

JUST A MINUTE

Some channels are configured by their authors so that they cannot be used as screen savers. Those channels will not appear in the list of channels on the Screen Saver Settings dialog.

Figure 12.1.

Begin setting up channel screen savers on the Screen Saver tab of the Display Properties dialog.

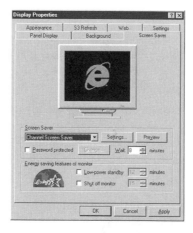

Figure 12.2.

The Screen Saver Properties dialog lists all the subscribed channels you may use as screen savers.

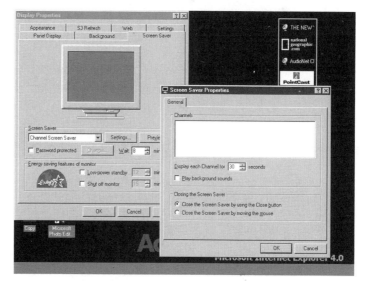

6. In the Screen Saver Properties dialog, check the check box next to the channel(s) you want to use as screen savers.

7. If you select multiple channels, select the number of seconds to display each channel (before switching to the next) in the Display Each Channel box.

8. If you want to enable the playing of any background sounds in the channel, check the check box next to Play Background Sounds. (Some folks like to keep this box unchecked, so their channels don't make noises at them all the time.)

9. Choose one of the two options under Closing the Screen Saver:

    The top option, Close the Screen Saver by using the Close Button, enables you to use your mouse to do stuff in the channel without shutting off the screen saver. When you do want to close the screen saver, you click a close button that always appears on it.

    The bottom option, Close the Screen Saver by moving the mouse, closes the screen saver if you move the mouse. However, you can still do clicking stuff in the channel by pressing and holding the Alt key while moving the mouse, which keeps the screen saver active.

TIME SAVER

> Regardless of your choice in the Closing the Screen Saver section of the Screen Saver Properties dialog, pressing any key (besides Alt) always closes the screen saver.

10. Close the Screen Saver Properties dialog by clicking OK.

11. Back on the Screen Saver tab, choose settings for the screen saver, such as the number of minutes to wait before the channel appears.

 12. Click OK to close the Display Properties dialog.

Subscribing to Desktop Items

In many ways, subscribing to a desktop item is a lot like subscribing to a regular channel. As more and more desktop items become available, you'll be more likely to come across them during your Web travels. While viewing a page that describes a desktop item, you'll see a link or a button labeled "Add to My Desktop." Clicking that link or button installs the desktop item.

Because items are new, the best place to find them today is Microsoft's Active Desktop Gallery (see Figure 12.3), where a number of fun items are offered for your enjoyment and experimentation. You can reach the Active Desktop Gallery by browsing to `www.microsoft.com/ie/ie40/gallery/`.

You can open the Gallery also by clicking the New button on the Web tab of the Display Properties dialog, as described next.

12

Figure 12.3.

Go to the Active Desktop Gallery to pick up new items.

To Do: Add a Desktop Item

JUST A MINUTE

In case you don't like the item you add, don't worry; later in this hour, you learn how to delete items from your desktop or disable them temporarily.

1. Right-click the desktop and choose Properties from the context menu. This opens the Windows Display Properties dialog.
2. Click the Web tab (see Figure 12-4). The Web tab lists all the items on your desktop. Observe that the channel bar is listed; it's your only item, before you add others.

Figure 12.4.

Use the Web tab of the Display Properties dialog to manage desktop items.

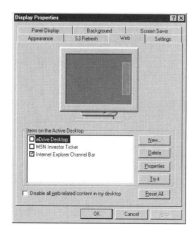

12

3. Click the New button. A dialog opens, informing you that you're about to go to the Active Desktop Gallery.

4. Click Yes. Internet Explorer 4 opens and connects to the Internet (if necessary), and then opens the Active Desktop Gallery. The Gallery lists links leading to descriptions of available items.

5. One by one, click each link to learn more about each item. After reading about each item, click the Back button to return to the main list.

6. Decide which item you'd like to try, and open its description. In the description, you'll see a button labeled Add to My Desktop.

7. Click the Add to My Desktop button. The Channel Subscription wizard opens, just as it does when you subscribe to a regular channel (see Hour 7).

8. Complete the wizard as you would for a regular channel. Note that the wizard's update scheduling options are the same as for a regular channel, but that you are not given the option to install the item as a channel screen saver.

9. When you finish subscribing, close Internet Explorer 4. The item may not appear on your desktop immediately; if it doesn't, right-click the desktop and choose Refresh to make it appear.

You can drag a desktop item to any convenient position on your screen.

TIME SAVER

Customizing the Channel Bar

If you're an experienced Windows user, you've probably figured out by now how to move, resize, and otherwise fiddle with your channel bar. But just in case you haven't figured it all out yet, here are some ways to make the channel bar more useful and attractive.

Moving the Channel Bar

To move the channel bar anywhere on your desktop, point to the very top border of the channel bar and wait a second. The border thickens, especially at the top, where close and minimize buttons also appear (see Figure 12.5). Click and hold on that top area of the channel bar border, drag the channel bar where you want it, and release.

Note that the borders don't go back to their original thickness for a few seconds after you release the channel bar in its new position.

Figure 12.5.

To move the channel bar, point to its top border, click, and drag.

Sizing the Channel Bar

You can adjust the size of the channel bar just as you would adjust a window's size.

When you have too many buttons to fit on the channel bar at its current size, scroll arrows appear so you can scroll buttons into view. If you don't like scrolling, you can lengthen the channel bar so that all the buttons appear at once. Or if you want a shorter bar, you can shorten it and use the scroll arrows.

You size the channel bar by dragging its borders (except the top border, which is for moving the channel bar). To make the channel bar taller or shorter, you drag the bottom border up or down. To make it wider or narrower, drag either side border in or out.

To drag a border, point to it carefully, so that the pointer becomes a two-headed arrow. Click and hold, and drag to size the channel bar.

Changing the Order of Buttons

As you subscribe to new channels, each new button is added to the bottom of the channel bar. On the channel bar, the older a channel is, the higher its position.

But you can change the order of the buttons in the channel bar in any way you like. To change any button's position in the order, click and hold on the button, drag to the position where you want to move the button, and release.

Deleting Microsoft's Buttons

When you unsubscribe to a channel, as you learn to do later in this hour, the channel's button is removed automatically from your channel bar. However, the buttons Microsoft put on your channel bar to get you started aren't real subscriptions (unless you've deliberately subscribed to them), so they can't be removed by unsubscribing.

12

Sometimes, when you delete a channel, its button doesn't disappear from the channel bar. If that happens, use the following procedure to remove it.

If and when you decide you no longer need Microsoft's buttons, you can delete them from the channel bar easily. Right-click the button you want to delete to display its context menu (see Figure 12.6), and then choose Delete from the menu. The button goes to the Recycle Bin.

Figure 12.6.

To delete a button, right-click it and choose Delete.

Subscribing to Web Pages

A channel is a Web page, but not every Web page is a channel. A regular Web page lacks the smart technology that lets a channel automatically update its content on your PC.

Still, Microsoft wants you to be able to use any Web page like a channel. To make this happen, it's built a Web crawler into Internet Explorer 4. When you've subscribed to a Web page, Internet Explorer regularly checks that page for new information, and downloads new content when necessary. This enables you to always know when a favorite page changes, and it also gets all the new content onto your hard disk so you can review it offline, anytime.

That sounds like channels, and it is, only not as smart. For example, the Web crawler can't distinguish minor changes that constitute no real change from real changes, whereas a channel is smart enough not to bother you with insignificant changes. Also, when the main Web page you subscribe to does not change, but an important subpage (another page linked to the main page) changes, you may not get an update. Channels are smart enough to update you when anything relevant changes.

Following are a few other important differences between subscribing to a Web page and subscribing to a channel:

☐ Subscribed Web pages do not show up on the channel bar or the Channel list in the Explorer bar. You open a subscribed Web page from within Internet Explorer by choosing Favorites | Manage Subscriptions, and then choosing the page from the Subscriptions list (shown later in Figure 12.7).

☐ Subscribed Web pages cannot be used as channel screen savers.

☐ Subscribed Web pages are always displayed in the regular Internet Explorer browser window, never in full-screen view (unless you specifically choose full-screen view by clicking the Full Screen button).

Updating subscribed Web pages manually, however, is the same as updating channels (see Hour 7). In fact, when you update from within Internet Explorer (Favorites | Update All Subscriptions) or from the desktop (right-click and choose Active Desktop | Update Now), you update all your channels, desktop items, and subscribed Web pages in a single operation.

To Do: Subscribe to a Web Page

1. In Internet Explorer 4, browse online to the page you want to subscribe to. Macmillan's Web site, for example, is www.mcp.com.

2. From the menu bar, choose Favorites | Add to Favorites. The Add to Favorites dialog opens.

3. In the dialog, choose a subscription option as you would for a channel.

4. Click OK.

JUST A MINUTE

You delete a Web page subscription exactly as you do a channel subscription. See the next section.

To Do: View a Web Page You've Subscribed To

1. In Internet Explorer 4, choose Favorites | Manage Subscriptions. The Subscriptions list appears, as shown later in Figure 12.7. The list shows all channels and Web pages to which you've subscribed.

2. In the list, click the page you want to view.

12

Removing Channels and Subscriptions

Adding channels, items, and subscribed Web pages is all well and good, but eventually you'll decide it's time to separate the wheat from the chaff and blow away a few things. Here's how.

TIME SAVER

> If you ever delete a channel, a Web page subscription, or a desktop item, and decide later that you want it back, simply subscribe again as you did the first time. Channels don't hold grudges.

Unsubscribing to a Channel or Web Page Subscription

To unsubscribe to a channel or Web page subscription, you use the Subscriptions list.

Unsubscribe to a Channel or a Web Page

1. Open Internet Explorer 4 (online or off).
2. Choose Favorites | Manage Subscriptions. The Subscriptions list appears (see Figure 12.7). Observe that the subscribed Web pages in the list are preceded by little globe icons, whereas the subscribed channels are preceded by little satellite channel icons.

Figure 12.7.

Use the Subscriptions list to open subscribed Web pages and to delete Web page and channel subscriptions.

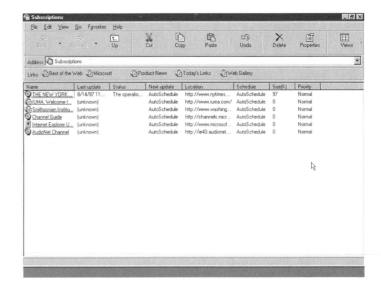

3. To delete a subscription, click it once in the list to highlight it, and then press the Del key. A warning appears, cautioning you that you're about to delete the channel or Web page subscription permanently. (It's a paranoid warning. You can always resubscribe later.)

4. Click Yes to clear the dialog and delete the selected channel or Web page subscription.

After you delete:

☐ Any deleted Web page subscriptions disappear from their spot in the Favorites menu, and Internet Explorer no longer checks them for new content.

☐ Any deleted channels disappear from the channel bar and the Channels list in the Explorer bar.

JUST A MINUTE

Sometimes channel buttons don't disappear immediately after a channel has been deleted. But they should disappear for sure the next time you restart Windows. If not, remove them, following the procedure described earlier under "Deleting Microsoft's Buttons."

Removing a Desktop Item

Desktop items don't show up on the Subscriptions list, so you can't kill 'em from there. Instead, you can delete them from the Web tab of the Display Properties dialog.

Note that you don't have to actually delete a desktop item to get it off your desktop. You can simply disable it, which clears it from your desktop and prevents further updates. If you want to restore it later, you can reenable it and save the hassle of resubscribing.

To Do: Remove a Desktop Item

1. Right-click the desktop and choose Properties from the context menu. The Windows Display Properties dialog opens.

2. Choose the Web tab (see Figure 12.4, shown earlier). The Web tab lists all items on your desktop.

3. Click the item to select it.

4. Disable or delete the item:

   To disable it, click its check box to remove the check mark. If and when you want to restore the item, simply return to the Web tab and check the check box.

   To delete it, click the Delete button.

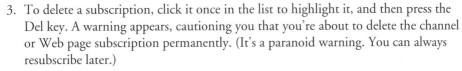
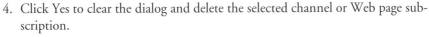

12

JUST A MINUTE

The item may not disappear from your desktop immediately; if it doesn't, right-click the desktop and choose Refresh.

Summary

As you can see, there's a lot more to channels than the simple sign-up-and-wait steps you learned in Hour 7. You can use them as screen savers and use desktop items to keep your favorite content up front and frequently updated. You can also subscribe to Web pages, to get some of the same benefits you get from true channels.

Q&A

Q How come a Web page subscription is not as smart as a channel?

A How come my sister Shirley is so dumb she let that orthopedic surgeon get away and married the actor with the bad teeth? Who knows about these things?

Actually, channels are written using a new language, called CDF (channel definition file), which uses server push technology. In effect, server push enables the channel itself to determine what's new and what's not, and to deliver that automatically upon request from Internet Explorer 4. That way, the content provider can tell Internet Explorer exactly what's new; Internet Explorer does not have to figure that out for itself.

A Web page subscription relies on a different technology, client pull, in which Internet Explorer must go out and search the Web site and determine what's new and what's not. Client pull works, but Internet Explorer simply can't guess what's new as accurately as a content provider can tell it what's new, through channel technology.

Q Ever since I started subscribing to channels and Web pages, browsing the rest of the Web has become deadly slow. What's wrong?

A Channel technology offers the greatest benefit to folks who have full-time, dedicated Internet connections. Channels can be updated on and off throughout the day, often when the user isn't doing anything else on the Net.

But for those who browse through a dial-up connection that's only open for a short time each day, channels present something of a problem. Each time you go online, Internet Explorer has a ton of catching up to do. It has to send its Web crawler out to check for new content on your subscribed Web pages. If the scheduled time for channel updates has passed, Internet Explorer has to check for new channel content as well as download that content if you use the download content option.

12

All this activity drains resources from your PC and your Internet connection that would otherwise be dedicated to your browsing activities. The problem gets worse when you add more subscriptions, when you schedule them to be updated often, when those subscriptions tend to have lots of new content often, and when you're not online very often. Also, Internet Explorer must work harder with Web page subscriptions than with channels, so Web page subscriptions affect your system more heavily, in general.

There's not much you can do about it, except to restrain yourself. Don't subscribe to more than you need to, and keep scheduled updates to a reasonable minimum. You might also want to connect to the Internet each day for five minutes or so before actually doing any browsing, to give Internet Explorer a chance to get its daily updating and downloading out of the way.

Quiz

Take the following quiz to see how much you've learned.

Questions

1. Which of the following can be used as a screen saver?
    a. One or more channels
    b. One or more subscribed Web pages
    c. One or more desktop items
    d. All of the above

2. From the Subscriptions list, you can delete
    a. Desktop items
    b. Channel and Web page subscriptions
    c. Microsoft's sample channel bar buttons
    d. *The New Yorker* and *Reader's Digest*

3. If a desktop item does not appear immediately after you subscribe to it, make it appear by
    a. Subscribing again
    b. Restarting Windows
    c. Banging your PC hard with a wooden mallet
    d. Right-clicking the desktop and choosing Refresh

12

4. Which is the smartest?

    a. A channel

    b. A Web page subscription

    c. Larry King

    d. Bullwinkle

Answers

1. a. You can't use Web page subscriptions or desktop items in the channel screen saver.

2. b. Only your channel and Web page subscriptions appear on the list.

3. d. Refresh updates the desktop.

4. Among Internet technologies, a. Choices c and d are a matter of opinion.

Activity

Look over the Favorites list you've accumulated up to this point. Do you visit any pages in the list daily? Several times a day? Do you visit some pages frequently, but find they don't often have new content? If you subscribe to these pages, you'll get the news automatically, and you won't waste time browsing to them when there's nothing new to see. Give it a try.

PART
IV

Using Outlook Express for E-Mail and News

Hour

Hour 13

Getting Started with E-Mail

Sending and receiving e-mail using Outlook Express is much the same as sending it the old fashioned way. You create something to e-mail and then e-mail it, or you go to your e-mailbox to get e-mail you have received.

With Outlook Express, your e-mail is delivered a lot faster than regular mail, and you can go to your e-mailbox without leaving your computer. All you miss is the taste of the stamp and envelope flap, and of course the paper cuts on your fingers and tongue from licking and sealing the envelope.

At the end of the hour, you'll be able to answer the following questions:

☐ How do I move among Outlook Express's various folders to perform different messaging activities?

☐ How do I display a message so I can read it?

☐ How do I compose and send an e-mail message?

☐ How do I receive messages others have sent to me?

☐ How can I reply to a message I've received, or forward that message to someone else?

☐ When someone sends me a message with a file attached to it, how do I open and use that file?

JUST A MINUTE

You use Outlook Express not only for exchanging e-mail messages but also for reading messages on Internet newsgroups and contributing to those newsgroups. In this hour and in Hour 14, you learn about using Outlook Express for e-mail. In Hour 15, you learn about using it for newsgroups.

Figure 13.1.

Outlook Express, your all-purpose Internet Explorer messaging partner.

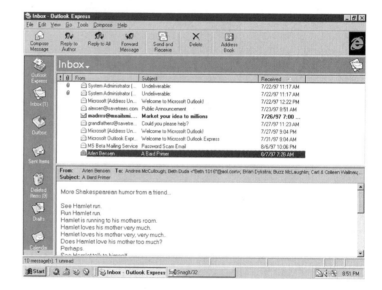

Getting Around in Outlook Express

Before jumping right into sending and receiving messages, orient yourself in Outlook Express by learning how to open the program, move among its *folders* (message lists), and display messages.

13

Opening Outlook Express

You can open Outlook Express in a variety of ways. Some are just general ways of opening the program; others are designed to get you straight into a particular activity within Outlook Express. Following are the principle ways to open Outlook Express:

☐ On the desktop, click the Mail icon that appears there after you install Internet Explorer 4.

☐ On the taskbar, click the Launch Mail quick launch button.

☐ From the Start menu, choose Programs | Internet Explorer | Outlook Express.

☐ From within Internet Explorer, click the Mail button on the toolbar to drop down a list of options (see Figure 13.2), and then click Read Mail.

☐ From within Internet Explorer, choose Go | Mail.

Figure 13.2.

You can easily open Outlook Express from within Internet Explorer.

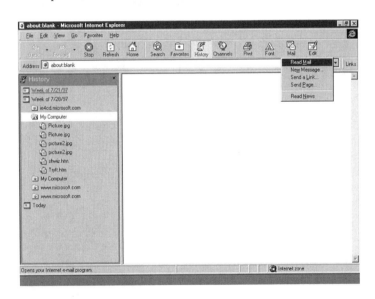

When you use any of these options, Outlook Express opens to its Inbox folder—the main folder for performing e-mail activities. From the Inbox folder, you can easily jump to any other folder or activity in Outlook Express.

13

TIME SAVER

Outlook Express is a component of Internet Explorer 4, but it does not *require* Internet Explorer. When you use Outlook Express, Internet Explorer can be open or closed. Also, Outlook Express is very smart about connecting to the Internet when necessary to complete a task you've started. So you need not be online when you open Outlook Express.

Depending on your configuration, when you open Outlook Express, it may immediately begin attempting to connect to the Internet or a dialog may appear, asking whether you want to connect. It's important to understand that, when working with e-mail, you need to connect to the Internet only to send and receive messages. You can compose new messages and read messages entirely offline. If you don't want to go online when Outlook Express tries to take you there, just click Cancel on whatever dialogs appear.

JUST A MINUTE

If you have other e-mail software on your PC, such as Microsoft Exchange, Internet Mail, or Netscape Communicator, a wizard opens the first time you open Outlook Express, asking whether you want to import the messages and address book entries stored by those programs into Outlook Express. You'll have the opportunity to check or uncheck a check box for each program, to specify whether or not you want to import messages. Just follow the wizard through a few easy dialogs to complete the import.

Choosing a Folder

Outlook Express divides messaging activities into a family of folders. In each folder, you see a list of messages you can display or work with in other ways. The folders are

- ☐ Inbox: Lists messages you have received.
- ☐ Outbox: Lists messages you have composed but not yet sent.
- ☐ Sent Items: Lists copies of all messages you've sent, for your reference.
- ☐ Deleted Items: Lists messages you've deleted from any other folder.

The Deleted Items folder does for e-mail what the Recycle Bin does for Windows: It holds messages you've deleted, giving you a chance to retrieve them if you change your mind. After you delete the messages from the Deleted Items folder, they're gone for good.

☐ News: Lists newsgroups to which you've subscribed (see Hour 15).

You use the panel along the left side of the Outlook Express window to switch among the folders (see Figure 13.3). The left side of the Outlook Express window contains either of two tools for moving among folders:

☐ Outlook bar: Also known casually as the "button bar," this bar (see Figure 13.3) shows an icon you can click to open each Outlook Express folder. The button bar contains more buttons than can be seen at once in the window, so a little arrow always appears at the top, the bottom, or both the top and bottom of the button bar; click the arrow to scroll other buttons into view.

☐ Folder list: The Folder list shows the same choices as the button bar, only in a text list rather than as a list of icons.

You can choose whether your copy of Outlook Express shows the button bar, Folder list, or both by making selections from the Window Layout Properties dialog.

In Outlook Express, choose View | Layout to open the dialog. In the dialog, insert a check mark next to Outlook bar to display the Outlook bar. Insert a check mark next to Folder list to display the Folder list. You can use this dialog also to customize Outlook Express's appearance in a number of other ways.

Because most people prefer the button bar, that's what you'll see throughout this hour, and that's what you'll be instructed to use most of the time in the To Dos. But using the Folder list is the same as using the button bar. For example, to open the Inbox folder, you can click the Inbox icon in the button bar, or click the word Inbox in the Folder list.

13

Figure 13.3.

Use the button bar to move among the Outlook Express folders, each of which lists a different set of messages.

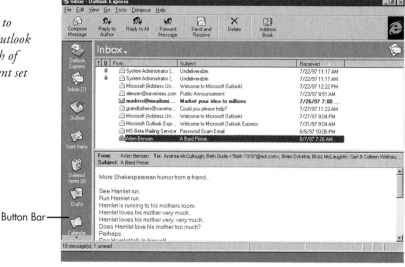

Button Bar —

The Outlook Express toolbar changes depending on the kind of folder you're in. When you're in an e-mail related folder, you'll see e-mail tools, such as the Send and Receive button. When in a newsgroup-related folder, you'll see newsgroup tools, such as Subscribe. Tools that apply to both activities, such as Compose Message, always appear.

JUST A MINUTE

Displaying a Message

From the list displayed by each folder, you can display any message. You do this in either of two ways:

☐ Single-click the message in the list to display it in the preview pane (see Figure 13.4) in the bottom of the Outlook Express window.

☐ Double-click the message in the list to display it in its own message window (see Figure 13.5).

In general, the preview pane is best when you're simply scanning messages, and need to move quickly from one to the next. Use a message window to read a long message, or to read a message you will reply to or forward (as described later in this hour).

13

Figure 13.4.

Single-click a message in a folder to display the message in the preview pane.

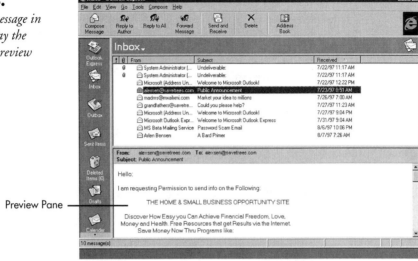

Preview Pane ————

Figure 13.5.

Double-click a message in a folder to display the message in a message window.

Message Window ————

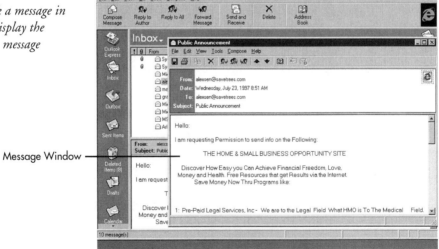

To Do: Get Around in Outlook Express

1. On the taskbar, click the Launch Outlook Express button. Outlook Express opens. (If dialogs appear to take you online, click Cancel in them so you can work offline for now.)

2. The Inbox folder now appears. You have at least one message there: A Welcome from Microsoft. If you chose to import messages from your other e-mail programs, your Inbox contains messages you received with those programs.

3. In the button bar, click Outbox. (If your copy of Outlook Express shows the Folder list instead of the button bar, click the word Outbox in the Folder list.) The Outbox folder opens. (It's empty; you've haven't composed any messages yet.)

4. In the button bar (or Folder list), click Inbox. The Inbox folder reappears.

5. Single-click the Microsoft message in the list. The message is displayed in the preview pane.

6. Double-click the Microsoft message. The message is displayed in its own window.

7. Click the X button in the message window's upper-right corner to close the message.

Composing and Sending a Message

To send e-mail in Outlook Express, you need to start with something to send:

- An original note or letter
- An e-mail you want to reply to
- An attachment
- An e-mail you want to forward

 Attachment: A file—any type of file—that's sent along with an e-mail message so that the recipient can open it and use it. You learn in this hour how to use an attachment someone sends to you, and you learn in Hour 14 how to send an attachment.

After you have something to say, you're ready to go. The following To Do shows how to compose a simple e-mail message.

To Do: Compose a New Message

1. Switch to an e-mail folder, such as Inbox, and click the Compose Message button on the toolbar. The New Message dialog opens (see Figure 13.6).

Figure 13.6.
Compose e-mail in the new message dialog.

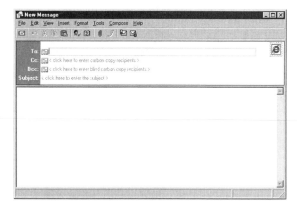

2. The edit cursor is already in the To line (near the top of the window), waiting for you to type the e-mail address of the person to whom you want to send a message. Type the e-mail address in the To line. To send the same message to multiple recipients, enter all the e-mail addresses in the To line, putting a semicolon (;) after each message except the final one.

> To "cc" (carbon copy) your e-mail to recipients other than your primary addressee, just click the Cc: line under the To line and enter one or more e-mail addresses there, separating multiple addresses with a semicolon (;). A copy of the letter will be sent to each address.

3. Move the edit cursor to the Subject line by clicking in the Subject line where you see < click here to enter the subject >. Type a concise, meaningful subject for your message. The subject line will appear in the message list of the recipient to help explain the purpose of your message.

After you've entered the To and Subject lines, the message is fully addressed; all that's left is typing the message itself, the body.

Body: The body of a message is the text, which you compose in the large pane of the New Message window. The address information you type—To, Cc, Subject—is called the *header* of the message, to distinguish it from the body.

4. Click in the large panel of the New Message window and type your message, just as you would in a word processor.

TIME SAVER

> You can use Windows copy and paste tools to copy text from other Windows applications to create the body of the message. For example, if the text you want to use already appears in a Word document, you can use copy and paste to copy it from Word into the body of your message.

13

JUST A MINUTE

> As a general rule, you cannot use text formatting (fonts, bold, italic, underlining, and so on) in an e-mail message. For now, stick to simple text. In Hour 14, you learn how to do some fancy message formatting. But you learn also that many e-mail recipients cannot display such messages, so it's important to stick to straight text when you do not know the e-mail capabilities of your recipients.

After your message is fully addressed and composed, send it by clicking the Send button (the little envelope) in the toolbar of the New Message window. When you click Send

☐ If you're already online, the message is sent immediately to everyone in the To and Cc lines.

☐ If you're not already online, Outlook Express connects you to the Internet, and then sends the message immediately to everyone in the To and Cc lines.

If the message is sent successfully, a copy of it appears in your Sent Items folder for your reference.

Sometimes, though, Outlook Express may have trouble sending a message; for example, if your ISP's mail server is down or overloaded, the message may not get through. When that happens, Outlook Express displays a message to inform you that the message could not be sent, and then it copies the message to your Outbox folder, so you can try to send it again later. (To learn how to send messages from your Outbox folder, see "Receiving Messages" later in this hour.)

Just a Minute

If you find that your messages always go straight to the Outbox, even when you click the Send button, your copy of Outlook Express is configured to send all messages first to the Outbox. That's not really a problem; the messages in your Outbox will all be sent automatically the next time you attempt to receive messages, as described later in this hour.

But if you'd prefer to send messages on their way without a stopover in the Outbox, reconfigure Outlook Express as follows: Choose Tools | Options | Send, and check the check box next to Send Messages Immediately.

Time Saver

When you're composing several messages offline, as you complete them you need not connect and send, disconnect, connect and send, disconnect, and so on. Instead, as you complete each message, you can save it in your Outbox folder instead of sending it right away. You can then send all the messages in the Outbox folder at once, the next time you go online, as described later in "Receiving Messages."

To save a message in your Outbox folder instead of sending it immediately, compose and address the message as usual, but don't click the Send button. Instead, from the menu bar of the New Message window, choose File | Send Later.

Receiving Messages

To receive messages others have sent to you, open any e-mail-related folder in Outlook Express (Inbox is a good choice) and click the Send and Receive button on the toolbar.

JUST A MINUTE

As always, Outlook Express knows when to go online. If you're offline when you click Send and Receive, Outlook Express connects you.

Outlook Express contacts your ISP's mail server, and checks for any new messages addressed to you. If there are none, the words "No new messages on server" appear in the status bar at the bottom of the Outlook Express window. If there are new messages, Outlook Express copies them to your PC and stores them in your Inbox folder, where you can read them.

TIME SAVER

When Outlook Express finishes retrieving your e-mail, you can disconnect from the Internet. You do not have to stay online to read the mail because it has been copied to your PC.

Why, you may wonder, is the button for retrieving e-mail named "Send and Receive," when it appears you're only receiving? Well, when you click Send and Receive, Outlook not only retrieves new e-mail but also automatically sends all messages waiting in your Outbox folder.

Any Outbox message that is successfully sent is removed from the Outbox folder and copied to the Sent Items folder. If Outlook Express cannot send a message successfully, the message remains in the Outbox folder; Outlook Express will attempt to send it again the next time you click Send and Receive.

Replying and Forwarding

Outlook Express provides you with easy ways to accomplish two popular ways of working with messages you have received: reply and forward.

NEW TERM **Replying and forwarding:** Replying means sending a message back to someone from whom you have received a message to respond to that message. Forwarding is passing a copy of a message you've received to a third party, either because you want to share the message's content with the third party or because you believe that, although the message was originally sent to you, the third party is a more appropriate recipient for it.

13

For example, when Maxine receives the frequent, praiseful e-mails from grateful readers, she forwards them to her agent, so the agent can use them as leverage in signing Maxine to ever-more-lucrative book, TV, and movie deals. When Maxine receives a complaint (which almost *never* happens), she replies to the complaint, explaining to the reader that his or her troubles were caused, depending on the situation, by the editor or the printer or Microsoft or a computer virus or an Act of God or the reader's glasses. Or Disney.

To reply or forward, you always begin by opening the original message. From the message window's toolbar, you then click one of the following buttons:

- Reply to author: Creates a reply to the person who sent you the message.
- Reply to all: Creates a reply to the person who sent you the message and to everyone else to whom the message was sent when it was sent to you.
- Forward message: Creates a new message containing the entire text of the original message, ready for you to forward.

Whichever button you click, a new message window opens. In the body of the message, a complete quote of the original message appears (see Figure 13.7).

 Quote: A quote is all or a portion of a message you've received. A quote is included in a reply to indicate what you're replying to. It's included in a forward to carry the message you're forwarding.

In either case, the quote is preceded by a summary of the header information of the original message (see Figure 13.7), showing who sent you the message and when it was sent. The quote appears in smaller text than anything you type in the message, to differentiate the quote from whatever you may add to the message.

In a reply or forward, you may edit the quote, cutting out any parts that aren't relevant and inserting your own comments above, below, or within the quote.

Figure 13.7.

A reply or a forward includes a quote of the original message.

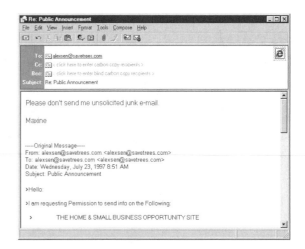

13

In the message window of a reply, the To line is automatically filled in for you, with the address of the person from whom you received the message (or multiple addresses, if you chose Reply to All). The Subject line is filled in with the original message's subject, preceded by Re: (*re*garding, or *re*ply to), to indicate that your message is a reply to a message using that subject. To complete the reply, all you have to do is type your comments above, below, or within the quote, and then click Send.

In the message window of a forward, the To line is empty, so that you can enter the address of the person to whom you want to forward the message. (As with any message, you may enter multiple To recipients, and Cc recipients as well.) The Subject line is filled in with the original message's subject, preceded by FW: (forward). To complete the forward, address the message, type your comments above, below, or within the quote, and then click Send.

Using Attachments You've Received

In Hour 14, you learn how to attach files to messages to send files to folks. But right now is as good a time as any to learn what to do with a file attachment someone sends to you.

In the Inbox message list, when you see a paper clip icon at the start of a message's line in the list, that message includes an attached file. If you open that message, you'll see one or more file icons in a panel at the bottom of the message (see Figure 13.8). Each file icon is a separate file attached to the message.

Figure 13.8.

An e-mail message that includes an attached file.

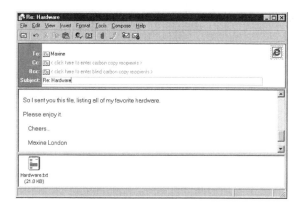

From within the message, you can use that file in several ways. Begin by pointing to the file icon and right-clicking. A pop-up menu like the one in Figure 13.9 appears.

Figure 13.9.

*Opening an attachment
to received e-mail.*

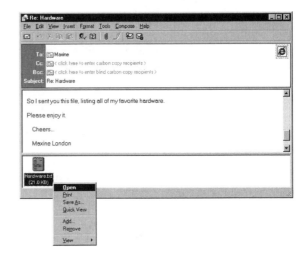

From the menu, choose

☐ Open, to open the file in the Windows program that's assigned to handle files of
that type. For example, if the attached file is a Word document, it opens in Word
(or WordPad, if you don't have Word).

☐ Save As, to open a standard Windows Save As dialog you use to save the file
separately from the message. Use this option to "break out" the file from the
message, so you can use it like any other file.

☐ Quick View, to quickly view the file's contents in a window you cannot use to edit
the file. Note that the Quick View option appears only when Windows has a
viewer configured for the file type of the attached file.

Summary

Outlook Express has a lot to it, and we've only scratched the surface. You'll spend two more
hours—Hours 14 and 15—with Outlook Express, and even then you won't know all of it.

Then again, in this single hour you've learned everything you really need to know to perform
90% of all the e-mail tasks most people ever do: getting around Outlook's folders, composing
and sending mail, receiving mail, replying, forwarding, and even dealing with file attachments. Most of the rest of Outlook's e-mail features are just for show-offs.

13

Q&A

Q What's the Bcc line in the header about?

A The Bcc line works exactly like the Cc line, except that it sends a "blind" carbon copy.

Everyone who receives a message from you can see in the message header who else got the same message, either as a To or a Cc recipient. But Bcc recipients don't show up in the header, so the only people who know that the message was copied to a Bcc recipient are the Bcc recipient and you. Use Bcc when your messaging relates to something you're doing that's especially private or sneaky.

Q I see a little open book icon on the toolbar. What does it do?

A That icon opens the Outlook Express Address Book. When you send e-mail to many different people, it can get tricky to remember all those e-mail addresses. Instead, you can click the Address Book button, and fill in a simple form for each person with whom you exchange e-mail, listing that person's name, e-mail address, and other information.

While filling in the form, you can assign a nickname to that person. When you've assigned a nickname, you can type that nickname in the To, Cc, or Bcc line to address mail to that person. For example, suppose I send e-mail to Ellen Woronicz at the address `ellenworonicz@earthnetenterprises.com`. I can create an Address Book entry for Ellen, and assign her the nickname Ellen. From then on, when I want to send her e-mail, all I type in the To line is `Ellen`. The Address Book takes care of the rest.

Quiz

Take the following quiz to see how much you've learned.

Questions

1. Outlook Express handles

    a. E-mail

    b. Newsgroups

    c. Exchanging files

    d. All of the above

2. To use Outlook Express, you must first open Internet Explorer and connect to the Internet.

    a. True

    b. False

13

3. The Outbox folder holds messages that

    a. You've thrown out

    b. You've composed but not yet sent

    c. Contain *out*rageous statements

    d. Contain ideas that are not "in"

4. When a subject line in a message you've received begins with "RE:", the message must be

    a. A *re*pulsive one

    b. A *re*cent one

    c. A *re*ply to a message you sent to someone

    d. A *re*publican one

Answers

1. d. Outlook Express handles all types of messaging.

2. b. False. You may use Outlook Express with Internet Explorer closed, and either on or offline.

3. b. It's b, of course.

4. c. It must be c, but of course any message might also be a, b, or d, or all four. (A repulsive, recent, republican message might indeed demand a reply, mightn't it?)

Activity

Do you have some e-mail addresses of friends, family, and associates? Send all of them an e-mail greeting today, so that they will have your e-mail address. Then check your e-mail often for their replies.

Hour # 14

Doing More with E-Mail

Most folks never do more with e-mail than what you learned to do in Hour 13. But you want your 24 hours' worth, and Maxine always aims to please. So here are ways to make cooler, more powerful use of Outlook Express for e-mail activities.

At the end of the hour, you'll be able to answer the following questions:

☐ How can I send a file to someone by attaching it to an e-mail message?

☐ How can I create and send e-mail messages containing fancy formatting, such as fonts or pictures?

☐ How can I configure Outlook Express to automatically perform certain actions on certain messages, such as storing all messages from a certain person in a certain folder?

Attaching Files to Messages

If you can find a file, you can attach it to an e-mail message. An attachment can be any type of file found in your computer (such as `.exe`, `.wav`, `.doc`, `.bmp`, or `.zip`) or any combination of files. After you attach the file, it can be changed up to the time you send the e-mail.

You might send an attachment for a number of reasons:

- ☐ To send a lengthy document or spreadsheet file
- ☐ To send a picture, a graphic, or a movie or sound file
- ☐ To send an entire program

Attaching a file to your e-mail is the electronic equivalent of attaching a report to a note. When attaching the report to a note, you use a paper clip. As you know from Hour 13, Outlook Express uses a paper clip to indicate that a message includes one or more attached files.

JUST A MINUTE

Observe in Figure 14.1 that under the label of the icon is the size of the attached file, reported in parentheses. It's important to pay attention to that number.

E-mail messages are small files, by design; that's why e-mail (without any attachments) is sent or received generally pretty quickly. However, file attachments dramatically affect the time required to send a message and the time it takes your recipient to receive it. Think carefully about this issue before sending any file over 100 KB.

Figure 14.1.

When you attach a file, it appears in the bottom of the New Message window.

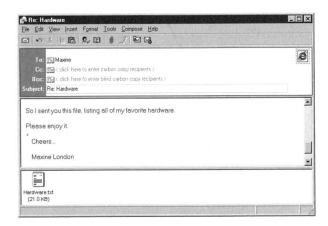

To attach a file, begin by addressing and composing the message itself. It's courteous to include in the message a description of what the file is and why you sent it, but doing so is not required.

When the message is ready, click the Insert File button (the paper clip) on the New Message window's toolbar. The Insert Attachment dialog opens (see Figure 14.2). Use the dialog as you would any file selection dialog in Windows to browse to the disk and directory where the file is stored.

14

Figure 14.2.

Use the Insert Attach-
ment dialog to choose a
file to send.

When you locate the file in the Insert Attachment dialog, double-click the file (or single-click it, and then click Open). The Insert Attachment dialog closes, and a new panel opens at the bottom of the New Message window, showing the icon for the file.

The file is attached and will travel along with the message wherever and whenever you send it. You can click the Send button to send the message and attachment immediately, or choose File | Send later to send the message and its attachment to the Outbox folder, to be sent the next time you retrieve your e-mail.

JUST A MINUTE

Lots of otherwise nice people, when they learn to attach files, start sending giant file attachments to friends, containing any picture, video clip, or other bauble they consider cute. When the friends check their e-mail, the fat file attachment makes downloading new messages take half an hour, which gets annoying if it happens often—especially if they use e-mail for business.

So before you zap that half-megabyte video clip to your brother in Des Moines, ask yourself: Will he be so entertained by it that he won't mind the download time?

To Do: Attach a File

1. From an e-mail-related folder in Outlook Express, choose Compose Message. A New Message window opens.

2. In the To line, type your own e-mail address.

3. In the Subject line, type **File Test**.

4. Type a few words in the body of the message. (Suggestion: Every Good Boy Deserves Fudge.)

5. Click the Insert File button in the toolbar. The Insert Attachment dialog opens. By default, the dialog opens to the Windows folder.

To Do

14

6. Double-click the Media folder. The folder opens, showing, among other stuff, a collection of music and sound clips (see Figure 14.3).

7. Double-click a sound or music clip that looks interesting. The dialog closes, and an icon for the clip appears at the bottom of the message.

8. Send the message. After sending, stay online.

9. Wait a few minutes, and then click Send and Receive to retrieve your e-mail. You'll get the message and file attachment.

10. In your Inbox folder, open the File Test message you have received.

11. Right-click the message icon, and choose Open from the menu that pops up. The clip plays (be sure your speakers are on).

Figure 14.3.

Send yourself a music clip from the Media folder.

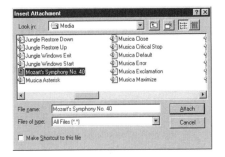

Formatting and Sending HTML Messages

In the final four hours of this tutorial, you learn how to use FrontPage Express—Internet Explorer's Web authoring program—to create Web pages. You learn how to format text with fonts and font sizes, use pictures and backgrounds, and more.

What you may not know is that you can use in an e-mail message the same kinds of formatting you create in FrontPage Express. You can send messages containing all kinds of fonts, colors, pictures—even multimedia.

The Downside of Fancy Messages

There's one hitch to sending fancy messages like this: Your recipient may not be able to display them.

When you create such a file, you do not create a regular e-mail message. You create a file in Web page format, HTML, and then send it through the e-mail system. To read the message, your recipient must use an e-mail program capable of displaying HTML files in addition to regular e-mail messages.

Outlook Express can display HTML files. In fact, when you click the Outlook Express button at the top of the button bar, you're looking at an HTML e-mail message supplied as a sample by Microsoft. Not only does the sample include graphics and fonts (see Figure 14.4), but it also includes links. You can click on the pictures in the message to start basic tasks in Outlook Express. Because Outlook Express has the capability, others can send you HTML e-mail messages.

Figure 14.4.

Using the HTML format, an e-mail message can be as fancy as a Web page.

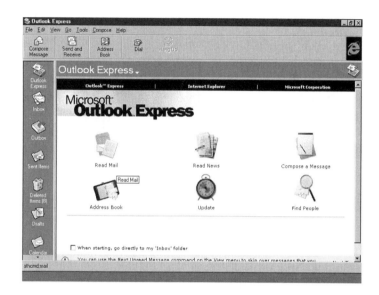

A few other e-mail programs support HTML messages, such as Netscape Messenger, the e-mail component of Netscape Communicator. But most e-mail systems do not support HTML messages.

The moral? Unless you happen to know that your intended recipient has an e-mail program that can show HTML messages, stick with plain text messages.

Creating HTML Messages

I won't get into all the specifics of formatting HTML documents now because you learn all that about seven hours from now. What I will show you here is how to specify that a message be sent in HTML format. You'll also see that when you specify that a message you're composing is to be HTML, the special HTML formatting tools appear automatically, so you may use them to format the message.

To create an HTML e-mail message, begin by opening the New Message window as usual. From the New Message window's menu bar, choose Format. At the bottom of the Format menu (see Figure 14.5), you can choose Rich Text (HTML) to compose the message in HTML format or Plain Text to create a regular e-mail message.

14

TIME SAVER

By default, Outlook Express automatically sends replies in the same format in which the message was received. If someone sends you an HTML message (which means the sender's e-mail program can display HTML), and you click Reply to Author to respond to it (see Hour 13), the message you create is automatically in HTML format.

Figure 14.5.

Use the New Message window's Format menu to choose between HTML and plain text format.

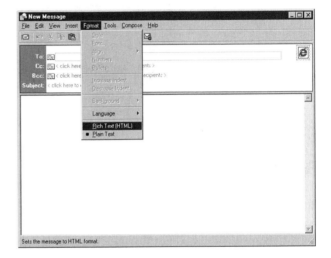

If you choose Rich Text (HTML) from the Format menu, a new toolbar appears between the header and body of the message (see Figure 14.6). The toolbar contains the same tools you use in FrontPage Express (see Hour 21) to use fonts and colors, align text, add pictures, and more. You may recognize some of these formatting buttons—such as those that apply bold, italic, and underlining—from your Windows word processor.

When you finish composing and formatting your HTML message, you send it like any other e-mail message.

14

Figure 14.6.

When you compose an HTML message, you get a new toolbar in the New Message window, used for applying HTML features and formatting.

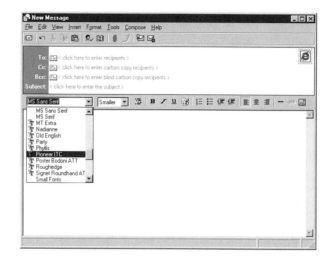

Organizing Mail with Inbox Assistant

Outlook Express includes a built-in e-mail manager, Inbox Assistant, which you can configure to automatically send e-mail received from selected addresses to particular folders, and to perform other e-mail management tasks. Using Inbox Assistant requires a little setting up, but after you do that work, Inbox Assistant can save you ten times the effort by managing your mail for you.

To open Inbox Assistant, click Tools on the Outlook Express menu bar and select Inbox Assistant. The Inbox Assistant dialog opens (see Figure 14.7).

Commands you've set up appear in the Description area. A check mark in the box signifies that the command is activated; no check mark signifies that the command is not activated. From this dialog, you can

☐ Add a new command—give Inbox Assistant specific instructions to sort your incoming e-mail

☐ Remove a command from the list

☐ Review or change the properties of a command—the specific instructions Inbox Assistant uses to sort the e-mail

14

Figure 14.7.

Use the Inbox Assistant main dialog as your starting point for managing your e-mail automatically.

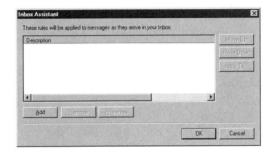

Adding a New Command

To add a new command for sorting e-mail, click the Add button. The Properties dialog opens (see Figure 14.8). Begin setting up the command in the top half of the dialog, by entering information that identifies the group of messages on which this command should be performed. Criteria include the following:

☐ To: Incoming messages addressed to the address you enter here (Probably you; otherwise, why would you have 'em?)

☐ CC: Messages whose headers include this address as a cc recipient (may or may not be you)

☐ From: Messages from a specific person or organization (this can be retrieved from your Address Book)

☐ Subject: Messages with a specific subject

☐ Message size: Messages greater in size than what you specify

After you specify the criteria, you can choose the action Inbox Assistant is to take with that mail:

☐ Move to: Move the e-mail to the folder you select (click on the Folder button and the Move To dialog will open with a folder tree to select from)

☐ Copy to: Copy the e-mail to both Inbox and the folder you choose

☐ Forward to: Forward the e-mail automatically to a person or a group in your address book

☐ Reply with: Reply to the e-mail with a saved e-mail file

☐ Do not download from the server: This will cause the file to stay on the server but not be downloaded

☐ Delete off server: This will delete all e-mail from the server before it can be down-loaded

When you have finished entering the actions, click OK to add the new command to the description list.

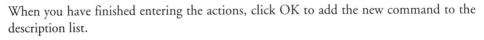

14

Figure 14.8.

Use the Inbox Assistant Command Properties dialog to specify which messages should be handled which way.

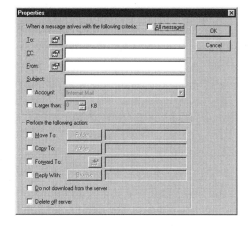

To Do: Give Inbox Assistant a Swing

1. In Outlook Express, choose File | Folder | New Folder to create a new folder for messages, and name it Test.

2. Open the Inbox Assistant.

3. Click Add to open the Properties dialog.

4. Type your own e-mail address in the To line and also in the From line. Specify that the action should be performed on all mail you receive from yourself.

5. In the action box, select Copy.

6. From the dialog that appears, choose your new Test folder.

7. Click OK. The new command appears in Inbox Assistant's Description list, checked to show that it's in force.

8. Click OK to close Inbox Assistant.

9. Send a message to yourself, then retrieve your e-mail to receive it. Observe that the new message is automatically copied to the Test folder.

Summary

Well, that's plenty about e-mail. As you can see, you can do a lot. Everything cool you can do, however, comes with a price. Using advanced e-mail techniques can limit your audience (not everybody can read HTML messages), add to your setup effort (setting up Inbox Assistant), or lengthen the time it takes to send messages (the added time it takes a file attachment to move through the Net). For each task, only you can decide when the ends justify the means.

14

Q&A

Q Why can't everybody's e-mail program show HTML?

A Well, the Internet e-mail system has been around for a long time, and a lot of e-mail programs are out there. Only very recently has the idea of using HTML as an e-mail format even come up. There simply hasn't been enough time for all e-mail programs to catch up.

And to be frank, how often do you really need fancy formatting in an e-mail message? Most of the time, plain text does the job fine. Because of that, there may be text-only e-mail programs for many years.

Q From my PC, I sent my buddy Peter a neat little Windows poker game in an e-mail attachment. He got it fine but says it doesn't work on his Mac. I checked, and he uses MIME. So what's the problem?

A Just because you can successfully send a file attachment doesn't mean your recipient can use it. Folks on the Internet use all kinds of computers. Because the Net is so adaptable, you can successfully send a file to almost anyone. But if that file is not compatible with the recipient's computer, the file still gets there but it won't work any better than if you'd walked it over there on a diskette.

Quiz

Take the following quiz to see how much you've learned.

Questions

1. In Outlook Express, a file attachment is indicated by a
    a. File cabinet
    b. Nail file
    c. Paper clip
    d. Stapler

2. The tools you can use in Outlook Express to format an HTML e-mail message are the same as those you'll learn to use in
    a. FrontPage Express
    b. LaunchPage
    c. PowerPage
    d. PageMaster

14

3. An HTML message can include

    a. Fonts

    b. Color

    c. Links

    d. All of the above, plus pictures

4. If you reply to a message you received in plain text format, the reply is automatically created as

    a. An HTML message

    b. A plain text message

    c. A chain letter

    d. A Dear John letter

Answers

1. c. The paper clip tells you an attachment is there.

2. a. I have no idea what options b, c, and d mean.

3. d. An HTML e-mail message can contain just about anything a Web page can contain.

4. b. A reply to a text message is automatically text; a reply to an HTML message is automatically HTML.

Activity

You haven't learned how to apply the HTML formatting tools, and you won't until Hour 21. But you're impatient. You're impetuous. You live on the edge. You answer to no one. Start an HTML message, and experiment with stuff on the formatting toolbar. (After all, you don't have to send it to anybody.) How much can you figure out on your own?

14

Hour 15

Understanding and Using Mailing Lists

You've already learned quite a lot about how to use e-mail for the most common tasks. You do, however, need to know about one more powerful e-mail tool—mailing lists. Mailing lists, often called *listservs,* have been around for a long time. They enable many people from all over to effectively communicate with each other.

By the end of this hour, you'll be able to answer the following questions about mailing lists:

- ☐ What is a mailing list?
- ☐ How do mailing lists work?
- ☐ Where can I find listservs?
- ☐ How do I get on a mailing list?
- ☐ How do I send and receive messages using listservs?

Listservs are a great way to talk to other people in a group setting. Before you start looking for the right listserv, however, you might find a little background information useful.

Exactly What Is a Listserv?

Soon after the advent of e-mail, users realized that it would be very helpful to have the ability to send e-mail to groups of people for collaboration and discussion. Thus, the first listserv was devised by the BITNET Information Center (BITNIC). This e-mail list server managed a large number of mailing lists, each one addressing a specific area of interest for network users and each having an independent set of list members. This service made the exchange of ideas and information between members very convenient.

How Listservs Work

It is easy to understand how a listserv works. Remember that you can use your e-mail client to assign an e-mail address (or addresses) to an easy-to-remember name called a nickname. Then you use that nickname to distribute e-mail to an individual or a group.

Well, listservs work much the same, only on a larger scale. A mailing list program runs on a computer and defines a unique e-mail address that distributes all e-mail sent to it. This listserv software automates the process of allowing people to add and remove their names from this giant "nickname" (called *subscribing* and *unsubscribing*), as well as a host of other functions.

After this listserv is set up, anyone who is subscribed to the listserv can send e-mail to it, and that e-mail will, in most cases, be automatically distributed to anyone on the mailing list (see Figure 15.1).

Figure 15.1.

A list server acts as a distribution point for messages to be sent to multiple subscribers.

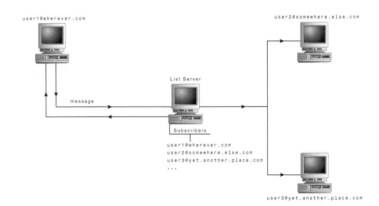

Listserv Personality

So who maintains these listservs? How can one person keep track of hundreds or thousands of subscribers on one listserv? Well, they can't. Many people don't realize that, for the most part, listservs are automated. After a listserv administrator has set up a listserv, he or she usually leaves it alone and lets it take care of itself.

15

The one exception to this rule is the *moderated listserv*. With a moderated listserv, a human being usually approves subscription additions and removals, as well as message submissions, before they are finalized. Listservs that are restricted to a certain population or deal with highly volatile issues are generally moderated.

 Moderated listserv: Just as a debate has a moderator to make sure both sides stick to the rules, some listservs have a human moderator who makes sure the rules of the listserv are being followed.

Finding the Right Listserv

Before you can use a listserv, you need to actually find a listserv that is of interest to you. You can find a listserv in basically three ways:

- ☐ Word of mouth
- ☐ E-mail
- ☐ The Web

Word of Mouth

Many people still find out about listservs from people they come in contact with who have similar interests. As people talk, e-mail each other, or surf the Web, they will usually find out about a listserv that interests them.

The List of Lists

If your Internet access is limited to e-mail (or even if it isn't), you can order a list of all available listservs.

To Do: Order a List of Lists

1. In Outlook Express, open a new message.
2. Address the message to LISTSERV@waynest1.bitnet.
3. Leave the Subject field blank. In the body of your message, type **LIST GLOBAL**.
4. Send the message.

Although you will receive a list of quite a few listservs, it is not exhaustive.

CAUTION

Lots of listservs are available. When you order the list of listservs, be prepared to read through a very long document to find the listserv you're looking for (see Figure 15.2).

Figure 15.2.

The list you receive will tell you about hundreds of listservs from A to Z.

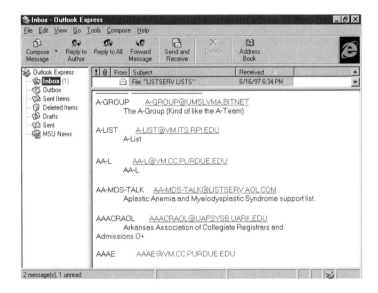

Listservs on the Web

In addition to using the search engines discussed in Hour 10, some excellent listserv search engines are available on the World Wide Web. A great place to start is CataList.

To Do: Check Out CataList

1. Use your Internet Explorer 4 browser to go to `http://www.lsoft.com/lists/list_q.html`.
2. In the Look for field, type a word or a phrase describing the type of list you're looking for (such as `education`).
3. Click to select the check boxes next to the listserv fields you'd like to search.
4. Click the Start the Search! button. For the search on education, CataList found quite a few mailing lists (see Figure 15.3).

None of these three methods gives you an exhaustive list of every available mailing list. Used in combination, however, you are sure to find some listservs to subscribe to.

Figure 15.3.

Looking for a listserv about education? CataList gives you 375 to choose from.

Signing On and Signing Off

The most important thing to know when using listservs is how to get onto them and then how to get off. If you know what you're doing, getting on (and off) is easy. This section describes a few points that will make your access of listservs easier.

Easy On

After you find a listserv, you're ready to subscribe to it. Most listservs are similar in how you subscribe and unsubscribe. Depending on where you located the listserv you want to subscribe to, you should have specific instructions on where to subscribe. In general, though, you'll need to complete the following.

To Do: Sign On to a Listserv

1. Using Outlook Express, address a new e-mail message to the e-mail address of the listserv or the listserv administrator.

2. Leave the Subject field blank. In the body of the message, type the subscribe message. (You usually type **subscribe** *Your Name*. Some lists require you to type **subscribe** *ListName Your Name*.)

3. If you have a signature attached to your messages, turn it off when sending this message.

4. Send the message.

CAUTION

> Monitor your e-mail closely for several days after subscribing to a listserv. It's not uncommon for high-traffic listservs to deliver dozens of messages to your mailbox every day. You'll probably want to think twice about staying subscribed to some of these listservs.

After you are subscribed, you usually are sent an e-mail message with basic information on the listserv. This message includes vital information about the listserv, so you should keep it.

One last note. If you subscribe to a moderated listserv, it may take a day or so for you to get a message confirming that you are on. You may even get a message from the moderator asking you to confirm that you really want to be on the list. It's usually a good idea to wait at least three days for a response before resubmitting a request to subscribe to a moderated listserv.

Easy Off

You might sign off a listserv for many reasons. Maybe it isn't exactly what you thought it would be, or maybe you're tired of it, or maybe there's too much traffic. Whatever the reason, you follow almost the same steps to get off a listserv as you do to get on.

To Do: Sign Off a Listserv

1. Address a new message to the e-mail address of the listserv or listserv administrator.
2. Leave the Subject: field blank. In the body of the message, type the unsubscribe message. (You usually type **unsubscribe *Your Name***. Some lists require that you type **unsubscribe *ListName Your Name***.)
3. If you have a signature attached to your messages, turn it off when sending this message.

4. Send the message.

CAUTION

> When unsubscribing from a listserv, make sure that you send the message from the same e-mail account you used when subscribing. Most listservs search for an exact e-mail address match when removing a subscriber. If you have trouble getting unsubscribed, contact the listserv administrator immediately.

Sending and Responding to Messages

Reading, sending, and replying to listserv messages involves the same basic steps as working with any other e-mail message. You should know about a few differences, though. This section describes these slight differences, along with a few handy rules.

Sending Messages to a List

Sending a message to an individual is no different than sending one to a listserv. The only difference is in who receives your message. You still fill in the To and Subject fields, as well as the body of the message. You should keep a few things in mind, however, when sending those messages.

To begin, after reading the listserv mail for a few days, you might want to start by sending a message of introduction to the listserv. Make this message brief, but include information about yourself that might be of interest to other subscribers. Remember, you are subscribing to the listserv to contribute information as well as get it. The only time you might not want to do this is if you have subscribed to a large listserv with lots of traffic.

TIME SAVER

> Make sure that you keep your contributions to the listserv reasonable. Remember, every time you send a message, you're sending it to everyone on the list. Don't dominate or flood a listserv with messages. Otherwise, you may find yourself on the receiving end of subtle (or not so subtle) hints to cease and desist.

Next, know that many times you will receive a copy of your message shortly after sending it. When you subscribe to a listserv, you receive a copy of all mail sent to the list, including your own. Conversely, don't be alarmed if you don't receive a copy of your mail right away, especially if you belong to a moderated list. Your e-mail might take a few minutes or a few days before it shows up in your mailbox.

Responding to Listserv Messages

CAUTION

> Before replying to a listserv, check to make sure your reply really should go to the entire list. Personal correspondence or off-topic mail should go to an individual, not to the list. Only mail of interest to those on the list should be sent to the list.

As with sending messages, responding to listserv messages is similar to replying to personal e-mail. You may need to pay special attention to one major difference, though.

When you reply to an e-mail message, you generally know that it will be returned to the person who sent it to you. With a listserv, this is not necessarily the case. Listservs are set up one of two ways:

☐ Replies are automatically sent to the list. This is how a majority of listservs are set up. In this case, you use the Reply to Author option to reply to the list and the Forward Message option to forward a reply to the individual who sent the message.

☐ Replies are automatically routed to the individual who sent the message. In this instance, you use the Reply to Author option to reply to the individual and the Forward Message option to forward a reply to the listserv.

So how do you tell which way the listserv you've subscribed to is set up? Easy. Simply compose a reply to a listserv message. When you do, look at the information in the To field. If a reply goes to the listserv address, as in Figure 15.4, the listserv is set up in the standard way. If the reply goes to the individual, the second method of listserv setup is being used.

Figure 15.4.

Most listservs are set to have replies automatically sent to the entire listserv.

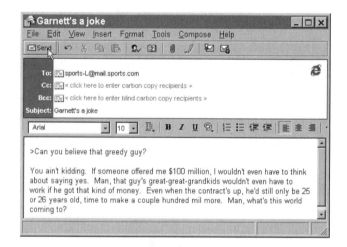

Listservs Helping Listsurfers

One of the best places to go for help in finding out what user options your listserv offers is to request help from the listserv itself. To get help, try the following steps with a listserv to which you are currently subscribed.

To Do: Find Help

1. Address a new e-mail message to the e-mail address of the listserv or listserv administrator. This will be the same address you sent your subscription message to (not the address you send regular messages to).

2. Leave the Subject field blank. In the body of the message, type **help**.

3. If you have a signature attached to your messages, turn it off when sending this message.

4. Send the message.

5. After a few seconds, you should get a message that looks something like Figure 15.5. Again, the amount of time it takes you to get this message back could vary.

15

Figure 15.5.

Most listservs offer help online.

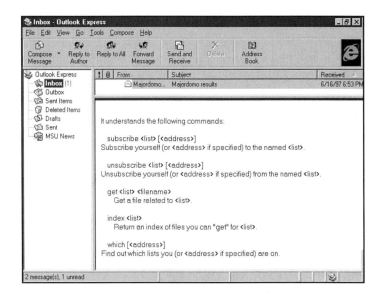

Table 15.1 lists the most common listserv commands. You use these commands in the body of a message you send to the listserv administrator address.

Table 15.1 Common listserv commands.

Command	Purpose
SUBSCRIBE	Subscribes you to a list
UNSUBSCRIBE	Unsubscribes you from a list
LIST	Shows all listservs served from a particular server
REVIEW or WHO	Shows the list of users currently subscribed
HELP	Sends the help message
INFO	Sends information on the list
INDEX	Shows a list of documents available for GET
GET	Retrieves documents from the listserv
SET ACTIVE	Makes your subscription active
SET INACTIVE	Suspends your subscription until the next SET ACTIVE command
SET DIGEST	Sends you a digest of listserv messages instead of individual messages once a day

Depending on the listserv you use, other or different listserv commands may be available as well. The SET commands can be particularly useful, as can the GET command. Feel free to experiment with the different settings to see what style of listserv participation best fits your needs.

Summary

In this hour, I gave you a lot of information about listservs. You should now understand that listservs are basically mass mailing lists that enable you to communicate with people who are interested in the same things you are. You also learned many ways to find the right listserv for you.

In addition, you learned some of the ins and outs of sending and replying to listserv messages, including how to watch particular headers to see to whom replies to the listserv go. Finally, I gave you some pointers about how to get help from the listservs themselves.

Q&A

Q It seems that listservs are everywhere, and I could easily start getting hundreds of messages a day. Is this true?

A The simple answer is yes. You can easily become "oversubscribed," just as many people subscribe to too many magazines.

Q How do I avoid oversubscribing?

A You can avoid this situation in a couple of ways. First, make sure that you stay subscribed to only the listservs you really read. If you find yourself automatically deleting most listserv messages without reading them, it's time to unsubscribe. Second, go to Hour 16 to find out about an alternative to listservs available on the Internet—newsgroups.

Q I'm still confused about the difference between a listserv administration address and the listserv address. Can you explain it again?

A Sure. The listserv administration address is the one to which you send commands such as SUBSCRIBE, UNSUBSCRIBE, and GET. This address may be something like majordomo@somewhere.com or listserv@somewhere.else.com. The address that you send listserv mail to usually looks more descriptive, such as sportsL@somewhere.com or edulist@somewhere.else.com.

Quiz

Take the following quiz to see how much you've learned.

15

Questions

1. One of the advantages of listservs is that they all work the same.

   a. True

   b. False

2. What is a "must do" after you subscribe to a listserv?

3. Which listserv command retrieves a file listing for a listserv?

   a. Search

   b. Get

   c. Index

Answers

1. b. False. Although they are all similar, you will find some important differences in how they work.

2. Always check your e-mail regularly for several days after subscribing to make sure you can handle the mailing list's traffic.

3. c. Index

Activity

Go to at least two different sources to find at least three listservs. Subscribe to all three. Then find the one you use the least and unsubscribe to it. If you find them all wonderfully helpful, great! You've hit the jackpot!

Hour **16**

Reading and Using Newsgroups

You've taken a look at e-mail and what it can do for you. To communicate with a much larger audience, you can try Usenet and its accompanying newsgroups. In this hour, you learn how to tap into this large resource and answer the following questions:

☐ What exactly are Usenet and newsgroups?

☐ How do you get started using News with Outlook Express?

☐ How do you find and subscribe to newsgroups?

☐ What are the basics of reading from and posting to newsgroups?

☐ How do you unsubscribe from newsgroups?

Newsgroup Basics

Before you can really understand how to use newsgroups, you need to understand two things. First, what is Usenet? Second, what are newsgroups really like?

Usenet Defined

The first thing most people ask is, "What does Usenet mean?" The name is modeled after Usenix, the UNIX users' conference series. Usenet was supposed to mean UNIX *Users Network* because all the early sites were UNIX machines, and many early discussions were about the UNIX operating system.

NEW TERM **UNIX:** Believe it or not, UNIX is not an acronym for anything. UNIX is an operating system developed in 1969 by Ken Thompson and Dennis Ritchie (allegedly so they could play games!). UNIX, a very powerful and portable operating system, expanded and became the foundational operating language of the Internet.

What you probably really want to know is how Usenet works. News is transferred across the Internet in two basic ways. The first is by means of listservs, which were discussed in Hour 15. The second is to have a machine dedicated solely to storing and serving news (see Figure 16.1).

Figure 16.1.

Usenet lets you go to the news instead of the news coming to you.

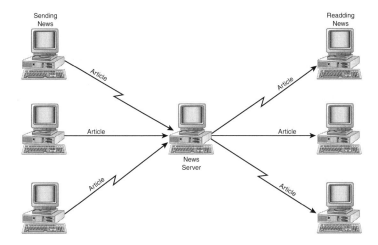

This second method, which is how Usenet works, enables you to read from and post to the news server using a news client such as Outlook Express. You then read what you want, when you want—instead of having tons of listserv mail jamming up your mailbox. These news servers organize, distribute, and keep track of thousands of messages—a task that a listserv simply can't duplicate.

NEW TERM **Post:** This is a message to a Usenet newsgroup. When you submit messages (also called articles) to newsgroups, you are said to be *posting.*

Newsgroups Defined

Many people have a difficult time distinguishing between Usenet and newsgroups. To clarify the difference, think about the publishing industry. The *publishing industry* is an all-encompassing, umbrella enterprise. *Publications,* such as *The Wall Street Journal,* are the actual "stuff" that the publishing industry consists of.

In this sense, think of Usenet as the encompassing structure, and newsgroups as the underlying electronic publications that make the industry. Just as there are thousands of magazines on thousands of topics, so too are there thousands of newsgroups on thousands of topics.

Newsgroup Organization

Newsgroups are organized into hierarchies that are similar to the folder structure on your hard drive. For instance, you might have a `Docs` folder on your hard drive, under which are other folders such as `Personal`, `Business`, and so on. As Figure 16.2 shows, this is exactly how newsgroups are organized.

Figure 16.2.

Newsgroup hierarchies are similar to other structures comprised of different levels.

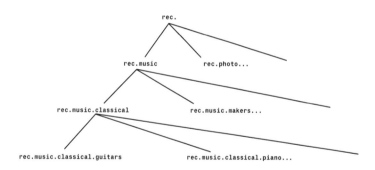

Newsgroup have eight major hierarchies, as follows:

- [ ] **comp.** is comprised of newsgroups having to do with *comp*uters.
- [ ] **soc.** contains newsgroups that deal with *soc*ial issues.
- [ ] **rec.** are the *rec*reational newsgroups.
- [ ] **sci.** is comprised of newsgroups about various topics in *sci*ence.
- [ ] **talk.** is the discussion hierarchy. In these newsgroups, you can talk about almost anything.
- [ ] **misc.** is the catch-all *misc*ellaneous newsgroup hierarchy.
- [ ] **news.** is the smallest hierarchy, and contains only a handful of newsgroups dealing with issues surrounding Usenet and newsgroups themselves. This hierarchy has excellent information for beginners.
- [ ] **alt.** deals with almost any issue under the sun and is considered the *alt*ernative hierarchy.

UsenEtiquette

Before diving in and starting to use the news, you should be aware of the etiquette that responsible people commonly observe when using Usenet. Although the following list of rules is brief, it will help you a lot as you begin to use newsgroups. Many rules that apply to e-mail apply to using newsgroups, too.

- [ ] Lurk before you leap. Lurking, the act of reading a newsgroup without posting, is a great way to find out what's appropriate for a certain newsgroup. You should lurk for several days before beginning to post.

- [ ] The war of the newsgroups. In Usenet, perhaps more than anywhere else on the Internet, it is vital that you think carefully about what you're going to write before you write it.

- [ ] No spam. Spamming, or posting the same article to multiple irrelevant newsgroups, is a definite Usenet no-no. As a rule, you should eliminate this abusive use of cross-posting from your Usenet repertoire.

- [ ] Free advertising? Another way to bring yourself lots of grief is to shamelessly advertise your business on Usenet.

- [ ] Obey the law. Most copyright laws apply to Usenet and other electronic media. If you're tempted to post the text to John Grisham's latest thriller, be aware that you would be liable for the same consequences that any other copyright violator faces.

Getting the News

In Hour 3, you used the Internet Connection wizard to give Internet Explorer all the information necessary to read newsgroups. If you need to go back and review that information, do so now. Otherwise, let's go use some news!

Signing Up

When you start Outlook Express, you should see an icon in the outlook bar with the Friendly Name of your news server. When you click on the icon, Outlook Express will attempt to connect to your server. Because you probably haven't subscribed to any groups yet, you will be asked whether you would like to view a list of available newsgroups. Click Yes to continue.

CAUTION

If you are connecting to news over a modem, this process could take 10 minutes or more depending on how many newsgroups your server carries. Be patient; you shouldn't have to do this very often. Figure 16.3 shows an example of what you'll see after you're connected.

16

Figure 16.3.

Outlook Express lets you choose the newsgroups you want to subscribe to.

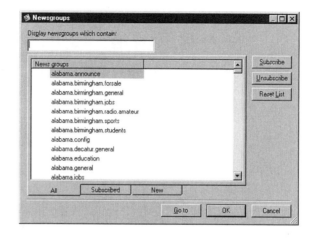

Take a moment to quickly scroll through some of the groups. Quite a few, aren't there? At this point, you can simply double-click on any group to subscribe to it. However, it's pretty apparent that it could take quite a while to find a group that you're interested in by simply scrolling through the list. That's why Outlook Express gives you the option of searching for newsgroups.

To Do: Search for Newsgroups

1. Suppose you are interested in a newsgroup about skiing. Type the word **skiing** in the Display Newsgroups Which Contain field, but do *not* press Enter.

2. In a few seconds, a listing of all newsgroups that matched your search appear. Take a moment to look at the listing.

3. Double-click one of the groups to subscribe to it.

4. Click the Subscribed tab to see that Outlook Express automatically updates the newsgroup you've subscribed to.

5. Feel free to repeat this process for several topics of interest to you.

6. After you have located and subscribed to some groups, click OK.

If you want to preview a group instead of subscribing to it, single-click on the group name and then click the Go To button. When you have returned to the main newsgroup window, your screen might look like Figure 16.4.

Figure 16.4.

In addition to displaying your newsgroups, you're offered a handy navigation menu.

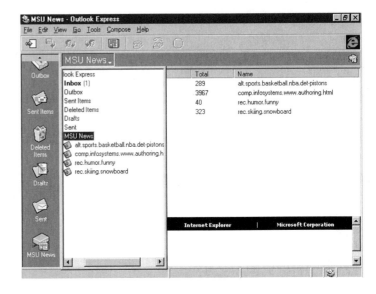

TIME SAVER

Quite often, newsgroup names do not contain an easily recognizable English name. Always be willing to search for different variations of what you're really looking for. For instance, if you're trying to find a group on education, try searching for ed, educ, edu, k12, or any other abbreviated phrase that you think might be appropriate.

One last note before moving on. You can view the complete list of newsgroups at any time. If you are using another Outlook Express function, such as e-mail, simply right-click on the Outlook Bar icon for your news server and select Newsgroups from the resulting pop-up menu. If you are reading newsgroups, just click on the Newsgroup button on the toolbar.

Setting 'Em Up

Before actually reading your groups, you should do a few things to make your newsgroup experience almost hassle-free. Notice that, for each newsgroup, Outlook Express displays the group name, the total number of articles your server has for that group, and how many articles are unread.

This last category is important. You should set up Outlook Express so that you aren't constantly wading through the same articles again and again and again. Your first step to ensure this is to choose Tools | Options | Read and select the Mark All Messages as Read When Exiting a Newsgroup check box.

16

Just a Minute

When choosing this option, don't worry about losing the ability to retrieve an article that's been marked as read. Simply choose Edit | Mark As Unread and all articles on the server will be displayed again.

You should complete one more important step before you proceed. Double-click on any newsgroup. (You're not going to read the newsgroup yet.) Choose View | Current View | Unread Messages.

Now, the next time you view the group, you will see only those messages you've never seen before. After you have properly set these two important configurations, you're ready to go.

Reading the News

Reading newsgroups with Outlook Express is easy. Simply double-click a newsgroup, and Outlook Express displays a two-paned window. The top half of this window displays a particular article's header and the bottom half displays the text of the selected article.

Reading Articles

After you have the newsgroup displayed, use the article window scroll bar to browse the article headers. When you've found one you want to read, just click it and the article will be displayed in the bottom pane.

Just a Minute

As with other Windows applications, you can save an article to text by choosing File | Save as. You can also cut or copy any or all of the article, and then copy it to any other Windows 95 application that makes use of text.

If you're the kind of person who wants to read an article in its own window, you can with Outlook Express. Simply double-click an article instead of single-clicking, and the article will be displayed in a separate window.

Reading Threads

As you scrolled through the list of articles in your newsgroup, you may have noticed that some articles had a small plus sign next to them. This sign indicates the first article of a thread. Just like many cloth threads make up a piece of clothing, so too do many article threads make up a newsgroup.

Threads: These are a series of articles all dealing with the same topic. Someone will reply to an article, and then someone else will reply to the reply, and so on. This organization of original topic articles and replies make up a newsgroup thread.

To expand a thread to view all its articles, click the plus sign. You see a number of indented articles beneath the original article heading (see Figure 16.5). You can click on these articles to read them. To collapse a thread after you've read it, simply click on what is now a minus sign next to the first article.

Figure 16.5.

Threads are the conversational building blocks of most newsgroups.

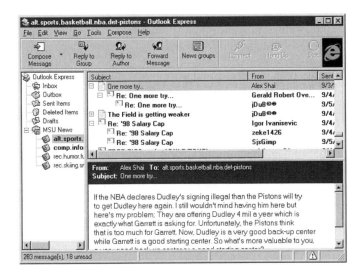

Posting and Replying to News

Finally, it's time to post some news. First, a piece of advice. Go back to your listing and subscribe to the alt.test newsgroup. This newsgroup is set up to accept test messages. If you make a mistake posting or replying to articles on this group, no one cares. After practicing here a while, you can go post some real articles to those groups you've been lurking on.

Posting Articles

Outlook Express enables you to post new articles from either the main newsgroups window or the article display window. If you try to post a new article from the main newsgroups window, you must click on one of the newsgroups to post a new message. Here's how you can post your first article.

16

To Do: Send a Test Message

1. Either click on the Compose Message button from the toolbar or choose Compose | New Message.

2. In the Subject field, type a short subject for your message.

3. Click in the body of the article composition window and type a short message. It should look something like Figure 16.6.

4. Finally, click on the Post Message button (see Figure 16.6).

Figure 16.6.

A newsgroup article looks almost identical to an e-mail message.

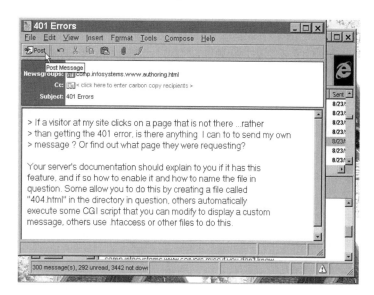

Congratulations! You have posted your first article to Usenet. Your article will appear the next time you choose Tools | Download This Account and read `alt.test`.

JUST A MINUTE

Although you were warned earlier in this hour against posting messages to multiple newsgroups, sometimes it's appropriate (for example, when posting a basketball question to several different basketball newsgroups). To do this, click the name of the newsgroup in the Newsgroup header. In the resulting dialog, select the groups to which you want to post. Click Add, and then click OK.

Replying to the Group

You can reply to a post you've selected in the article listing window in one of two ways. The first is to reply to the entire newsgroup, also called posting a reply.

To Do: Post a Reply

1. Either click the Reply to Group button from the toolbar or choose Compose | Reply to Newsgroup.

2. Because all header information should be filled in, move your cursor to the message body.

3. In the body of the message, notice that the original article is included, with each line preceded by an include mark (>). As with e-mail, you can select and edit the original article's text, and add your own text to the reply.

4. After your reply is complete, click on the Post Message button to post your reply.

CAUTION

Before composing your reply, make sure it will not be cross-posted to many groups. If you *are* replying to an article that has been cross-posted, double-click the Newsgroup icon in the reply header. The Pick Newsgroups dialog appears (see Figure 16.7). Click the name of each newsgroup that shouldn't be cross-posted, and then click the Remove button. Click OK when you've finished removing the groups.

Figure 16.7.

Outlook Express lets you choose which newsgroups to send messages to.

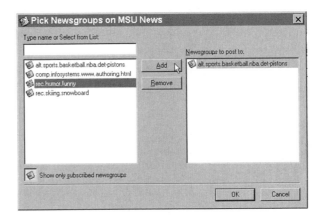

Replying to a Person

In addition to replying to the group, you can compose a reply directly to the person who posted the article via e-mail. You will want to do this if you want to get into detail that you feel is inappropriate to the group or if you want to pursue something that is off-topic to the newsgroup.

16

Composing a personal reply is almost identical to replying to the group. You either click on the Reply to Author button from the toolbar or choose Compose | Reply to Author. Next, choose the appropriate Internet Mail profile when asked. When the Outlook Express e-mail composition window appears, compose your reply as you would any other e-mail. Finally, you click the Send button to deliver your message.

More Replying Options

You should know about a couple more options before you're finished. To adjust who you send your message to, you can modify the Newsgroup: and Cc: headers while composing a post or use the following options in Outlook Express:

- [ ] Forward. This option accomplishes the same thing as a Reply to Author. The only difference is that you must supply the e-mail address of the recipient.

- [ ] Reply to Newsgroup and Author. This option, which enables you to post your reply to both the author and the group, is available from only the Compose | Reply to Newsgroup and Author menu item.

Unsubscribing from Newsgroups

We've saved the easiest for last. Unsubscribing to newsgroups is easy with Outlook Express. When you decide you just don't use a particular group any more, simply right-click on the newsgroup name from the main newsgroup listing window and choose Unsubscribe From This Newsgroup in the resulting pop-up menu. That's all there is to it.

Summary

In this hour, you learned exactly what Usenet and newsgroups are and how they work. In addition, you learned some of the ins and outs of newsgroup etiquette. You now know many of the most common mistakes to avoid.

You also discovered how to browse, find, and subscribe to newsgroups. Most importantly, you learned how to read, post to, and reply to newsgroup articles.

Q&A

Q I'm not sure I understand why it's so terrible to do some advertising and cross-posting on Usenet. Can you explain a little more?

A Sure. First, a vehicle already exists for disseminating commercial information—it's called the World Wide Web. Second, there are a lot of newsgroups and a lot of articles in those newsgroups. Someone is paying for all this traffic. Needless replication of posts and lots of useless posts only adds to the costs a server administrator absorbs, and then immediately passes on to you, the user.

Q **What if I'm interested in a newsgroup, but can't find it on my news server. What do I do?**

A Probably the best thing is to ask your Internet service provider if such a group exists. If it does, it won't hurt to ask them to add it to their server. Another avenue is to find a related newsgroup, lurk a while, and then ask whether such a newsgroup exists.

Q **I have limited time and don't want to spend too much of it online to access newsgroups. Do you have any advice for me?**

A Yes. Begin by subscribing to a moderate number of groups (no more than 20 to 25), possibly including two or more groups dealing with each topic. Then, browse each group for a week or so and weed out those groups that have too much traffic or information that isn't useful to you. Most people settle on 5 to 10 groups that they read on a regular basis.

Quiz

Take the following quiz to see how much you've learned.

Questions

1. Which of the following newsgroups does not belong to the `soc.` hierarchy?

    a. `comp.soc.women`

    b. `soc.culture.indian`

    c. `soc.penpals`

2. If you were trying to find out some information about a particular breed of hunting dog, would you

    a. Find `rec.hunting.dogs` and immediately ask your question.

    b. Lurk on a couple of dog groups, and then cross-post your question to the entire `rec.pets.dogs...` hierarchy.

    c. Look on a few groups to try to find information on hunting dogs, and then post your question to `rec.hunting.dogs` if you couldn't find anything.

3. Which of the following gives newsgroups their conversational nature?

    a. Posts

    b. Articles

    c. Threads

16

Answers

1. a. `comp.soc.women` belongs to the `comp.` hierarchy
2. c. It's always a good idea to look a little on your own before jumping into a newsgroup.
3. c. Threads

Activity

It's time for the rubber to meet the road. After lurking on some groups for a while, post an original article to a newsgroup and get involved in one additional thread by replying to an article. Hint: the `alt.quotations` newsgroup is a great place for this. People are always looking for the source of quotations and discussing other interesting topics.

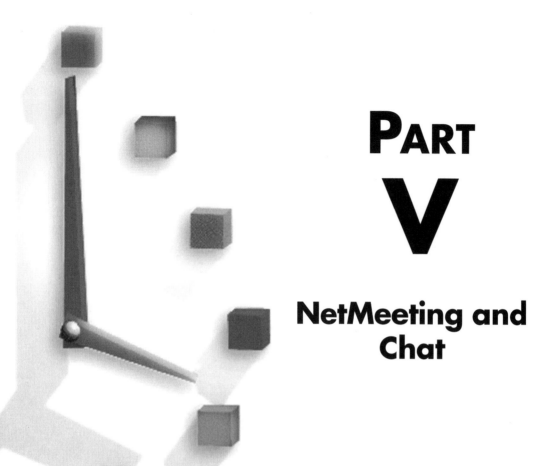

PART V

NetMeeting and Chat

Hour

Hour 17

Understanding Live Online Communications

In the four hours of the tutorial that begin now, you'll discover the ways Internet Explorer 4 supports live online interaction.

By *live,* I mean you're live at your PC, one or more persons with whom you're conversing are live at their PCs, and you're all communicating right then—in the moment—back and forth, just as if you were on the telephone (except that the conversation may involve typing and reading rather than talking and listening).

This is a dramatically different mode of communication than anything you've experienced up to this point. Although you may not have thought about it this way, everything else you've performed online has been an exchange of files. When you surf the Web, all you really do is download and display files from Web servers. When you send e-mail, you send files, and when you browse newsgroups, you receive files. Because the information in the transaction is all contained in files, communications need not be live; someone sends you an e-mail at 4:00, you read it at 8:00, and you respond Tuesday.

When communications are live, though, no files are waiting patiently for your attention. An ongoing stream of interaction exists between you and other parties, and if you go for coffee, you'll miss something. To put it the way they'd put it on the S.A.T.:

> "Live online communications are to all other Internet activities as phone calls are to exchanging voice recordings on tape."

Before getting into your first live conversations, it's important for you to appreciate that live communications have their own set of advantages and drawbacks that are quite different from those you encounter in other Internet activities. In this introductory hour, you discover the issues and methods involved in live interaction, so that you may approach Hours 18, 19, and 20 from an informed perspective.

At the end of the hour, you'll be able to answer the following questions:

☐ In what ways does Internet Explorer support live online communications?

☐ What are the pitfalls I should watch out for when communicating live?

☐ What other ways are there to communicate live on the Internet, besides those included with Internet Explorer 4?

How Does Internet Explorer Support Live Interaction?

In its full installation, Internet Explorer 4 includes two live communications tools: Microsoft Chat and NetMeeting.

Microsoft Chat: The Internet features a family of servers called *Internet Relay Chat* (IRC) servers that serve as hosts for live online chats in which participants type their statements and read the statements made by others. Anyone with a chat program, typically called a *chat client*, can use that program to communicate with an IRC server and join in a chat.

Because IRC is standardized, anyone, anywhere, on any type of computer can join in a chat. The other participants may themselves be using different kinds of computers as long as everyone in the chat uses an IRC-compatible chat client, of which there are many. Microsoft Chat is one.

Like any IRC program, Microsoft Chat can get you into chats on IRC servers. Unlike other chat clients, Chat displays the conversation as a comic strip (see Figure 17.1), putting participants' statements in the word balloons of onscreen comic characters. Microsoft thinks this makes chatting more fun. You learn how to use Chat in Hour 18.

17

Figure 17.1.

Microsoft Chat gets you into online chats, in comic style.

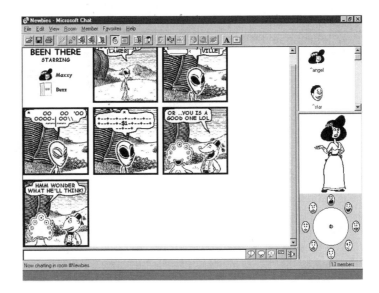

NetMeeting: Microsoft NetMeeting is an online conferencing system. You can use NetMeeting to establish a conference—using the Internet as the communications medium—among two, three, or more participants.

Between you and just one other participant, you can have a voice or a voice and video conference. Voice conferences use your PC's sound card; an attached microphone records your voice to send to your partner, and its speakers play the partner's voice for you. Because you do this through the Internet, you can, in effect, use NetMeeting to have the equivalent of a long-distance phone call, but you won't pay long-distance charges; you pay just your regular Internet charges. With computer video cameras attached to each partner's computer, the conference can include a fuzzy, jumpy video of each partner's face.

JUST A MINUTE

> For obvious reasons, the major long-distance phone companies are lobbying to get Internet phone conversations like those enabled by NetMeeting banned. "Reach out and sue someone."

Although voice and video conferences support only two participants at a time, any number can join in a NetMeeting-based text chat. A text chat in NetMeeting looks very much like an IRC chat session, with multiple participants typing and reading each other's statements. During conferences, participants can also use such NetMeeting tools as the Whiteboard, which lets participants draw or jot notes for all others to see. You learn how to use NetMeeting in Hours 19 and 20.

Figure 17.2.

NetMeeting lets you have online voice, video or text conferences.

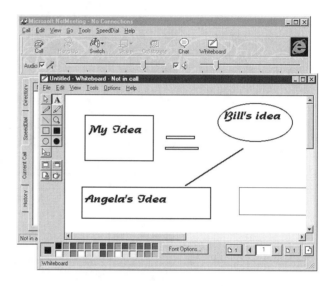

An essential distinction between Microsoft Chat and NetMeeting highlights the core issue of live communications: Chat supports an Internet standard (IRC), and therefore enables you to converse with many other people using many other IRC clients. NetMeeting is a closed system. All participants in a NetMeeting conference must use NetMeeting; they cannot use any other conferencing software. This severely limits the range of people with whom you can have a conference or an Internet phone call.

What Are the Problems with Live Communications?

Live communications bring with them a whole set of challenges and considerations that are different from those related to Web, e-mail, and newsgroup traffic—the rest of the Internet toolset.

Little Standardization

The distinction between Internet Explorer 4's two live tools—NetMeeting and Chat—illustrates the pervasive problem with live communications: a lack of standardization.

Most Internet activities are fairly well standardized. The Web uses a standardized set of file types and communications protocols, and because of that, you can use virtually any Web browser to visit virtually any Web site (although a site's use of leading-edge technologies, such as Java, may limit you to browsers that support those technologies). E-mail is standardized, so you can exchange e-mail through the Internet with anyone else, no matter what e-mail program they use. And any newsreader can get you into any newsgroup.

17

Among live activities, however, only IRC is standardized. Other activities, such as NetMeeting-style conferencing, are not standardized. To participate in such activities, everyone in the conversation must use the same program. That wouldn't be such a big deal if there were a single, widely adopted program that ran on every type of computer. But there isn't. The conferencing arena alone, for example, has at least three competing, mutually incompatible programs: NetMeeting, Netscape's Conference, and Internet Phone.

Until (and unless) a standard emerges, your best bet is to equip yourself with all popular options. That way, you'll be able to communicate with a broader range of partners. Some of the other popular options are described later in this hour.

Long Time Online

You can do a lot on the Web without spending much time online. And you can dramatically reduce the time you spend online with Web pages or channels by downloading the content and reading it offline. You can do the same with newsgroups and e-mail.

Live communications, however, requires a live connection at all times. And just as with the telephone, people sometimes find themselves starting conversations, losing all track of time, and spending hours and hours online. For some, this is not a problem; especially for those who have unlimited Internet accounts (see Hour 2). But those who pay for the Net by the minute, or those who should not tie up their phone line for so long, often find that they must make a choice between their Internet relationships and their real lives.

Privacy Problems

More so than the Web, more so than newsgroups, live communications expose you to potential Internet predators and violations of your privacy.

Although plenty of decent people use live communications, you must understand that IRC servers—and now NetMeeting directory servers—are prowled by sexual deviants looking to make trouble for you. A great deal of sexual and fetishist traffic exists on IRC and NetMeeting servers. Some of it—if you ask Maxine—is harmless fun between consenting adults. But there are also maladjusted folks wandering into other regions of the chat landscape looking for someone to bother.

The main reason you must watch out for this is that live communications programs—including Microsoft Chat and NetMeeting—generally allow you to enter a lot of personal information about yourself in the program, including such stuff as your real name, e-mail address, mailing address, and even telephone number. Depending on the programs involved, any information you enter in the dialogs may be accessible to others you communicate with. Typically, when someone accesses this information, nothing appears on the screen to tell you it's happening.

The programs tend to encourage you to enter this information, on the principle that communications are friendlier when everyone knows everyone else's life story. But in

17

Maxine's opinion, you must never supply more information to one of these programs than is absolutely required for the program to operate. If an online relationship develops, and you want to let someone know more about you, you can arrange to do that privately through e-mail, not in a live session where others may see it.

And if the program requires information that you're not comfortable divulging, don't use that program. After you lose your privacy, it's very hard to get it back.

Hardware Crunch

Being a text-only system, IRC exacts light demands on your PC. That's part of why IRC is so successful; even folks with old, underpowered, or obsolete computers and slow Internet connections can go chatting on IRC because all that's moving across the wire is text, the least demanding kind of data.

All other types of real-time communications are hardware intensive and communications intensive, and therefore demand serious hardware and Internet connections. For example, it's unlikely you could conduct a NetMeeting voice conference successfully without at least a 486 DX2 PC, 12 MB of RAM, an Internet connection running at 28.8 Kbps or faster, and a 16-bit sound card capable of full-duplex audio. You could try an audio/videoconference on that system, but you'd get pretty weak results: choppy, slow video and broken-up sound. A Pentium, 24 MB of RAM, and a 33.6 Kbps connection are the reasonable minimums for video-conferencing, regardless of the program you use to support the show.

"So what," you might say, "My system and connection are fast enough for all that." Fine... but what about your conferencing partners? Everyone in the group needs to have sufficient hardware and a fast connection. Do all your friends have as high-end a setup as you do?

Internet "Addiction"?

Lastly, the much reported "Net addictions" that can afflict some people can be associated with any Internet medium: the Web, e-mail, newsgroups, and so on. But by far, users of IRC and other live tools are the most susceptible. Whether that's because the medium itself is addictive or because the medium attracts addictive, lonely personalities is up for debate. But one can't ignore the data: Live communications are where the addicts wind up.

That's not a reason to eschew live communications. But it is a reason to keep an eye on yourself and your online behavior as you begin using these tools—especially if you know yourself to be an addictive personality. If you begin to notice that online activities are taking over your life, cut the cord before you get in too deep, or seek help.

17

Ironic though it may seem, you can find online some good resources for learning about, and coping with, Net addictions. A good starting place is Yahoo!'s directory of Internet Addiction resources (see Figure 17.3) at www.yahoo.com/Health/Mental_Health/Addition_and_Recovery/ Internet_Addiction.

Figure 17.3.

Yahoo!'s directory of Internet Addiction resources.

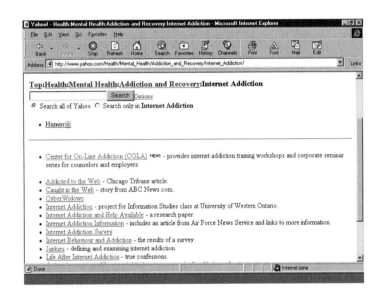

What Other Live Options Are There?

If you dig live communications, you're not always going to find that those with whom you want to converse have the same software as you. To broaden the range of folks you can chat with, you'll need to acquire and install other software besides Internet Explorer's Microsoft Chat and NetMeeting. Here are some of the more widely used options, plus information about *Web chats*, a little-used alternative to IRC.

By the way, a good place to learn more about live Internet interaction is the Voice FAQ (see Figure 17.4) at www.northcoast.com/savetz/voice.faq.html.

In the Voice FAQ, you'll learn about efforts underway to devise and promote standards that may, one day, lead to live Internet voice and video that works as well as the Web and e-mail work now. You'll also learn more about the wide variety of live communications software tools available for all systems.

Figure 17.4.

The Voice FAQ, where you can learn more about live communications.

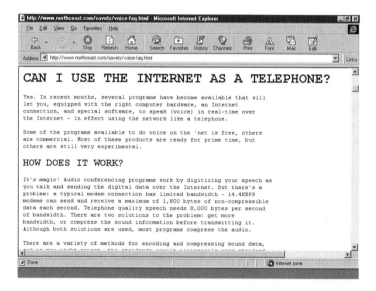

Speak Freely

Speak Freely is a voice conferencing program for Windows and UNIX systems that enables users of these different systems to intercommunicate. It features four different *compression modes*, which may enable voice communications over slower Internet connections.

You can learn more about Speak Freely at its home (see Figure 17.5): `www.fourmilab.ch/netfone/windows/speak_freely.html`.

Figure 17.5.

Here you can learn more about the Speak Freely voice conferencing software.

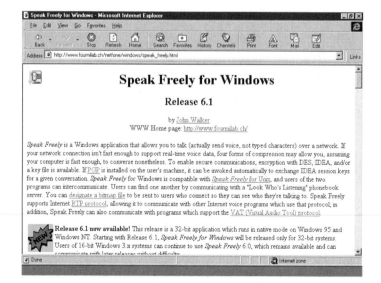

17

CU-SeeMe

Developed at Cornell University (the *CU*), CU-SeeMe is a widely used voice/videoconferencing system, with capabilities similar to those in NetMeeting (except for the lack of a whiteboard tool like NetMeeting's). Not only is it widely used in Windows, but it's available for the Mac, too.

You can learn more about CU-SeeMe at its home (see Figure 17.6): `www.fourmilab.ch/netfone/windows/speak_freely.html`.

Figure 17.6.

All about CU-SeeMe, a voice/videoconferencing system created by an Ivy Leaguer.

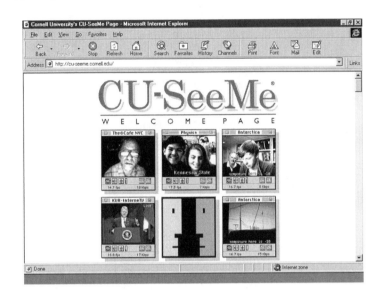

WebPhone

A product of an outfit that used to be called the Internet Telephone Company but is now called NetSpeak, WebPhone turns your browser into a voice conferencing system. It includes a cool looking interface that looks like a cellular phone, and includes NetMeeting-like features such as text chatting. It also has unique features, such as a multiple-lines capability and voice mail.

You can learn more about WebPhone at NetSpeak's home (see Figure 17.7): `www.itelco.com`.

Figure 17.7.

NetSpeak's Home, where you can learn more about WebPhone.

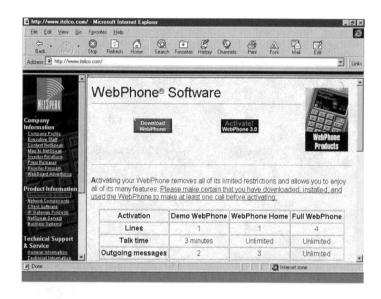

Netscape Conference

In case you didn't already know, Microsoft's chief rival in Internet software, Netscape, has an Internet software suite that's similar to Internet Explorer 4 and its components. Netscape Communicator includes a browser, e-mail software, newsgroup software, and a voice/video conferencing program, Netscape Conference (see Figure 17.8), which is nearly identical to NetMeeting, despite the fact that the two programs cannot communicate with one another. Conference even includes a Whiteboard tool that's very much like NetMeeting's.

You can learn more about Conference at Netscape's home page: `home.netscape.com`.

Figure 17.8.

Netscape Conference, the voice/videoconferencing component of Netscape Communicator.

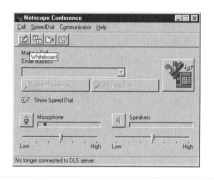

Web Chats

As an alternative to IRC, Web pages sometimes host text-based chats centering on particular topics. Because the Web and browsers are not designed for chatting, each of these chats generally requires a different player program or plug-in to enable the browser to join the chat. When you find a page about an upcoming Web chat, you'll also usually find a link for downloading any software required to participate in it.

The Yahoo! search service, for example, hosts frequent Web chats on all sorts of topics. You can learn about upcoming chats by visiting Yahoo!'s home at www.yahoo.com. Although some browsers must download a plug-in to participate in a Yahoo! chat, Internet Explorer users can simply log into the chat, as instructed by the Yahoo! chat page (see Figure 17.9). When they do, the plug-in is automatically downloaded and installed in Internet Explorer by Yahoo!.

Figure 17.9.

Setting up Internet Explorer to enter a Yahoo!-hosted Web chat.

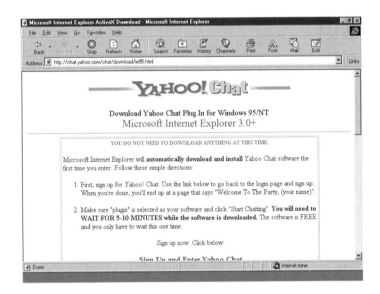

Summary

I hope this hour hasn't turned you off regarding live communications. It can be a very useful tool. But I do hope that, before diving into live communications in Hour 18, you now appreciate the problems associated with live conversations. They're terrific when used smartly, but easily abused. Keep sharp.

Q&A

Q You mentioned something about the importance of a "full-duplex" sound card for voice conferencing. I live in a duplex, here in Flushing. (My landlord lives in the other unit.) Does that mean I have a full duplex sound card? Or is it half-duplex because I live in only one side of the house? My kids play with Duplo... Does that help?

A Full-duplex means that the card can handle playing audio and recording audio simultaneously. Half duplex means that the card can do only one of these at a time.

With a full-duplex sound card, the conversation is more like a real telephone call because you can interrupt and hear the other person while you're speaking (and vice versa). With half-duplex audio, the call is more like a CB radio or a cheap speakerphone: One talks, the other listens, and then the other talks. Most newer PCs have full-duplex sound cards. But older (and cheaper) PCs may have only half-duplex capability.

Quiz

Take the following quiz to see how much you've learned.

Questions

1. Which of the following Internet activities is not standardized?

   a. Web surfing

   b. Voice conferencing

   c. IRC chatting

   d. E-mail

2. When configuring a live communications program, you're presented with a dialog that asks you to enter information about yourself. You should

   a. Fill in every blank.

   b. Enter details about an alternate identity.

   c. Skip the dialog.

   d. Enter as little information as the program will accept, and never enter anything that you wouldn't want made public.

3. Which activity generally requires the fastest PC and Internet connection?

   a. Voice conferencing

   b. Videoconferencing

   c. Web chatting

   d. IRC chatting

4. Choppy, halting sound in a voice conference is generally a sign that

   a. Your Internet connection is too slow to support voice conferencing.

   b. Your PC is too slow to support voice conferencing.

   c. The PC or connection of your conversation partner is too slow to support voice conferencing.

   d. Any of the above.

Answers

1. b. There's no standard yet for voice conferencing.

2. d. Never reveal more than you have to when describing yourself to an online communications program.

3. b. Video can bring a network to its knees.

4. d. Any of the choices—or any combination of them—can cause choppy sound or video.

Activity

Think about the types of live communications available. Which attract you? Which don't? Does the anonymity of text chatting appeal to you, or are you drawn to the up-front reality of voice/videoconferencing? The answers may affect how you approach the next two hours of this tutorial.

17

Hour 18

Chatting with Microsoft Chat

Feel the need to reach out and touch someone, "live" and (almost) in person? Microsoft Chat puts you online in a live conversation with other Internet users, anywhere in the world.

At the end of the hour, you'll be able to answer the following questions:

☐ What is Internet chatting, also known as Internet Relay Chat (IRC)?

☐ How is Microsoft Chat different than a typical chat program?

☐ How do I join an online chat session?

☐ How do I choose the identity by which I will be known in the chat?

☐ How do I enhance my contributions to the chat with expressions, gestures, and other touches?

☐ How do I exit one chat and enter another?

JUST A MINUTE

You may as well know right here that a substantial amount of chat traffic on the Internet is dedicated to sex chats of various persuasions and fetishes. There are many sex chat rooms, and sex-chat-oriented chatters often wander into non-sex-oriented rooms looking for new friends.

If that's okay with you, fine. But if you have an aversion to such stuff, tread carefully in Chat. If you have a severe aversion to it, it's best to stay out of Chat altogether.

Understanding Internet Chatting

When you're in an Internet chat, everything you type appears on the screen of everybody else participating in that particular chat. Thousands of different chats are underway at once, each in its own chat room. When you join a chat, you enter a room, and from then on you see only the conversation that's taking place in that room.

Chat room: A space where a single conversation is taking place. In Internet chat parlance, a chat room is sometimes known as a *channel.*

In most chat rooms, the conversation is focused around a given subject area. In a singles chat room, participants chat about stuff singles like to talk about. In a geology chat, people generally talk about rocks and earthquakes.

Everything the other chatters type appears on your screen, as shown in Figure 18.1. Each participant's statements are labeled with a nickname to identify who's talking. Those participating in a chat (known as *members*) choose their own nicknames and rarely share their real names. In a chat, you can be whoever you want to be, and so can everyone else.

Nickname: Your nickname, which you choose yourself, is how you're known to others in a chat. Your nickname appears on every statement you make, so everyone knows who's talking.

Figure 18.1.

An Internet chat is conducted as an ongoing volley of typed statements between participants sharing a chat room.

About Microsoft Chat

To chat, you must have a program called a chat client. Internet Explorer 4's own chat client, included in the Full installation (see Hour 1), is called Microsoft Chat, and it's a very unusual animal.

Like any chat client, Microsoft Chat—henceforth to be known simply as *Chat* with a capital *C*—lets you communicate with chat servers. You can view the list of chat rooms, join a chat room, read what everyone says in the chat room, and make your own contributions to the discussion. What's different about Chat is the way it displays the conversation.

NEW TERM   **Chat server:** A chat takes place on a chat server, more properly called an *IRC server*. (IRC stands for Internet Relay Chat, the full formal name for Chat.) Just as you need a Web browser to communicate with a Web server, you need a program called a *chat client* to communicate with a chat server.

Like the chat client shown earlier in Figure 18.1 (which is really just Chat in its text mode, which you'll learn more about later), most chat clients show the text of the conversation, a line at a time, and label each line with the speaker's nickname. Chat, however, displays the conversation like a comic strip (see Figure 18.2), using little cartoon characters to represent members and showing the member's words in cartoon word balloons. Folks at Microsoft think this approach makes chatting feel more human, more fun. In its first versions, Chat was actually named "Microsoft Comic Chat."

NEW TERM   **Balloon:** The little bubble you see in comics in which the words and thoughts of characters appear.

Figure 18.2.

Microsoft Chat makes the chat look like a comic strip, with a different cartoon character for each participant.

It's important to understand that chat servers support any IRC client, so most folks you'll end up chatting with probably don't use Microsoft Chat. Many use ordinary text IRC clients; they see your statements labeled with your nickname but don't see your comic character.

On your display, Chat converts all statements in a chat—even those made by users of text-only clients—into comics. Other Chat users in the room with you appear as their chosen cartoon character. For users of other chat clients, Chat automatically uses an unused character.

Joining a Chat Room

Now that you understand what chatting is all about, it's time to hit a server and see it for real. On the way, though, you'll perform some automatic configuration that Chat needs to operate properly.

TIME SAVER

Before opening Chat, you can be online or off. If you're offline when you begin, Chat connects to the Internet automatically. Also, the Internet Explorer 4 browser need not be open for you to use Chat, although it won't hurt anything if it is open.

18

To Do: Start Chat and Display the Chat Rooms List

1. Click the Windows Start button and choose Programs | Internet Explorer | Microsoft Chat. The Connect dialog opens, as shown in Figure 18.3.

Figure 18.3.

The Connect dialog connects you to a selected chat server.

2. Select the Show All Available Chat Rooms option, and then click OK. After you're online, a list of all chat rooms available on the server appears. You are now connected to a chat server and ready to chat—except that, as a new user, you have not yet selected a nickname and a comic character, as described next.

Choosing an Identity

Before you can join in a chat, you must create a nickname. And because of Chat's unique presentation style, you must choose a comic character too. In addition, you can select a background that appears behind the characters in each panel of the comic, as you see it on your screen.

After you choose a nickname, character, and background, Chat remembers them for future sessions. You do not need to choose them again, unless you want to change them.

To Do: Choose Your Chat Identity

1. Choose View | Options. The Options dialog appears.

2. Choose the Personal Info tab (see Figure 18.4), if it is not already open.

3. Click in the Nickname box and type a nickname for yourself. Your nickname should be one word, using no spaces or punctuation, and it should also be unusual to reduce the chances that another member has chosen the same nickname. If you attempt to enter a room where someone is already using the same nickname as you, Chat prompts you to change your nickname before entering.

18

Figure 18.4.

On the Personal Info tab, you type a nickname.

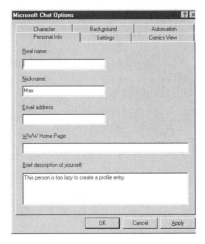

JUST A MINUTE

On the Personal Info tab, you can enter other information besides your nickname, such as your real name and e-mail address. Think carefully before doing so, however. Whatever information you supply here can be seen by other members whose clients (like Chat) can display member profiles. If you want to keep your anonymity, enter your nickname and nothing else.

4. Click the Character tab. This is where you select your character.

5. Select the character you want to play by clicking a name in the Character column (see Figure 18.5). Note that someone else in the chat may use the same character as you. Chatters can share characters, but not nicknames.

   The Preview column shows what the selected character looks like—what *you* will look like to other Chat users if you stick with that character.

TIME SAVER

When choosing a character in the Character tab, you can click the faces in the emotion wheel (beneath the character preview) to see what the character will look like when you apply to it a given emotion when making a statement. You learn about choosing emotions later in this hour.

6. Click the Background tab. This tab (see Figure 18.6) enables you to select from several cartoon backgrounds to use when chatting.

7. Choose a background. When you select an entry in the Background column, the background appears in the Preview column.

8. Click OK.

18

Figure 18.5.
Click a name in the Character column, and you see the character in the Preview column.

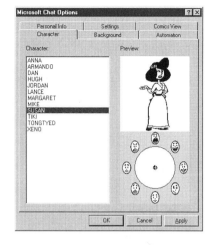

Figure 18.6.
On the Background tab, choose the background to go behind the characters in each panel of the chat.

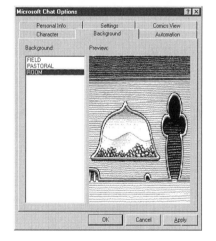

Entering a Room

To enter a chat room, you select a room from the chat room list. Figure 18.7 shows the list of chats available on Microsoft's chat server. Each server has its own list, and the lists change often.

TIME SAVER

The chat room list reappears after you finish selecting your identity. But you can open the chat room list any time you're connected to the server by clicking the Chat Room List button on Chat's toolbar.

In the list, the name of each room begins with a hash mark (#). The name of the room is followed by the number of members currently in the room, and sometimes also by a description of the conversation that usually takes place there.

Figure 18.7.

To enter any room in the list, double-click its name.

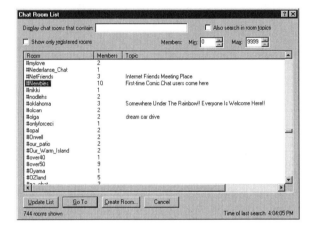

On most servers, there's a chat room specifically set up to practice chatting, called #Newbies. Give it a try.

To Do: Enter a Chat Room

1. Scroll down the chat room list (it's organized alphabetically) until you see the room #Newbies.

2. Double-click #Newbies. The Chat window opens, as shown in Figure 18.8, and you're in the chat.

Observe that the Chat window is broken up into five sections, or *panes* (covered clockwise from upper left):

☐ The biggest pane is the viewing pane, where you see the chat session as it progresses.

☐ The small pane in the upper right is the member list pane, which lists all members in the current chat room.

☐ The pane showing your character is the self-view pane, which reminds you of who you are.

☐ The ring of faces is the emotion wheel, from which you can select your character's facial expression.

☐ The small text box at the very bottom of the window is the compose pane, where you type your statements.

18

TIME SAVER

Instead of double-clicking the chat room name, you can click it once to select it, and then click the Go To button in the chat room list.

JUST A MINUTE

When you first arrive in a room, you won't see any comic panels right away. The server shows you only what's been said *since* you entered the room. After you enter, statements begin appearing, one by one, as members make them.

Figure 18.8.

Chats happen in the chat window.

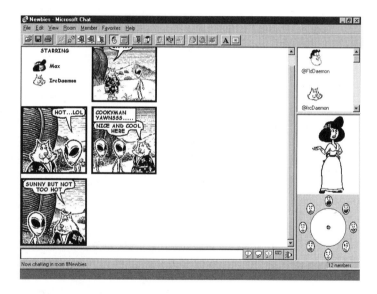

JUST A MINUTE

Often in a chat with three or more members, the conversation appears out-of-order, not following the logical order of a conversation. That jumbling happens because each member's words take a different amount of time to reach the server, and because some members take more time composing their statements than others. But once you've used Chat for a while, you get used to the jumbling, and your brain learns to sort out the conversation intuitively.

18

Contributing to the Conversation

Now that you're in a room, you can just *lurk* (listen in) to the conversation, or you can contribute to it by sending your statements for all others to see. Note that you are not obligated to add anything to the conversation. In fact, just lurking in a chat room is a great way to learn more about chats before diving in.

When you contribute, you can choose the style of the comic word balloon in which your words will appear to you and to other Chat users. You choose the style of the word balloon by clicking a button next to the compose pane, which is the text box at the bottom of the Chat window in which you type all your statements.

For example, for a particular statement, you can choose a think balloon so that the words appear in the balloon style generally used in comics to represent what the character is thinking. (Snoopy, for example, can't speak, so all his words appear in thought balloons.)

JUST A MINUTE

Keep in mind that while you're typing and editing your statements, no one sees them but you. A statement is sent to the chat only when you press Enter. That gives you a chance to choose your words carefully and correct typos before committing your statement to the chat.

To Do: Add Statements to a Chat

1. Enter a chat room that interests you, and follow the conversation until you understand what's being talked about.

2. When you are ready to contribute, simply begin typing. Anything you type while in a chat room appears automatically in the compose pane, the text box at the bottom of the Chat window. As you type, you can use the Backspace, Delete, Insert, and arrow keys to edit your statement and correct mistakes.

JUST A MINUTE

When wording a statement, keep in mind that Chat automatically gives your character certain gestures based on words in the statement (see "Gesturing," later in this hour).

3. When your statement is worded the way you want, press Enter. After a few moments, your statement appears as part of the scrolling conversation displayed in the chat window. It appears at the very same spot in the list in the display of everyone else in the room.

18

Those in the room using regular chat clients see your statement labeled with your nickname, so they know you said it. Those in the room using Microsoft Chat see your chosen comic character speaking the words in a *say balloon,* the type that surrounds words that comic characters say aloud. The say balloon is the default balloon style, the one Chat uses automatically when you don't select a different balloon style.

4. Type a statement that's more a thought than a statement—an opinion perhaps. Before pressing Enter to submit the statement, click the Think button (second from the left) in the compose pane. Then press Enter. Chat users see your character thinking the words in a thought balloon, the type that surrounds the thoughts of comic characters.

5. Think of a statement your character might whisper, rather than say aloud. Type the statement, click the Whisper button (third from the left), and then press Enter. Chat users see your character whispering the words in the type of balloon that surrounds the whispers of comic characters.

Showing Emotions

The emotion wheel in the lower-left corner of the chat window lets you change the expression of your character's face when making a statement.

JUST A MINUTE

> Because some members in the room might not be using Chat and there-fore can't see expressions, be sure your words alone carry your meaning.

To Do: Change Expressions

1. Get into a chat.

2. Type a statement, but don't press Enter.

3. Select a face from the emotion wheel. The character in the self-view pane changes to show how your character will appear if you commit to using the selected expression. As long as you don't press Enter, you can choose a different expression until you find one you like.

TIME SAVER

> To choose your character's normal, *neutral* expression, click the + at the center of the emotion wheel.

4. When the self-view pane appears the way you want it to, press Enter to submit your statement.

Gesturing

If you watch a chat for awhile, you'll notice that the characters are not static. They change body position and gestures, panel to panel. The gesturing is selected automatically by Chat, based on words you use in your statements. For example, if a statement contains the word *I,* when speaking that statement your character will appear to point to himself or herself.

You can use other member's nicknames to control to whom the gesture is made. For example, if you say "Hi," your character appears to wave to the group. If you say "Hi, Eloise," your character appears to wave at the member using the nickname Eloise.

Table 18-1 describes the gestures that Chat applies. Observe that some gestures are based on words used to *begin* a statement and others are based on words *within* the statement.

JUST A MINUTE

When a statement both begins with a gesture word and contains a gesture word, Chat applies the gesture for the beginning word.

Table 18.1. Gestures used automatically by Chat characters.

Statement Begins With	Character's Action
I	Points to itself
You	Points to another member
Hello or Hi	Waves
Bye	Waves
Welcome	Waves
Howdy	Waves

Statement Contains	Character's Action
are you	Points to another member
will you	Points to another member
did you	Points to another member
aren't you	Points to another member
don't you	Points to another member
I'm	Points to itself
I am	Points to itself
I'll	Points to itself
I will	Points to itself

18

Switching Rooms

Often, you'll find that not much is going on in a chat room you enter, or that the conversation has taken a turn you don't care to follow. At such times, all you have to do is leave the room you're in and enter a different one.

JUST A MINUTE

When you leave the room, a message appears in the chat to inform everybody that you're gone. You can't "sneak out" without anybody knowing, as you can in life when a conversation turns ugly.

To Do: Switch to Another Room

1. While in a room, click the Leave Room button on Chat's toolbar.

2. Click the Enter Room button on the toolbar to open a dialog like the one in Figure 18.9. Observe that the dialog features an optional place to type a password. Some chat rooms are set up for private conversations; to enter, you must type a password. Most chats are public, though, so you generally ignore the password box.

Figure 18.9.

To enter a new room, click Enter Room and type the name of the room.

3. Type the name of the room. Be sure to include the hash mark (#) at the beginning of the room name, as in #Newbies.

4. Click OK.

TIME SAVER

If you don't know the name of the room you want to go to, click the Chat Room List button on Chat's toolbar to open the chat room list, and then choose a room from the list.

Summary

Chat's fun, as long as you stay among those whose reasons for chatting are the same as yours. Like a carnival or a circus, Chat is an entertaining place with a seedy underbelly, one to be enjoyed with caution. But if you're careful, you can have blast with Chat.

Q&A

Q Maxine, you seem a little negative about the crowd one might meet when chatting. Do I really need to be all that concerned?

A First off, let me point out that I'm fine with whatever my readers want to do. If you're attracted to the racy side of chat, have fun. But for those who are put off by sex chats and such, it's important to understand that chatting has become the preferred domain of such traffic, far more so than the Web or newsgroups. Chat is also the principal medium through which lonely people may develop unhealthy Net "addictions."

I encourage all my readers to try Chat. But go in with your eyes wide open. And don't assume that because you're not in a sex-oriented chat room, the conversation won't turn that way. For example, on Microsoft's server, a number of different channels are supposedly set up as practice areas for Chat (each room name begins "#Microsoft..."). I had planned to take the figures for this hour from one of those rooms, but in each one I visited, characters were making statements that a nice, family publisher such as Sams would never permit in its publications.

Quiz

Take the following quiz to see how much you've learned.

Questions

1. To start Microsoft Chat, open your Start menu and choose

    a. Microsoft Chat

    b. Programs | Internet Explorer | Microsoft Chat

    c. Settings | Control Panel | Chat Clients | Chat

    d. Programs | Microsoft Chat | Now

2. When you share a chat room with members using chat clients other than Microsoft Chat

    a. Everyone sees the session as comics

    b. Everyone sees the session as text

    c. You see the session as comics (including statements made by non-Chat users), but they see it as text (including your statements)

    d. Chat users cannot share a room with non-Chat users

18

3. To make a statement appear as a "thought" to other Chat users

    a. Click the Think button before submitting the statement

    b. Use the word *think* anywhere in the statement

    c. Think really really hard while typing it

    d. Include the command [IDEA] in the statement

4. Be careful what you include on your Personal Info tab because

    a. Wrong information can crash Chat

    b. The Internal Revenue Service monitors the tab, which is scary

    c. Direct-marketing people at Microsoft monitor the tab, which is *really* scary

    d. That information may be accessed by others you chat with

Answers

1. b. Only b opens Chat.

2. c. Remember that only you and other users of Microsoft Chat see the comics; all others see just the text.

3. a. This choice is the only one that works, and is also not stupid like the others.

4. d. Don't give others the chance to learn more about you than you care to tell.

Activity

Open the chat room list, and spend some time scrolling through it and reading the names and descriptions of chats on the server. Make notes of the names of any chats you'd like to check out, and be sure to visit one or two new chats each time you go exploring.

18

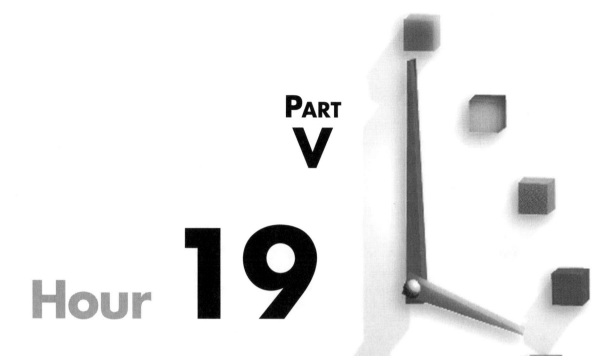

PART V

Hour 19

Getting Started with NetMeeting

NetMeeting is Internet Explorer 4's component for live, real-time audio and visual conferencing.

With NetMeeting (see Figure 19.1), you can have a voice conference with anyone else on the Internet who uses NetMeeting. Depending on what you pay for Internet service and how far away your caller is, using NetMeeting for such "Internet telephone" calls may be substantially cheaper than using the telephone because the call costs you nothing beyond what you already pay for your Internet account.

But NetMeeting does much more. You can have a text-based chat (like a chat client), draw and type messages on a collaborative whiteboard, and more.

In this hour, you'll learn the basics of setting up NetMeeting and using it for voice calls.

At the end of the hour, you'll be able to answer the following questions:

- What can I do with NetMeeting?
- What hardware do I need to have a voice conference?

□ How do I set up and configure NetMeeting?

□ How do I move among the activities in the NetMeeting window?

□ How can I customize my personal information in NetMeeting?

□ How do I start a conference by accepting a call from someone else?

□ How do I start a conference by calling?

In Hour 20, you'll go further, learning how to use the whiteboard, have a video conference, and use speed dialing.

JUST A MINUTE

To have a voice conversation through NetMeeting, everyone in the conversation must have not only NetMeeting and an Internet account, but also a sound card, a microphone, and speakers (or headphones) installed on their computers.

Figure 19.1.

NetMeeting lets you talk to people all over the world.

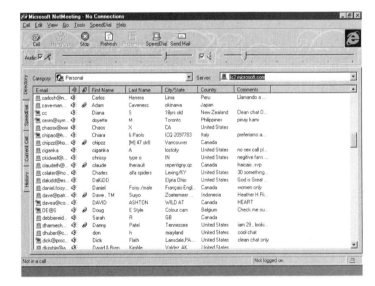

Starting NetMeeting for the First Time

The first time you start NetMeeting, it launches the NetMeeting Setup wizard to help you get NetMeeting configured (see Figure 19.2). Work your way through the steps to configure NetMeeting.

CAUTION

Close all programs (except Windows, of course) before beginning the following procedure.

To Do: Set Up NetMeeting

To Do

1. Open NetMeeting from the Start menu by choosing Programs | Microsoft NetMeeting or by choosing Programs | Internet Explorer | Microsoft NetMeeting. The wizard opens, as shown in Figure 19.2.

Figure 19.2.

The NetMeeting Setup wizard helps you get started.

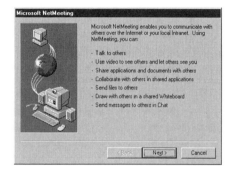

2. Read the introductory message, and then click on the Next button to get started. The dialog shown in Figure 19.3 appears.

   The first thing you need to decide is whether you want to log on to a NetMeeting directory server when you start the application and, if so, which one. In most cases, this is a good idea because the directory server is where you will probably find the people you want to talk to. The server can also list your name in the directory so that other people on the Internet know you're online and can call you.

   I suggest leaving the Log On to a Directory Server When NetMeeting Starts check box checked, and leave the What Directory Server You Would Like to Use? list set to ils.microsoft.com for now. You can change both options later if you need to.

Figure 19.3.

The NetMeeting Setup wizard helps you configure NetMeeting.

19

3. Choose your server options, and then click Next. The dialog shown in Figure 19.4 appears.

   NetMeeting wants to know some things about you. This information will show up on the directory server that you chose in the preceding dialog whenever you are logged on.

4. Type the information that you want to have listed, and click the Next button to continue.

CAUTION

Before the Setup wizard will let you continue to step 5, you have to enter at least your first and last name and your e-mail address in the dialog shown in Figure 19.4.

As with Chat (see Hour 18), it pays to be discreet and cautious when using personal information in NetMeeting. Directory servers are cruised by some lonely, creepy people to whom you may not want to reveal too much about yourself. In the dialog shown in Figure 19.4, consider using a phony name and e-mail address, just to preserve your privacy.

Figure 19.4.

Enter the information you want NetMeeting to use for you on the directory server.

5. On the next screen (see Figure 19.5), you decide which category in the directory to list yourself in: personal use, business use, or adults-only use. Choose the option that is appropriate for how you intend to use NetMeeting, and then click the Next button to continue. A dialog informing you that you're about to configure your sound card for NetMeeting opens.

6. Click Next. A dialog opens, listing your sound card as the *wave device* (sound card) that NetMeeting will use for recording (sending your voice to others) and playback (playing others' voices to you).

19

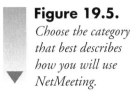

Figure 19.5.

Choose the category that best describes how you will use NetMeeting.

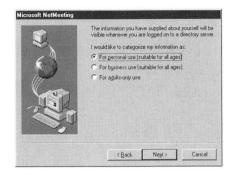

7. If the device listed is your sound card, click Next. Otherwise, use the drop-down lists to select the correct devices, and then click Next. The dialog shown in Figure 19.6 opens. Here you tell NetMeeting what type of connection to the Internet you have.

Figure 19.6.

Choose the type of connection to the Internet you have.

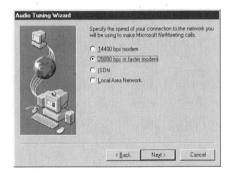

8. Click on the correct option, and then click Next. A dialog appears in which you help NetMeeting set the microphone level so that the people you talk to can hear you clearly.

9. Click the Start Recording button, and then immediately begin reading the paragraph that begins "Microsoft NetMeeting enables you to...", speaking clearly and as loudly as you would speak during a voice call in NetMeeting. NetMeeting records your voice for about nine seconds, using its strength to set a recording level for future NetMeeting sessions. (See Figure 19.7.)

10. When the Tuning Progress indicator reaches the end, NetMeeting stops recording. Don't worry if you haven't finished reading the paragraph; just click the Next button to continue.

11. A final dialog appears, reporting that you've configured NetMeeting. Click Finish to close the wizard.

Figure 19.7.
*Set your micro-
phone level so you
can be heard
clearly.*

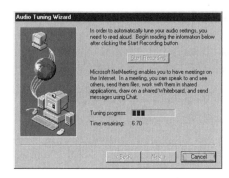

NetMeeting starts and logs on to the directory server you chose. After you're logged on, you see a list of other users who are logged on to the same server. You can scroll through the list (which is sorted by e-mail address) and find your name in there. Now anyone who wants to talk to you can find your name on the list and call you up.

Getting Around in NetMeeting

NetMeeting has a simple interface that's easy to figure out. In the main screen (shown earlier in Figure 19.1), the biggest section is the list of people logged on to the directory server that you chose. To its left are tabs that enable you to change what you see in the main view.

Above the directory listing are the Category and Server drop-down lists. Above those lists is the audio level adjustment toolbar. Finally, the toolbar and menus are at the top of the window, as with most Windows applications.

This section is a quick tour of each of these areas, one at a time.

The Directory Listing

When you first start NetMeeting, you see a list of people. These are the people in the Category you selected and on the server you selected when you ran the NetMeeting Setup wizard. Because I chose `ils.microsoft.com` as my server and put myself in the For Personal Use category, I can see the list of everyone who made the same choices.

In this list, you see eight columns:

E-mail	The person's e-mail address
Audio	A small yellow speaker in this column means that this person can talk to you
Video	A small gray video camera in this column means that this person can send live video over the Internet
First Name	The person's first name

19

Last Name	The person's last name
City/State	The city and state that this person is currently in
Country	The country that this person is in
Comments	Comments, if any, that this person entered in the comments field

Keep in mind that all this information, other than that in the Audio and Video columns, is entered by the person using NetMeeting. Some people choose not to reveal their true identities or locations. You shouldn't accept the information listed here as 100% accurate.

By default, the listing is sorted by e-mail address, but you can sort it by any information you like. To sort the entries by a different column just click on the column header. For example, if you want the entries sorted by country, you can click on the Country heading above the listings.

The Category and Server Lists

Above the directory listing are the Category and Server drop-down lists. These control who shows up in the directory listing. When you start NetMeeting, by default it logs you on to the server you chose in the NetMeeting Setup wizard and displays the category you chose for your entry.

If you want to see the entries on a different server, just click the down-arrow to the right of the Server drop-down list and choose the server that you want to use.

TIME SAVER

Dropping down the server list on the main screen does not log you on to a different server. It only shows you the listing of who is logged on to that server. You will not find your name in the list after you change servers.

Similarly, to see the list of people in a different category than yourself, just choose the category you want to see from the Category drop-down list. Setting the Category field to, say, Business, will let you see the list of people who have designated that their information is For Business Use.

JUST A MINUTE

As with changing the Server field, choosing another category to view doesn't change the category that your information is listed under. I'll show you how to change your category in the section, "Changing Your Personal Information."

19

The Tabbed Call Windows

To the left of the directory listing are four tabs:

- Directory
- SpeedDial
- Current Call
- History

The Directory tab contains the Category and Server fields and the directory listing. The first time you start NetMeeting, the Directory tab is the one you see. Clicking on the other tabs enables you to see different information pertaining to calls you can make, the current call, or calls you've received.

 Current call: Current call is how NetMeeting describes the conference in which you are currently engaged. It's the "current call" whether it's a voice conference or a video or text conference (see Hour 20).

You can use the SpeedDial tab the same way you would use a SpeedDial button on your telephone. This tab keeps a short list of people you call regularly so you don't have to search for their names in the main directory listing. You can also have on the same SpeedDial list people who frequent different servers so that you don't have to keep changing servers to find the person you want to call.

After you've added someone to your SpeedDial list, NetMeeting starts on this screen instead of the Directory screen, because you're more likely to want to call the person whose number you've saved than someone you haven't talked to before.

The Current Call tab, as the name implies, shows a list of the people in the current call. You will always find at least two names in this list if you're in a call, or none if you're not. Also, if you or another person is sending video, you'll see it in the video boxes on the right side of the screen on this tab. I'll be talking about the Current Call tab in each of the other hours in this part of the book.

Finally, the History tab holds a list of all the calls you've received from other people. The caller's name, the date and time of the call, and whether you accepted, rejected, or ignored the call are all listed on this tab.

The Audio Level Controls

Using the audio level controls, you can change the level of your voice and the voice of the other person on the call (see Figure 19.8).

19

Figure 19.8.

The audio level controls enable you to adjust the volume of your voice and the voice of the person you're talking to.

Just drag the slider for either the microphone (your voice) or the speaker (the other person's voice) to the left to lower the level or to the right to increase the volume. In most cases, you won't need to adjust the microphone level because that should have been set automatically by the NetMeeting Setup wizard. You can change the speaker volume to suit your taste for each individual call, however. You can also use the check boxes on the audio level controls to temporarily mute yourself or your conversation partner.

Changing Your Personal Information

Earlier in this hour, you entered your personal information in NetMeeting. You also learned that you have to be careful about how much information to reveal, and whether to use real or phony information (to protect your privacy).

So it stands to reason that you may want or need to change that personal information from time to time. Here's how.

To Do: Change Information about Yourself

1. From NetMeeting's menu bar, choose Call | Change My Information. The Options dialog opens (see Figure 19.9).

Figure 19.9.

To change your personal information, choose Change My Information from the Call menu.

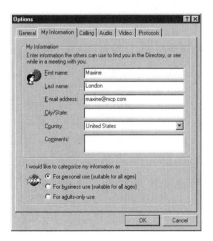

19

2. In the My Information section, change any fields you want.

3. In the I Would Like to Categorize My Information As section, choose the category that your listing belongs in.

4. If you want to change the server that you log on to when you start NetMeeting, click the Calling tab of the Options dialog (see Figure 19.10). The first item in the Directory section shows the directory server you are currently using. Select the one you want to use from the drop-down list.

5. When you have made all the changes to your information that you want, click the OK button at the bottom of the Options dialog.

Figure 19.10.

Change your directory server on the Calling tab of the Options dialog.

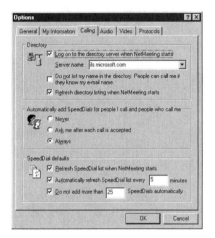

Answering a Call

To talk to someone on the Internet with NetMeeting, you have to call someone or someone has to call you. Here I cover answering a call; in the next section I cover making a call.

When someone calls you, the first thing that happens is you hear the phone ring. It's not really the phone ringing, though; the sound is coming out of the speakers of your computer. Next, you'll notice at the bottom right side of your screen a NetMeeting dialog that says who is calling. It also has two buttons: Accept and Ignore. If you don't want to talk to the caller, click the Ignore button. To answer this call, click the Accept button.

After you accept a call, the NetMeeting window switches automatically to the Current Call tab. Here you'll see the name of the caller and your name, along with a little information. To the right of each name are several columns:

Audio   A little yellow speaker in this column means that this person can talk over the Internet

19

Video   A small gray video camera in this column means that you should also
             see live video in the Remote Video frame to the right (see Hour 20).

Chat   A small white and blue rectangle in this column means that the chat
             window is open (see Hour 20).

TIME SAVER

> When you're talking to someone over the Internet, be sure to keep your microphone about five to ten inches from your mouth for best results. If you hold it too close, your voice will be distorted. If it's too far away, it will not pick up enough of your voice to transmit properly.

It may take a few seconds for NetMeeting to complete the connection between your computer and the caller's. After it has finished, though, you can talk to the other person just as if you were using a telephone. Feel free to talk to the caller for as long as you like. No one is paying a long-distance bill for this conversation; you and the caller are simply paying whatever you pay for Internet access.

During the call, you can use any special features of NetMeeting, including the Whiteboard and text-based chat (both are covered in Hour 20).

When you finish talking to the caller, one of you has to hang up. In NetMeeting, this means clicking the Hang Up button on the toolbar. You can hang up at any time, just like you can on the telephone. And just like on the telephone, common courtesy dictates that you should wait until the conversation is over before you do.

Placing a Call

Calling someone with NetMeeting is actually easier than using the white pages and a telephone. You don't need to remember or dial anyone's phone number, you just have to double-click a name in the directory list. After you've connected with someone, you can have NetMeeting automatically save the listing for you — no more writing down phone numbers on scraps of paper and then looking them up again after you lose them.

Let me show you the basic steps involved in calling someone. Suppose I want to call my sister Shirley. All I have to do is log on to the directory server where she is listed and find her name in the listing (see Figure 19.11).

Now I just double-click her name. When she answers, NetMeeting switches over to the Current Call tab. After a few seconds during which the computers connect, we'll be able to talk just like we would over the telephone.

19

Figure 19.11.

Find the person you want to call in the directory listing.

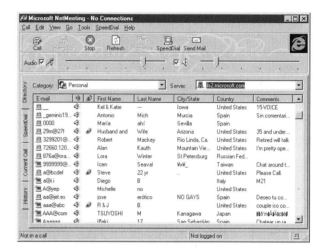

If for some reason Shirley doesn't want to talk to me when I call (she may still be fuming about that totally innocent thigh remark I made at Thanksgiving), she can click on the Ignore button in the NetMeeting dialog that announces my call. (But she better not, if she knows what's good for her!)

If she does click Ignore, I see a dialog telling me that she didn't accept my call. The dialog asks me whether I want to send her a message instead. If I click the Yes button, NetMeeting opens a new message window in Outlook Express (see Hour 13), preaddressed to Shirley. All I have to do is type a subject and compose a message to her—letting her know how *completely* childish she's being—and then click the Send button. The next time Shirley checks her e-mail, she'll find the message. And then she'll reply with a lavish apology and an invitation to her Memorial Day picnic.

JUST A MINUTE

The same dialog appears whether the person you're calling clicks Ignore or simply doesn't respond. So when you get that message, do not assume that the person you're calling refused your call. He or she may simply be away from his or her PC.

Summary

As you can see, NetMeeting is terrifically useful to those who need to converse or collaborate with others who also use NetMeeting. To everybody else, it's *bupkis*. But if you've been hooked by this hour, wait till you learn how to make NetMeeting take off in Hour 20.

19

Q&A

Q **In the columns on the Current Call tab, I see some you didn't mention, such as Sharing. What's that about?**

A NetMeeting is so full-featured that it includes a number of capabilities that exceed the target user level and space restrictions of this book. In addition to conferencing, NetMeeting can be used to allow conference participants to share applications and to transfer files. If you want to learn how to use these features, consult NetMeeting's Help file.

Q **How do I know your sister Shirley is being unreasonable? After all, I wasn't at your Thanksgiving. Maybe she's right to be mad at you. After all, it's never nice to comment on someone's thighs.**

A She *got* to you, didn't she? *Didn't* she! You call her and tell her I'm not budging until she apologizes. Or at least until her birthday.

Quiz

Take the following quiz to see how much you've learned.

Questions

1. You can open NetMeeting from the Start menu by
   a. Choosing Programs | Microsoft NetMeeting
   b. Choosing Programs | Internet Explorer | Microsoft NetMeeting
   c. a or b
   d. None of the above

2. You store your name and e-mail address on a directory server so that
   a. You can be billed a monthly NetMeeting usage fee
   b. You can receive great merchandise offers
   c. Other NetMeeting users can more easily find you and connect with you
   d. You can be mailed a monthly NetMeeting directory

3. The first time you open NetMeeting, the NetMeeting Setup wizard opens automatically to
   a. Install NetMeeting
   b. Collect identification and server information
   c. Configure your sound card for use in voice conferences
   d. b and c

19

4. To have a voice conference through NetMeeting, both participants must have

    a. A telephone

    b. At least four years of college

    c. NetMeeting, a sound card, a microphone, and speakers (or headphones)

    d. A video camera

Answers

1. c. In most configurations, you can open NetMeeting either way. Some people may see only one of the two choices on their PCs. (No points off if you see only one!)

2. c. Listing yourself on a directory server helps others find you.

3. d. NetMeeting makes you configure before it lets you call.

4. c. No sound card, no talk. Life is like that.

Activity

E-mail your friends, and ask whether they have NetMeeting. When you find one that does, arrange a time for a voice conference, and give NetMeeting a spin.

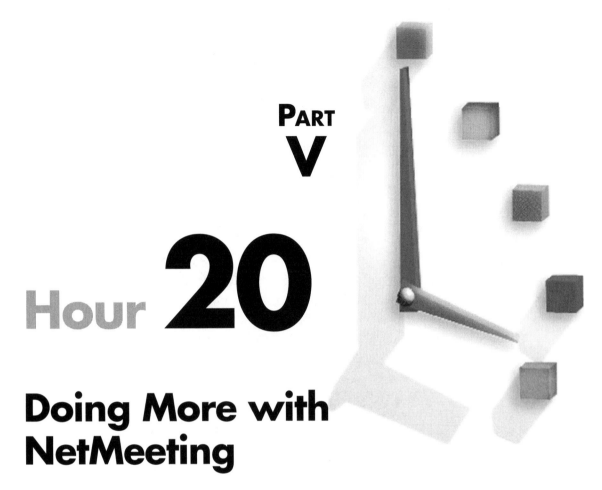

Hour **20**

Doing More with NetMeeting

Let's be perfectly honest here: A lot of Internet Explorer users will ignore NetMeeting entirely. And among those who use NetMeeting, many will never do more than the stuff you learned in Hour 19.

With that in mind, this hour has been included for two reasons. First, for those hardy few who want even more NetMeeting than Hour 19 provided, here's the rest—stuff like videoconferencing, using SpeedDial, and using NetMeeting's Whiteboard tool.

And second, without this hour, the "24 Hours" part of this book's title would have to be changed to "23 Hours," and Maxine would get stuck with the bill for all the extra typesetting.

At the end of the hour, you'll be able to answer the following questions:

☐ How can I create and use SpeedDial entries?

☐ What hardware do I need to have a video conference?

☐ How do I participate in a video conference?

☐ How can I have a text-based conversation through NetMeeting?

☐ How can my conversation partners and I collaborate by drawing together on the NetMeeting whiteboard?

Using SpeedDial

With your SpeedDial list, calling someone is even easier than usual. You simply choose a name from the SpeedDial menu without worrying about which directory server someone is using. But first, you must have added the person to your SpeedDial list.

Adding People to Your SpeedDial List

Every time you accept a call from someone, NetMeeting adds that person to your SpeedDial list. This provides you with an easy way to call that person back if you need to.

You can add people to your list by clicking the SpeedDial button on NetMeeting's toolbar. A dialog opens (see Figure 20.1) in which you can fill in the address and directory information required to reach the person. After you add a person in this way, you can dial that person in a snap, any time, from the SpeedDial list.

Figure 20.1.

Click the SpeedDial button to add someone to your SpeedDial list.

Calling Someone on Your SpeedDial List

To call anyone on your SpeedDial list, choose SpeedDial from the menu bar and then choose the name from the SpeedDial menu (see Figure 20.2).

If that person is running NetMeeting at the time you call, the person's computer will ring to announce that you're initiating a call.

If the person you're calling isn't connected to the Internet or running NetMeeting, you will see a dialog saying that NetMeeting couldn't find that person. All you can do is try again later or e-mail the person to arrange the call for a specific time.

Figure 20.2.

Choose someone from your SpeedDial list to initiate the call.

Using NetMeeting for a Video Conference

Using video in NetMeeting is almost completely automatic. If you have a video camera hooked up to your PC, NetMeeting will automatically use it. All you have to do is say "Cheese!"

TIME SAVER

You can get a color video camera for your computer for under $200. Several companies make them; you can probably find one at your local computer store or in a magazine advertisement. The simplest cameras even hook up to your computer's printer port so you don't have to open the computer's case.

To check whether your camera is working, switch to the Current Call tab in NetMeeting. With a camera installed on your system, you'll have two video frames at the right side of the window: My Video and Remote Video. Both should have the Microsoft NetMeeting logo in them until you click the Play/Stop button at the bottom of the My Video frame. That will start your video playing in that frame. When you've seen enough, click the Play/Stop button again to turn it off.

Another thing to notice is that the video frames can be detached from the NetMeeting window. Just click the title bar of the frame you want to move and drag it to where you want to see it. To put it back in the NetMeeting window where it came from, just drag it back there. It will stick in place when you drop it.

20

Having a Video Conference

If someone who has a video camera turned on calls you, you will automatically see it in the remote video frame. Also, if you have a video camera hooked up and running properly, it will begin transmitting as soon as you answer a call. It's all automatic: Just hook up the cameras, initiate a NetMeeting call as usual, and you have a video conference.

TIME SAVER

If you want to temporarily stop sending your video, click the Play/Stop button in the My Video frame. The person on the other end will see the last frame of the video that you sent until you start transmitting again by clicking the Play/Stop button.

You can pause incoming video in the same way, by clicking the Play/Pause button in the Remote Video frame to force it to pause.

Changing Your Video Options

NetMeeting offers several options pertaining to using video.

To Do: Manage Your Video Preferences

1. Choose Tools | Options to open the Options dialog, and then click the Video tab (see Figure 20.3).

Figure 20.3.

Set your video options on the Video tab of the Options dialog.

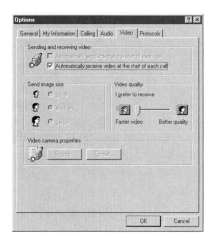

20

2. The first section, Sending and receiving video, lets you specify whether you want video to start automatically at the beginning of your calls. You can decide separately for incoming and outgoing video. If you want the video to start automatically when the call begins, check the check box.

JUST A MINUTE

Video uses a lot of *bandwidth*, meaning it imposes a heavy burden on your Internet connection, which was not really designed for the demands of video transmission. While in a video conference, your voice will probably come across choppy or with static because there's simply not enough bandwidth to carry both video and a clear audio signal.

If you use NetMeeting to communicate with coworkers through a company intranet, you may not see this problem due to the superior bandwidth some intranets supply. But on some intranets, the problem may be as bad as on the Internet—or worse.

3. The Send image size section lets you decide whether you want to send a small, medium, or large image to the caller. Just click the option that suits your taste.

JUST A MINUTE

Keep in mind that the larger the image you send over the Internet, the more bandwidth it requires. If you are connecting to the Internet using a modem, consider sending a smaller image to maintain a higher quality transmission.

4. The next section deals with the quality of the video you receive. Because of bandwidth limitations, you have a direct tradeoff between faster video and a higher quality image. Moving the slider closer to Faster Video will give you a smoother picture with more frames per second, but the frames will be somewhat blurrier with a lower resolution. Sliding towards the Better Quality end of the scale will show you a higher resolution picture but the video will be choppier, showing fewer frames per second. Place the slider at whichever position on the scale suits you.

5. The Video camera properties section has two buttons: Source and Format. These buttons enable you to set properties specific to your video card and video camera. Because each camera has different properties available to set, I won't go into much detail here. Some properties you might be able to set, though, are hue, saturation, brightness, contrast, and the size and resolution of the image taken by the camera.

6. When you've made all the settings you want to right now, click OK. NetMeeting saves your changes and uses those settings the next time you have a video conference.

20

Feel free to change the settings in this dialog until you get optimal performance from your system. The only way to really know what works best is through trial and error, as long as you keep in mind the bandwidth of your connection to the Internet.

Text Chatting in NetMeeting

If you don't have a microphone or a sound card, you can still use NetMeeting. With the text-based NetMeeting Chat tool, you can communicate with people all over the world even if one of you doesn't have a multimedia computer.

JUST A MINUTE

> Don't confuse NetMeeting's Chat tool with Microsoft Chat (see Hour 18). Microsoft Chat is an all-purpose chat client for communicating on IRC servers with others—who may use any client they want—around the world. NetMeeting's Chat tool is simply a text-based way to have a conversation with another NetMeeting user.

The Chat tool is NetMeeting's real-time, text-based communications facility. You can use it any time you need to type something to the other participants in a meeting. The tool enables you to have a NetMeeting conference with another NetMeeting user who lacks multimedia capability. (However, considering the type of computer Internet Explorer 4 and NetMeeting require, such a situation would be rare.) The Chat tool is also handy because

☐ Only two people at a time can share audio and video in NetMeeting. If you have three or more people in a meeting, you *must* use the Chat tool to communicate with everyone at the same time. Anyone in the meeting can see the Chat window, the Whiteboard, and the Shared Applications, but only two at a time can hear voice and see video.

☐ If you use NetMeeting over a relatively slow Internet connection, such as a modem, you might find that the audio starts cutting out somewhat when you have an application open or when you're in a video conference. To make communication easier, you could use the Chat tool.

Chatting in a NetMeeting

The Chat tool is extremely easy to use, especially if you're already familiar with real chatting through Microsoft Chat (see Hour 18).

20

To Do: Use Chat with NetMeeting

1. While you're in a call, click the Chat button on the toolbar of NetMeeting's Current Call tab (see Figure 20.4).

Figure 20.4.

Click the Chat button on the Current Call tab to start Chat.

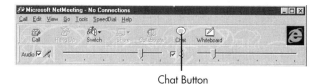

Chat Button

2. The Chat window appears, telling you how many people are currently in the meeting. The Chat window has three fields and a button:

   ☐ The list of messages that have been typed by anyone participating in the meeting

   ☐ The Message field, where you type your messages to the meeting

   ☐ The Send to drop-down list, from which you can choose who will see your message

   ☐ The Send button, which you press after you type a message that you want to add to the meeting

3. Any messages that anyone in the meeting sends will appear in the large message list field. The name of the person who typed the message is in the left column, and the message itself is in the right column. As each message is typed, it is appended to the bottom of the list, scrolling the list upward.

4. When you want to send a message, just type it in the Message field. Then press Enter or click the Send button. The message is sent to the meeting and appended to the bottom of the message list.

Using the Whiteboard

Whenever you're in a call with someone, you can bring up the Whiteboard tool (see Figure 20.5). The Whiteboard is basically just that: a white drawing board that everyone in the meeting can see and draw on. This is another leap forward in the long-distance workgroup collaboration process.

20

Figure 20.5.

Everyone in the NetMeeting can draw on the Whiteboard.

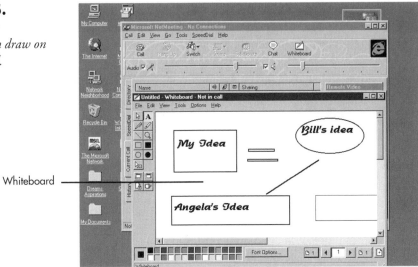

Whiteboard

Starting the Whiteboard

The Whiteboard is one of the most useful tools in NetMeeting. The Whiteboard, possibly even more than videoconferencing, makes NetMeeting so much better than a phone call. With the Whiteboard, you and anyone else in the meeting (as many people as you want) can see and work on the same thing.

Anytime you are in a call with someone, you can start the Whiteboard by clicking the Whiteboard button on the toolbar of the Current Call tab (see Figure 20.6).

Figure 20.6.

Start the Whiteboard by clicking the Whiteboard button on the Current Call tab.

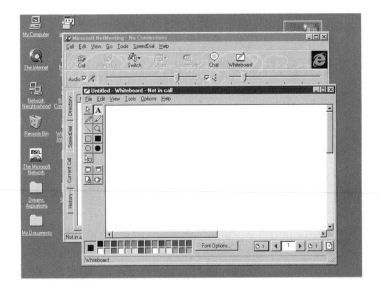

20

As soon as you start the Whiteboard, everyone in the meeting will be able to see it. Now all you need to do is start drawing, as described next.

Drawing

The first thing most people do when they discover the Whiteboard is try to draw something. In fact, most of the tools provided have something to do with drawing things.

The toolbar on the left side of the Whiteboard window (look back at Figure 20.5) holds them all, along with several other buttons that I'll describe a little later. For now, look at what you can draw on the Whiteboard.

To begin, select a drawing tool by clicking a button in the panel of buttons on the left side of the Whiteboard. Your choices of drawing tools are

 Pen: Draw freehand wherever you click and drag the mouse

 Line: Draw a straight line between the point you click the mouse and the point you release it

 Unfilled Rectangle: Draw the outline of a rectangle with one corner where you click the mouse and the opposite corner where you release it

 Filled Rectangle: Draw a solid rectangle with one corner where you click the mouse and the opposite corner where you release it

 Unfilled Ellipse: Draw the outline of an ellipse, starting where you click the mouse and ending where you release it

 Filled Ellipse: Draw a solid ellipse, starting where you click the mouse and ending where you release it

With these six tools, you can easily draw block diagrams or just about any simple picture for communicating your ideas to the other people in the meeting. You don't need to be a great artist to make useful drawings with the tools in the Whiteboard.

After you get accustomed to making shapes on the Whiteboard, you'll probably want to try changing colors. That's easy too. You'll find the color palette at the bottom left of the Whiteboard window (see Figure 20.7). The palette consists of the current color box at the left end of the palette and the grid of colored squares, each of which shows a color you may apply.

To change the color that you're drawing with, simply click the color you want to use. The current color box reflects your choice.

20

Figure 20.7.

Choose a color from the color palette.

JUST A MINUTE

Everything you draw on the Whiteboard is affected by the color you select, including all drawing objects and text. If you change the color to red for the pen, for example, everything you draw on the Whiteboard after that will also be red until you change the color again.

However, changing colors affects only what you draw or type *after* you make the change. Stuff you already created keeps its color.

You can also select the width of the line that you want to draw with. Whenever you have a drawing tool selected, the line width selection appears below the panel of drawing tools. Click the line width you want to use (smallest, small, large, or largest), and any lines you draw from that point on will be that size.

Typing Text

Drawing shapes on the Whiteboard is nice, but it's difficult to write a message or label something with the pen tool. Luckily, Microsoft added a couple of tools to help you work with text on the Whiteboard:

 Text: Type text on the Whiteboard in any font and any color

 Highlight: Draw over a word or an object on the screen to highlight it

First, let me show you how to type some text on the Whiteboard.

To Do: Type Text on the Whiteboard

1. Click the Text tool.

2. Choose the font that you want to use by clicking the Font Options button to display the standard Font dialog (see Figure 20.8). Here you can select a font, a font style, a size, and several effects for your text. When you've made your decision, click the OK button.

2. Choose the color you want to type with by clicking the color in the color palette at the bottom left of the Whiteboard window.

3. Click the Whiteboard where you want the text to appear.

4. Type whatever you want.

5. Click somewhere else on the Whiteboard or select a different tool when you're finished typing.

20

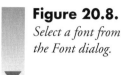

Figure 20.8.

Select a font from the Font dialog.

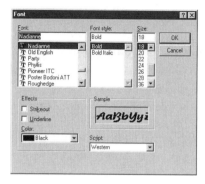

The text you type will show up on the Whiteboard, and everyone in the meeting will be able to see it. You can easily use this to label objects you've drawn or to explain ideas you have.

If you want to highlight a word or a phrase to emphasize a point, you can do that with the Highlight tool.

To Do: Highlight a Word or a Phrase

1. Click the Highlight tool.
2. Choose the color you want to use for highlighting from the color palette at the bottom left corner of the Whiteboard window.

TIME SAVER

> The highlighter comes up in bright yellow by default, which is a good color for highlighting things. You can change it to any color you want, but keep in mind that lighter colors work much better for highlighting. Darker colors are more likely to obscure the object you were trying to highlight.

3. Choose the width of the line you want to use to highlight from the line width selection below the toolbar.
4. Drag the mouse pointer over the object you want to highlight. The highlighter works just like the Pen tool, letting you draw freehand on the Whiteboard. Unlike the Pen tool, however, the highlighter doesn't completely cover the objects that you draw over. Instead, it highlights them the way a highlighter would on paper.

Summary

Is that enough NetMeeting for you? It is for Maxine. NetMeeting is great—if you're willing to invest the time to use it to its fullest, as this hour showed. If not, no big whoop. You still need to leave some long-term memory in your brain free for Web authoring, which you learn about in the next—and final—four hours of this book.

20

Q&A

Q I'm still fuzzy on this whole bandwidth issue. Why shouldn't I use all the voice and video I want? Isn't that what the Internet is for?

A Actually, people used the Internet for two decades without really trying to put voice, video, or even pictures through it. Modems and other hardware on the Net have become faster of late, but still, the system simply isn't up to the incredible amounts of data that live voice and video demand—you can't cram that much data through a wire at once and have everything work smoothly. It's the same reason we still don't have decent videophones, even 30 years after *The Jetsons*.

It's not that you shouldn't try. It's just that you have to be realistic about the expected results. If your sound or video seems choppy, your computer isn't busted and NetMeeting isn't crummy software. You're overtaxing the line.

Quiz

Take the following quiz to see how much you've learned.

Questions

1. To use video conferencing through NetMeeting, all you need is
    a. All the same stuff you need for voice conferencing, plus a computer video camera
    b. All the stuff in a, plus another user to conference with who also has all the stuff in a
    c. An appealing countenance
    d. An agent

2. You can use NetMeeting's Chat tool to go on Internet chats, just like Microsoft Chat.
    a. True
    b. False

3. When the Whiteboard in open, each person in the current call sees
    a. Only what he or she draws on it
    b. Nothing—the Whiteboard "whites out" NetMeeting
    c. A fun light show
    d. Everything anyone in the call draws or types on it

20

4. Callers are added to your SpeedDial list when

    a. You accept calls from them

    b. You click SpeedDial and enter their addresses to add them

    c. You type "SD" during a conference with them

    d. a and b

Answers

1. b. What's a video conference unless both you *and* your partner can send video to one another?

2. b. False. NetMeeting's chat is for chatting only with other NetMeeting users.

3. d. The Whiteboard shows everybody everything.

4. d. Choice c does nothing.

Activity

Find out which of your NetMeeting friends have video cameras. If several do, go shopping for a computer video camera or ask Santa for one. Why miss the fun?

20

PART
VI

Web Publishing with FrontPage Express

Hour

Hour 21

Getting Ready to Publish with FrontPage Express

After reading about all the great stuff on the Web, you might be a bit overwhelmed. Maybe you're thinking that the Web is simply too big and has no room for "the little guy." Well, you're wrong. Plenty of people publish their own personal Web pages through their university, employer, Internet service provider, or another source.

This hour gets you started on the road to publishing your own Web pages using FrontPage Express. By the time you are finished with this hour, the following questions will be answered:

- ☐ What is HTML?
- ☐ How will FrontPage Express help me publish on the Web?
- ☐ What is FrontPage Express like?
- ☐ How do I set up the Web Publishing wizard?

Cracking the Code

Before you look at FrontPage Express, it might be helpful to know something about Hypertext Markup Language (HTML). This knowledge will give you a better understanding of what Web sites are and a greater appreciation for FrontPage Express's flexibility and ease of use.

If you have ever used a word processor, you know it's easy to create and print text that is **bold,** *italicized,* or in a number of other formats. Although to you and your printer a word appears bold, for example, it may look different to the word processor (see Figure 21.1). Hidden codes in the word processor describe text and other objects so that they appear as you want them.

Figure 21.1.

The codes in the bottom panel reveal what the text in the top panel looks like.

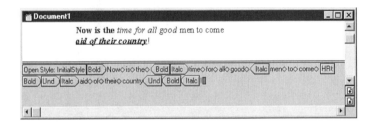

The word processor acts as a translator between you and the codes so that you see a nicely formatted document. Similarly, a Web browser is a translator between you and the HTML *tags* and code embedded in a Web page. Simple, isn't it?

 Tag: A tag is a piece of HTML code that tells a Web browser or a Web editor how to display information, such as text or graphics, that the tag modifies. For instance, the tags <B> and </B> around a word or a phrase make the text appear bold.

The Right Tool for the Job

One look at the FrontPage Express toolbar and you will understand why the word processor analogy makes so much sense. At first glance, FrontPage Express could almost pass for Microsoft Word. This familiar interface is one of the features that makes FrontPage Express so easy to use. Long-time users of Word or other major word processing programs will have little trouble getting a feel for how FrontPage Express works.

Standard Buttons

You can probably tell that the FrontPage Express toolbar contains many "universal" buttons. You use these standard buttons to

21

Create a document

Open a document

Save a document

Print a document

Preview a document

The five buttons next to these should also look familiar. These standard editing buttons enable you to

Cut text

Copy text

Paste text

Undo the last action

Redo the last action

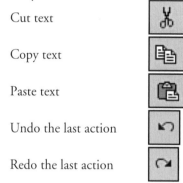

These ten buttons are almost universal and should pose no particular problems. If you aren't as familiar with them as you'd like to be, you might want to play around for a few minutes. Remember, holding your mouse over a button for a few seconds reveals a pop-up guide to what the button does.

TIME SAVER

Most functions in FrontPage Express have a keyboard shortcut. For instance, to cut text, you can simply press Ctrl+X on your keyboard. Knowing, and using, these shortcuts will save you hours of time. Refer to the menus in FrontPage Express for a function's corresponding keyboard shortcut.

21

More Buttons

Of the remaining buttons on the toolbar, several are covered extensively in later chapters. For now, I'll simply show you what some of the remaining buttons do.

Most of the buttons on the top row of the FrontPage Express toolbar are formatting buttons. These buttons enable you to align text, create lists, and change the size, appearance, and color of fonts. You will find yourself using the formatting buttons a lot!

FrontPage Express also has four browser buttons. These buttons are the same ones that appear in the Internet Explorer 4.0 toolbar (see Figure 21.2). Since the documents you create and edit in FrontPage Express are actual Web pages, FrontPage Express acts as a "mini-browser" to let you interact with your pages as you would on the Web.

Figure 21.2.
FrontPage Express performs some browser functions.

If you are creating and editing more than one Web page at a time (which is likely, after you get used to doing Web pages), you can use the FrontPage Express Forward and Back buttons to easily toggle from one page to another, just like you would in Internet Explorer 4.0.

The Refresh button gives you a chance to redisplay a Web page, while giving you the opportunity to save your work if you've made any changes. Lastly, use the Stop button to halt the display of a page.

JUST A MINUTE

Next to the Stop button is the Show/Hide button. At first glance, you might think that this button enables you to see only where paragraphs end. Don't be fooled: Selecting this option enables you to view page breaks, outlines, and other formatting elements.

Looking Over the Menu?

You can access many popular functions from the button bar. However, you can utilize many of FrontPad's capabilities only from the FrontPage Express menus or by using the corresponding keyboard shortcut.

21

TIME SAVER

Don't forget that right mouse button. Many menus and options can be displayed also by placing your cursor on an element and right-clicking.

Edit Commands

When you select the Edit menu, you'll notice that most of the standard editing functions are displayed. You'll notice also that the menu contains Find and Replace functions as well. Choose these two options to find or replace text in a Web page quickly and easily.

TIME SAVER

You've just authored the definitive Web page on the mathematician Pascale. Or was it Pascal? Oh, no, now you have to go change all those misspellings by hand! Actually, you don't. Simply choose Edit | Replace, type the wrong word in the Find What field and type the correct word in the Replace With field. FrontPage Express will find and correct all your mistakes for you.

Insert Here

The Insert menu also offers plenty of choices to help you. From formatting elements such as horizontal lines to marquees that enable you to insert your own HTML tags, the Insert menu gives you a lot of flexibility and choices.

And More Menus

The rest of the FrontPage Express menus primarily duplicate functions that you can find on the toolbar. Many menu items simply give you more extensive or advanced control over an element than the toolbar offers. For instance, choosing Format | Font gives you access to a menu of special styles. It might be helpful to click some of these so that you have a better feel for the capabilities of particular menu items.

JUST A MINUTE

You will see a tempting Help menu in FrontPage Express. It's just that— tempting. You will find little step-by-step help. (Otherwise, you wouldn't need this book, right?) For most FrontPage Express functions, read the rest of the chapters in this section for detailed information on how to get the most out of FrontPage Express.

21

The Publishing Wizard

This first thing you should do before working on your Web page is to make sure you have someplace to put it—makes sense, right? That's why one of your first tasks is to set up the FrontPage Express Web Publishing wizard. Using this tool, you will be able to quickly and easily upload your pages to your server.

Of course, this means you need an ISP that is giving you space on its server. Before proceeding, you need to know both the URL of your ISP and the directory on its server that you will be uploading files to. If you don't have all this information, you should contact your ISP to find out.

TIME SAVER

Most ISPs give users space in a particular directory on their server. Usually, this directory has the same name as the user's e-mail ID. For instance, if your e-mail address is jdoe@yourisp.com, the URL of your home Web page will probably be http://www.yourisp.com/~jdoe (and their FTP site is probably ftp.yourisp.com). Furthermore, the URL directory of /~jdoe usually corresponds to a directory on their server. In our example, this directory might be /home/jdoe/public/web/. It is very important that you know this information about your ISP before proceeding.

Starting the Wizard

The Web Publishing wizard will take you through the step-by-step process of setting up your server the first time you save a page to the Internet.

CAUTION

Depending on how your ISP is set up, some of the procedures in the next few sections might be slightly out of order. We recommend that you read all the way through the "Finishing Up" section before proceeding. That way, you'll know all the information that the wizard will expect from you from beginning to end, regardless of order.

To Do: Start Publishing

1. Connect to your ISP. (You can do it later, but it's easier if you do it now.)
2. Open FrontPage Express and type something in the blank page. (Don't worry what it is; you can change it later.)
3. Choose File | Save to display the Save As dialog.

4. In the Page Title field, type **Test Page**.

5. Click in the Page Location field, type the URL of your test page, and click OK (see Figure 21.3).

Figure 21.3.

This information gives the wizard something to go on.

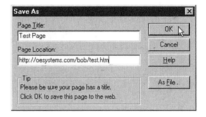

CAUTION

Depending on your ISP, you might be asked to provide your ID and password at some point during this process. In fact, you may be asked to provide them more than once. Whenever you are asked, type them both into the appropriate fields and click Next.

The wizard then informs you that you are ready to proceed with saving your Web page. Click on the Next button to proceed.

Taking the Next Step

Now you are ready to give the Web Publishing wizard some specific information.

To Do: Define Your ISP

1. Give your ISP a descriptive name. Call it whatever you want (for example, My ISP).

2. Click the Next button.

3. The wizard asks you to select your service provider if it can't determine one for you. Select the FTP option.

4. Click Next to continue.

Next, the Wizard asks you some information about your ISP's FTP server. You need to provide the following information:

☐ Your FTP server name. Your FTP server is usually just the term ftp. in front of your ISP's domain (for instance, ftp.yourisp.com).

☐ Your server's Web page subfolder (for example, /home/jdoe/public/web).

☐ Your root URL. You'll need to provide the URL that users on the Web will use to get to your home page (for example, http://www.yourisp.com/~jdoe), if you didn't already provide it in a previous step.

The screen that asks for all this information is pictured in Figure 21.4.

Figure 21.4.

The wizard must have
this vital information.

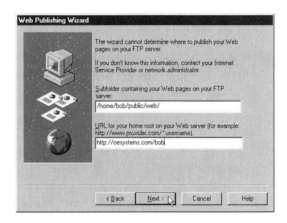

Finishing Up

You are now ready to finish. After providing all the information asked for in the previous three sections, the wizard tells you that it's ready to upload your files. Click the Finish button at this point, and you're finished, as shown in Figure 21.5.

Figure 21.5.

The Wizard tells you that
you've been successful.

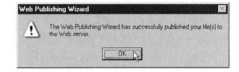

Take a Look

It's time to take a look at your work. Click OK when the wizard tells you that the upload is complete. Next, open Internet Explorer and type the URL of your Web page. Sure, it may be only a few random characters now, but just wait!

Publishing Future Works

As you modify pages or create new ones on your hard drive, publishing them is simple.

To Do: Publish Future Works

1. After you have modified or created a document, choose File | Save As (and make sure you're connected to your ISP).

2. Type the page title and page location, and click OK.

3. Click the Next button to proceed.

4. When asked, type your ID and password.

5. Press Enter, and your new page is automatically uploaded.

Repeat these easy steps every time you want to change your Web site or add information to it. Congratulations—you are a published Web author!

TIME SAVER

> Because uploading files is time consuming, always create and edit your Web pages in a folder on your hard drive first. Then, when you're ready to publish, upload them all at the same time. This not only makes it faster to create your pages but also serves to give you a backup copy of them.

Summary

In this hour, you were given an overview of HTML. You learned that browsers display information in much the same way as word processors do.

You also got a feel for the FrontPage Express interface and were given further confirmation that doing HTML will be as easy as using your word processor. Finally, you were told how to upload your Web pages using FrontPage's Web Publishing wizard.

Q&A

Q You make it sound too easy. Am I really going to be able to publish professional Web pages that easily?

A Well, let's not get carried away. Remember, professional Web designers have been at it for years. However, as you will soon see, you can produce appealing pages with FrontPage Express. Later, you may want to think about moving up to a more robust commercial product such as Microsoft FrontPage.

Q You skipped a lot of buttons on the toolbar. Any harm in experimenting with them now?

A Well, you won't get arrested if you do and it's not likely to hurt anything, but I suggest that you go through the next few chapters first. Unless you've already performed some HTML editing, it's a good idea to start out simple and move to the more complex later.

Q I've been using FTP for a long time and am just getting into HTML. Do I need to use the Web Publishing wizard, or can I use my trusty FTP client?

A After you configure the Web Publishing wizard, it's much easier to publish using it rather than using a separate FTP client. If you feel more comfortable using FTP, however, go ahead.

21

Quiz

Take the following quiz to see how much you've learned.

Questions

1. What does HTML stand for?

2. You can get to all the FrontPage Express options using a toolbar button or a keyboard shortcut.

   a. True

   b. False

3. Which of the following is not a requirement to publish your Web pages in FrontPage Express?

   a. Your FTP server's domain name

   b. Your user ID and password

   c. Your Web server's IP address

Answers

1. Hypertext Markup Language

2. a. True. You have to use the menu to get to certain options.

3. c.

Activity

Open your favorite word processor (Microsoft Word or Corel WordPerfect would be best) and type a paragraph of text. Format the text you just typed (use bold or underline, justify the text, and so on). Now go to FrontPage Express and try to duplicate the same paragraph of text with identical formatting. I think you'll find it's just as easy. Save the paragraph as a new page, upload it to your server, and view it. Looks just about like the word-processed document, doesn't it?

21

Hour 22

Web Publishing Basics

You are now ready to write some HTML. After reading most of this book, you should have collected lots of examples of what Web pages can look like. This hour shows you what you need to know to create a basic Web page.

When you have completed this hour, you will have the answers to the following questions:

- ☐ What are basic Web page properties?
- ☐ How can I use different page properties to customize my page?
- ☐ How can I add text and format it in my Web page?
- ☐ How can I add a marquee to my Web page?

Starting with Page Properties

Every Web page must have some basic pieces of information so that it can be read properly by a browser. Because your Web page will be viewed by many types of browsers on different types of computers displaying information on monitors set to different resolutions, it's important that your Web page be seen as you intend it to be seen.

This is where Page Properties come in. As you will soon see, many of these properties play a very important part in what your Web pages look like.

CAUTION

> It is important to remember here, as well as throughout the rest of the chapters in this section, that certain settings are readable by only certain types of Web browsers. All HTML you will produce in FrontPage Express can be properly displayed by Internet Explorer. Some tags, however, are ignored by browsers such as Netscape Navigator and Mosaic. It's always a good idea to view your HTML with a few different browsers to make sure it looks satisfactory in each.

General Controls

You must first set some general properties so that your HTML will contain certain information for browsers to read. Web page background color, text, and hyperlink colors as well as the title of your page are among the things you will set here. You'll start with some basic information.

To Do: Set Properties

1. Open FrontPage Express, and then open a new document by choosing File | New.
2. Next, click on File/Page Properties. Make sure the General tab is selected.
3. Press the Tab key until your cursor is in the Title field.
4. Type the title for your Web page to have. For instance, you could type My Home Page.
5. Click OK to return to the FrontPage Express editor.
6. Choose View | HTML to look at what you've accomplished (see Figure 22.1).

Figure 22.1.

You didn't type much, but FrontPage Express sure did!

```
< View or Edit HTML                                                     _ □ ×
<!DOCTYPE HTML PUBLIC "-//IETF//DTD HTML//EN">
<html>

<head>
<meta http-equiv="Content-Type"
content="text/html; charset=iso-8859-1">
<meta name="GENERATOR" content="Microsoft FrontPad 2.0">
<title>My Home Page</title>
</head>

<body bgcolor="#FFFFFF">

<p> </p>
</body>
</html>

○ Original  ● Current  ☑ Show Color Coding    OK      Cancel      Help
View or edit the current HTML
```

22

JUST A MINUTE

> You'll notice that you didn't fill in several of the fields. Many are quite advanced and beyond the scope of this book. If you want to find out how you use these settings, you might pick up *Teach Yourself HTML 3.2 in 24 Hours* by Dick Oliver (published by Sams.net).

Before going back to the Page Properties, you should save this basic file you just created. The process for this will be slightly different than saving it to the Web.

To Do: Save Your Page

1. Choose File | Save.
2. In the Save As dialog box, click on the As File button.
3. Locate the folder you'd like to save the file to and double-click on it.
4. Click in the File name field and type the name of the file. (Don't type .htm as part of the file name because FrontPage Express automatically appends it to the name you choose.)
5. Click OK.

You can now choose File | Page Properties to continue setting up your page. When you do, you'll see that the Location field has been filled in with the location of your newly saved page.

Add a Little Color

FrontPage Express also gives you the ability to create backgrounds, text, and links of different colors. Suppose you want your page to have a black background, white lettering, blue hyperlinks, aqua visited hyperlinks and silver active hyperlinks.

To Do: Add Some Color

1. From the Page Properties dialog box, select the Background tab.
2. Click and hold down the mouse button on the arrow next to the Background setting. Move the mouse to select Black, and then release the mouse button.
3. Repeat step 2, using the following settings and colors:

Text	White
Hyperlink	Blue
Visited Hyperlink	Aqua
Active Hyperlink	Silver

When you're finished, your screen should look like Figure 22.2.

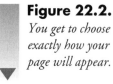

Figure 22.2.
*You get to choose
exactly how your
page will appear.*

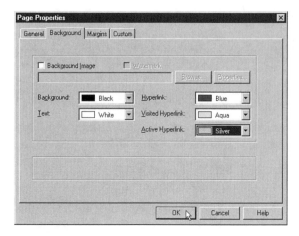

JUST A MINUTE

You can also use an image for your background. Simply click in the
Background Image check box and then browse for the image. Be careful,
though, because background images displayed on low resolution monitors
or used with certain colored text can make your page *very* hard to read.
Also, images are tiled to fit in the browser window and may not look right
when displayed this way.

Setting the Margins

Finally, you might want to set the margins for your Web page. As with word processing
documents, margins determine how much empty space will be at the top and sides of your
Web page. Most of the time, you shouldn't need to set this. However, there may be times
when you'd like to.

For instance, if you have an image you want to display at the top corner of your page, you
might want to set your margins to 0. Setting these margins is easy. From the Margin tab in
the Page Properties dialog box, click in each box to specify either a top or a left margin. Choose
the desired number of pixels for the margin, and you're finished.

JUST A MINUTE

You can set your margins to anything you want. It's not a good idea to set
them too big, though, because you want to make sure that those viewing
your Web page don't have to do a lot of scrolling to see all your content.

22

Putting in the Words

I had a professor in college who could make it through an entire two-hour lecture without changing his tone of voice. Every...word...sounded...exactly...the...same. It was one of the worst classes I've ever had in my life.

Regardless of how sophisticated a Web page may be, text usually comprises the majority of its content. This section helps you avoid becoming the Internet equivalent of my professor.

TIME SAVER

> FrontPage Express has auto word wrap, so don't press the Enter key at the end of each line of text. Otherwise, FrontPage Express will put a blank line before the next line of text. Instead, press Enter at the end of each paragraph.

To get started, go ahead and type a paragraph or two describing yourself, your interests, or whatever else you'd like to include that you think people might be interested in. This will be the basis for your home Web page. Of course, feel free to include just about anything you'd like.

JUST A MINUTE

> One tool that FrontPage Express doesn't have is a spell checker, so you might want to proofread your page now before moving on. You'll have to do it eventually anyway.

Spice It Up

So what can you do with your newly formed Web page? Well, before all is said and done, you'll be able to do just about anything you want to with it. For now, start out simple. However, even the simplest things can make your Web page look much better.

Heads Up!

Headers are one of the most used text formats. A header basically performs three functions:

- ☐ Controls the size of the text, depending on the size header you choose
- ☐ Automatically bolds the text to make it stand out
- ☐ Creates a blank line above and below the header text

If you don't have some text at the top of your page that you can turn into a header, you might want to add some now, since it's a great way of attracting attention to your page. Creating headers is easy.

To Do

To Do: Make a Header

1. Select the text you want to turn into a header.

2. Choose Format | Paragraph. The Paragraph Properties dialog box appears.

3. Click on the size header you would like to apply. Header 1 is the biggest (and is very big) and Header 6 is the smallest. In general, Header size 4 is about the same as regular bolded text.

4. Click on the arrow next to the Paragraph Alignment field. Quite often, headers are centered. You can choose any alignment you want.

5. Click on the OK button to view the result. (Figure 22.3 shows a centered size 3 header.)

Figure 22.3.

Headers can make text stand out.

TIME SAVER

After you have selected text, you can always right-click on the selection to display a pop-up menu of options. This is usually faster than using the menu bar.

Emphasize Your Words

The most common formats for text are **bold**, *italicized*, and underlined. These effects make certain words jump off the page in different ways. They can be effective in breaking up your page to be more visually appealing, but don't overuse them.

Adding these types of formatting to your text is even easier than applying headers. Simply select the text you want to format, click the B (for *bold*) button, the I (for *italicize*) button, or the U (for *underline*) button and you're finished.

22

CAUTION

It is generally not recommended that you underline text. First, many browsers don't display underlined text. Second, because many browsers are set to display hyperlinks as underlined text, underlining nonlinked text can confuse users.

If you know what formatting you would like text to be in before you type it, simply click on the appropriate formatting button before typing, type your text, and click the formatting button again to turn it off.

Size *Does* Matter

Suppose you want the first word on your page to be bigger than the rest for emphasis. What would you do? Well, you could apply a header size to the word. The header would automatically insert a line break after the word, though, so that won't work.

What you really need to do is to increase the size of the word. Again, FrontPage Express makes it easy. After selecting the text, click on the Size button from the toolbar (it's the one with the large *A* on it) one or more times until your text is as large as you'd like it to be. To make text smaller, select your text, and then click on the button with the small *A* on it instead.

What Type of Type?

Another thing you can do to spice up your page is to use a special font for your text. This can draw attention to your words, because many Web pages simply display text in a browser's default font. Making your text show up as a different font will certainly draw attention to what you have to say.

CAUTION

It's generally not a good idea to use unusual fonts for your text. People viewing your page need to have that font installed on their system for it to be displayed. In addition, many fonts make some text hard to read.

Choosing a special font is easy. Simply select the text you would like to apply a font to and click on the arrow next to the Font Type field on the toolbar. Scroll through the list until you find a font you'd like to use, and click on it.

After applying all these different formats, your page should look quite different than when you started. Figure 22.4 shows an example of what a page with these different formats might look like.

Figure 22.4.

This page is really
starting to look alive.

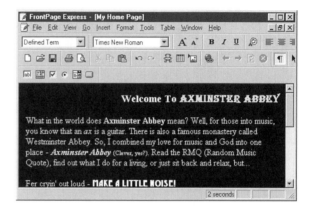

You can apply to your text other formatting, such as color and text alignment. As you become more familiar with FrontPage Express, you will begin using these options more and more.

Creating a Marquee

Whether it's the latest stock market numbers scrolling across CNN's screen or the latest stats zooming across the scoreboard at the game, marquees always grab your attention. A marquee, which is nothing more than scrolling information, presents textual information in a dynamic way.

You need to decide exactly what you'd like to scroll across your Web page. You might want to use a witty quote or a thought for the week. The first step is to open the Marquee Properties dialog box and type in your text.

To Do: Insert a Marquee

1. Choose the Insert | Marquee option.
2. The cursor should be blinking in the Text field. Type your text now.
3. Click OK and save your work.
4. Open Internet Explorer and view the file you just created.

CAUTION

> Be very careful of how much text you choose to display. As a general rule, don't type in more text than will fit on your screen.

Customizing Your Marquee

You have just created a simple, scrolling marquee. Now it's time to figure out how to make it even better. Editing a marquee is slightly different than creating one.

To Do: Improve Your Marquee

1. Return to your FrontPage Express document with the marquee you just created.

2. Click on the marquee to select it.

3. Choose Edit | Marquee Properties. The Marquee Properties dialog box in Figure 22.5 appears. (You can display this dialog box also by double-clicking on the marquee text.)

Figure 22.5.

This dialog box enables you to customize your marquee in many ways.

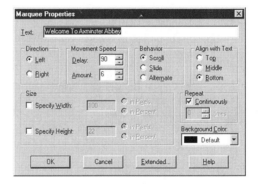

When you clicked on the marquee text in FrontPage Express, you might have noticed that a standard Object border appeared around the marquee. With FrontPage Express, you can adjust the size of your marquee, without going to the Marquee Properties dialog box, by simply pulling on the marquee border markers when you select the marquee.

Direction

The first decision you need to make is the direction in which you want the marquee to scroll across your screen. You can choose to scroll the marquee to the left or to the right of your screen by clicking on the appropriate Direction option.

Behavior

After determining which direction your marquee will scroll, you want to choose also where it's going:

- Scroll continually scrolls your marquee off one side of the screen and begins again on the original side.
- Slide causes the marquee to come to a stop at the edge of your Web page and stop.
- Alternate makes your marquee bounce back and forth across your screen.

Repeating

The Repeat setting goes hand-in-hand with the Direction and Behavior settings. The Repeat function tells a Web browser how many times text will scroll or oscillate across your page. You can have the marquee scroll or alternate across your screen continuously, or you can have your marquee scroll or alternate a specified number of times.

TIME SAVER

You may occasionally want your text to scroll across the screen once and then disappear. To do this, choose the Scroll behavior and a Repeat setting of 1 time.

Movement Speed

Movement Speed is perhaps the trickiest setting to adjust. This setting has two options:

- Delay tells FrontPage Express how long a period to wait between each "jump" of your text. It's not important to know exactly how long a particular number actually delays. What is important to know is that the smaller a number you use, the faster the text will scroll across the screen.
- Amount tells FrontPage Express how many pixels each "jump" should be. Again, exact numbers aren't important. You should, however, know that the text scrolls very smoothly if you use a small number. Using large numbers here makes the text very jumpy.

Adjusting the Size

You can set your marquee to an exact number of pixels. You can also set the size as a percentage using the Marquee Properties dialog box instead of clicking and dragging on the marquee border. To do so, use the following two options:

- Width. Click in the Specify Width check box, select whether you want the width to be a percentage or an absolute pixel width, and then type the number you'd like the width to be.

☐ Height. Click in the Specify Height check box, select whether you want the height to be a percentage or an absolute pixel height, and then type the number you'd like the width to be.

Align with Text

You can use the Align with Text option to line up the marquee with other text that might be on the same line:

☐ Top aligns the top of the accompanying text with the top of the marquee.

☐ Middle aligns the center of the marquee with the text.

☐ Bottom tells a browser to align the text with the bottom of the marquee.

Remember, the Align with Text setting aligns the *borders* of the marquee with the accompanying text, *not* the text within the marquee!

Background Color

You can also specify a background color for your marquee. This is helpful if you'd like to have your marquee appear as a banner along the top of your page. Setting a background color is no different than setting a color in your Page Properties. When you finish, you might have a banner marquee similar to the one pictured in Figure 22.6.

Figure 22.6.

This marquee uses page margins of 0, a back-ground color of navy and a marquee width of 100%.

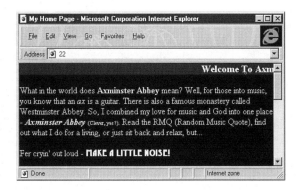

You can always apply formatting (such as bold, italics, color, or size) to marquee text. After clicking on the marquee, simply click on the appropriate button on the Formatting toolbar at the top of your screen.

Summary

In this Hour, you were shown how to set up your Web page's background by using Page Properties. You also discovered many ways to add and format the text in your Web page.

Lastly, you learned how to create a marquee on your Web page to add movement to your text. By putting these elements together, you have been given the tools to create a very effective text-based Web page.

Q&A

Q I noticed that you can add background sound in the Page Properties dialog box. Is this easy?

A Relatively easy, yes. Simply choose a sound file from your hard drive using the Browse button in the Page Properties dialog box. However, it is generally recommended that you use an audio utility to convert sounds into WAVE or AU format before including the sound. Also, remember that audio files can be quite large.

Q Can I get to most of the formatting options from one central location in FrontPage Express?

A Yes, you can. If you select the text that you want to format and right-click, a pop-up menu appears. Choose the Font Properties item and a dialog box is displayed allowing you to set the font color, type, alignment, and size, among other options.

Quiz

Take the following quiz to see how much you've learned.

Questions

1. Which of the following can you set using Page Properties?

    a. The size of your Web page

    b. An opening video clip for your page

    c. The background color of your page

2. You can make text on your page as big or as small as you want to.

    a. True

    b. False

3. Will all graphical Web browsers display marquees?

    a. Yes

    b. No

22

Answers

1. c. The other two choices are determined elsewhere.

2. b. False. There is a limit to how big or how small text can be displayed.

3. b. No. The marquee was developed specifically for Internet Explorer and cannot be displayed in all browsers.

Activity

I always think it's useful to know what's going on "under the hood." For this activity, I want you to try and figure out which HTML tags do what. Choose View | HTML and see whether you can figure out which tags create which effects on your Web page. Completing this exercise will help you know even more about HTML.

Hour 23

Beyond Web Publishing Basics

Now you're ready to move on to some of the elements that give most pages some real zip, in addition to a lot of functionality. You can use lists, hyperlinks, images, and tables to make your Web page even better and easier to use.

This hour will answer the following questions:

- [ ] What different types of lists can I add to my Web page?
- [ ] How can I put images into my Web page?
- [ ] In what ways can I use hyperlinks most effectively?
- [ ] How can tables help me display the contents on my page better?

Using Lists

One of the best ways to organize your text is using lists. Even the most aesthetically appealing text, when continually lumped into paragraph after paragraph, can become tedious to read. (Think of how hard it would be to use this book if there weren't plenty of lists to help you out.) Lists have a way of letting your readers know that they are looking at important, concise information.

You can include a list on your page in two basic ways. Unlike other types of formatting, lists are probably easier to create on-the-fly, as opposed to typing in the list text and then applying the list style to it.

Creating a List

Suppose that you want to include a list of your interests on your Web page so that people can easily find what interests you. How would you do it?

To Do: Make Your List

1. Position your cursor at the beginning of a blank line (this is where you want your list to begin).

2. Click on either the bulleted list button or the numbered list button on your toolbar.

3. Type the first item in your list and press the Enter key.

4. Repeat step 3 until you have typed all the items in your list.

5. After pressing Enter after your last item, you'll notice that there is an extra bullet or number at the end of the list. Simply press the Backspace or Delete key. FrontPage Express automatically deletes the extra element and moves your cursor down, ready to start typing a new paragraph.

When you're finished, your list might look something like Figure 23.1. You can create lists also from text you've already typed in by just selecting the text and choosing the type of list you want to create. Just remember that each item in the list needs to be on its own line before you start.

Figure 23.1.

This is a simple bulleted list.

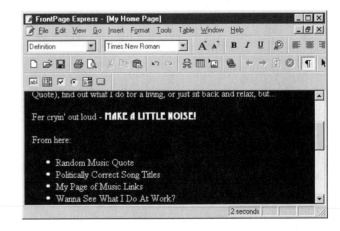

23

One of the most common reasons for creating lists is to provide a list of links to other Web pages on the Internet. Creating a list can make it easier for the people viewing your page to figure out what types of links they may be going to.

More Kinds of Lists

23

Now that you have a feel for how lists are made, you're ready to move beyond basic lists to make them more interesting.

To create these different types of lists, you need to use the FrontPage Express Format menu. Before continuing, select the list you've already created by highlighting it. Click on Format | Bullets and Numbering (or right-click and choose List Properties) to display the List Properties dialog shown in Figure 23.2.

Figure 23.2.

This dialog enables you to apply different formats to your list.

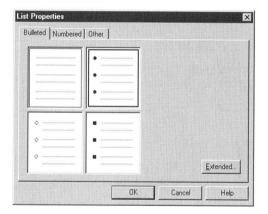

Choosing Your Bullets

What if you want to create lists using different types of bullets, either for variety or function? Doing so is easy.

To Do: Make Another List

1. Make sure your current list is highlighted and the List Properties dialog is open.

2. Select the Bulleted tab. FrontPage Express always automatically highlights the current type of list for you.

3. Click one of the selections that shows an alternative type of bulleted list.

4. Click OK and view your list.

5. Repeat these steps to try each different type of bulleted list.

You can convert a standard bulleted list to a list without any bullets. Simply highlight the list, and choose Format | Bullets. Then choose Numbering | Other and click the Menu List item. When you return to your Web page, you'll see that the bullets have disappeared.

Choosing Your Numbers

You have even more variety in the types of numbered lists you can create. Complete the following to experiment with numbered lists.

To Do: Make a Numbered List

1. Make sure your list is highlighted and the List Properties dialog is on your screen.
2. Select the Numbered tab.
3. Click one of the selections that shows an alternative type of numbered list.
4. Click OK and view your list.
5. Repeat these steps until you have tried all the different types of numbered lists.

Definition Lists

The lists that you have learned to create so far should be sufficient for most of your needs. However, you should know about one more type of list—the definition list.

Definition lists are quite common on the Web. By using a definition list, you can list a word or a phrase along with an indented definition or description of the word or phrase. An example should make this clear.

To Do: Create a Definition List

1. Position your cursor where you'd like to start the list.
2. In the Formatting toolbar, click on the Style drop-down field and select the Defined Term option.
3. Type the term or phrase you'd like to define, and press Enter.
4. Type your definition or description, and press Enter.
5. Repeat steps 3 and 4 with all your items. You should end up with a list similar to the one pictured in Figure 23.3.

23

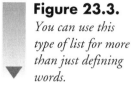

Figure 23.3.
You can use this type of list for more than just defining words.

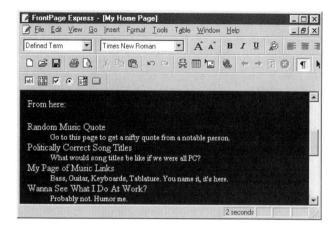

From There to Here and from Here to There

Dr. Seuss would have loved the Web. Oh, the places you can go! The great thing about it is that you can create a place others will want to go to simply because you've taken the time to create a page that links them to useful information.

Creating the Link

Unlike most other HTML elements, hyperlinks should be created using text that you have already typed on your page.

To Do: Create a Hyperlink

1. Select the text that you would like to turn into a hyperlink.

2. Choose Insert | Hyperlink.

3. Because most of your links will be to other Web pages, make sure the World Wide Web tab is selected in the Create Hyperlink dialog.

4. Click the Hyperlink Type menu and scroll down to select the http: option.

5. Click next to the http:// in the URL field and type the address of the site you want to link to. When you're finished, the dialog should look similar to the one pictured in Figure 23.4.

6. Click on the OK button.

Figure 23.4.

It's this easy to create
a hyperlink.

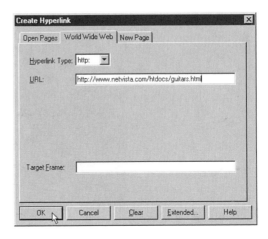

TIME SAVER

To create a hyperlink the easy way, go to the page you want to create a link to using Internet Explorer and copy the URL that appears in the Address field. When you return to FrontPage Express and open the Create Hyperlink dialog, you'll notice that the address is automatically placed in the URL field!

You can repeat these steps to create hyperlinks to e-mail addresses, newsgroups, ftp sites, and just about any other Internet site you want. You might want to use what you learned previously in the book about finding things on the Net to create a few hyperlinks now.

New Page Link

You should know how to use a few other tabs in the Create/Edit Hyperlinks dialog. The easiest is the New Page tab. This tab enables you to create a new page that your current page can link to.

For instance, suppose you created too many guitar links to be displayed easily on one page. You want to create an entirely new page on your site consisting of just guitar links.

To Do: Link to a New Page

1. Highlight the word you want the link to your new page to go to.
2. Choose Insert | Hyperlink.
3. Select the New Page tab.
4. Type the title and file name that you would like your new page to have.
5. Click the OK button.
6. In the New Page dialog, select Normal Page.
7. Click OK, and FrontPage Express displays a brand-new page for you to edit.

23

Linking to Open Pages

As you start to create more and more Web pages, you will no doubt want to create many links to those pages you create. The Create/Edit Hyperlink dialog has one more tab that makes this process easy.

The Open Pages tab makes linking to other Web pages quick.

To Do: Link to an Open Page

1. Suppose that your home page (named index.htm) has a link to your guitar page (named guitar.htm). Make sure both files are open.

2. While in index.htm, select the text (for instance, the word *guitar*) that you want to link to guitar.htm.

3. Choose Insert | Hyperlink | Open Pages to display the Create/Edit Hyperlinks dialog to the Open Pages tab.

4. Click the name of the page you want the hyperlink to point to.

5. Click OK. It's that easy!

Make Your Page Worth a Thousand Words

Graphics are Web page staples. They give you greater creativity and your user greater enjoyment. By using images in different ways, you can produce a livelier, more attractive Web page.

Getting the Picture

The first step is to insert the picture. FrontPage Express enables you to insert graphics in many formats, such as GIF, JPEG, BMP, TIF, and even clip art files.

CAUTION

Although you can insert many graphic file formats, only the GIF and JPEG formats can be viewed on the Web. When inserting images of different formats, you must save them as one of these two formats before they can be used on the Web.

To Do: Insert a Graphic

1. Click where you would like to insert your image.

2. Choose Insert | Image to display the Image dialog.

3. Click the tab that includes the location of the file you want to insert. (You will probably choose the Other Location tab.)

4. In the Other Location tab, click on the From File option or the From Location option. (If you clicked the Clip Art tab, simply select the category and file, and then click OK; you can skip steps 5 through 7).

5. If you clicked the From Location option, type the exact URL, including the name of the image file. If you clicked on the From File option, you can now click the Browse button to find a file. (The C:\Windows directory has a few bitmap images if you don't have any.)

6. Click the Files of Type menu and choose the All Files option so you can see all available graphics files.

7. Double-click the file you want to insert (see Figure 23.5).

Figure 23.5.

Find your image and put it in.

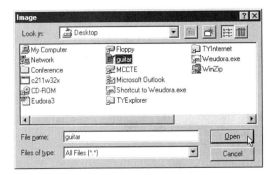

Getting the Picture Right

Now it's time to adjust your picture.

To Do: Adjust Your Picture

1. Right-click on the image and select Image Properties to display the Image Properties dialog.

2. Click the Appearance tab.

3. Click the Alignment pop-up menu to align your image with any accompanying text on the same line. A few of these choices are important:

   Top aligns the top of accompanying text with the top of the image.

   Middle aligns the text with the middle of the image.

   Bottom aligns the bottom of accompanying text with the bottom of the image.

   Left places the image at the left margin.

   Right places the image at the right margin.

23

4. Select the number of pixels of empty space you want above and below (vertical) and beside (horizontal) your image using the Vertical and Horizontal Spacing settings.

5. If you want to specify a size other than the image's size for display, select it in the Size area. (This is not recommended.)

6. When you are finished, click OK.

You can set the size of your image in the same way you adjusted the size of your marquee, setting the height and width as a specific number of pixels or as a percentage of the size of the Web page.

Caution

> It's generally not a good idea to set a size for most images. Doing so can cause a lot of distortion in the image when it's displayed on various browsers.

The General tab in the Image Properties dialog enables you to also set the image type to GIF or JPEG and a number of other settings that you generally don't need to worry about as a beginner.

Caution

> One last caution. If you use an image that isn't GIF or JPEG, FrontPage Express will ask you to save the image as a file when you next save your Web page. When prompted to do so, click Browse and give the image a file name with a .gif or .jpg extension (such as guitar.gif). You can then click Save and Yes and the image will be saved correctly.

Using Tables

It's difficult to find Web pages that don't use tables in one way or another. Whether you actually see them or not, they're there—helping the page to be more organized for easier navigation.

The first thing you need to do before creating your table is to think about how you want the elements on your Web page arranged. It usually helps to sketch out your Web page's layout on a piece of paper before creating the table.

Time Saver

> At the very least, it's a good idea to determine the general number of columns and rows in your table (for example, 3×2 or 4×4) before you begin. With FrontPage Express, you can easily go back and make your table more complex later.

23

Setting Up Your Table

You are now ready to begin. Just as when you began a new Web page, when you create a new table, you need to set some properties. To do this, click at the point you want to insert your table and select Table | Insert Table. The Insert Table dialog appears, as shown in Figure 23.6.

Figure 23.6.

Control all the vital parts of your table from here.

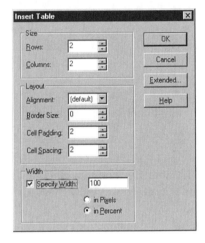

In the Size area, click the arrow buttons to set the number of rows and columns you would like your table to have. For now, start with a 2×2 table. If you want, you can also define how wide (in pixels) the border of your table will be (a border setting of 0 means there will be no table border) and how your table will be aligned on your page.

Finally, you'll want to define your table's width, either in pixels or as a percentage. Unless your table has specific data, it's always a good idea to use a percentage width. Finally, you can use your arrow keys to define the amount of *cell padding* and *cell spacing* in your table. When you're finished, go ahead and click OK so you can take a look at your newly created table.

 Cell spacing refers to the amount of space you want between each cell. **Cell padding** refers to the amount of space you want between the text and the inside edges of a cell wall.

Selecting Table Elements

It is very important that you be able to select various cells, rows, and columns in your table to set their properties. You can select table elements from the Table menu, but that can be very time-consuming. Selecting elements directly from your page layout is easy:

☐ Column. To select a column, position your mouse cursor above the column until it turns into a black arrow pointing down, then click.

23

□ Row. To select a row, position your mouse cursor to the left of the row until it turns into a black arrow pointing right, then click.

□ Cell. To select a cell, position your cursor just inside the left wall of the cell until the cursor becomes an arrow, and then double-click.

□ Table. To select an entire table, position your cursor anywhere to the right of the table and double-click.

Inserting Table Elements

As mentioned, you can customize your table in many ways. One of the most common ways to add complexity to your table is to insert various elements in or around it. Beginning with the standard 2×2 table you created earlier, you can choose the following options from the Table menu:

□ Insert Rows or Columns/Rows. If you want to add more rows, choose the number of rows to add and whether you want them added above or below the current cell.

□ Insert Rows or Columns/Columns. If you want to add more columns, choose the number of columns to add, and whether you want them to be added to the left or the right of the current cell.

□ Insert Caption. If you want to include some text that describes your table (called a caption), choose this option and type your text. After you have typed a caption, you can right-click on it to bring up the Caption Properties dialog. From there, you can put the caption above or below the table.

Inserting Cells

If you choose Table | Insert Cell, you will notice that an extra cell is added to your row so that your table no longer makes a square. You are definitely going to need to play around with the settings to get it right again. For instance, what if you added a cell to the bottom row of your table so that the top row has two cells and the bottom has three?

To Do: Adjust for Extra Cells

1. Click in the cell at the end of the shortest row and choose Table | Cell Properties.

2. For the Cell Span setting, set the Number of Columns spanned to 2. If you click OK at this point, you'll see that the table is once again square, but the cells are all different sizes.

3. Click in one of the cells in the row with three cells. Choose Table | Cell Properties and specify a width of 33%.

4. Repeat step 3 for the other two cells in the same row.

5. Finally, click in the first cell on the row with two cells and set its width to 33% as well. Figure 23.7 shows a table aligned in this manner with the appropriate width settings for each cell.

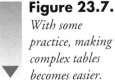

Figure 23.7.

With some practice, making complex tables becomes easier.

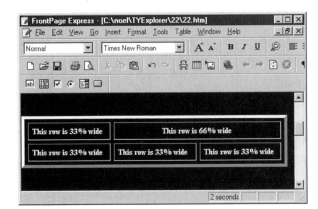

Doing More with Tables

The last thing you can do easily with cells is to either merge them or split them. To merge cells, simply select the cells (or row or column) that you'd like to merge and choose Table | Merge Cells. That's it.

Splitting cells is a little more complex. Once again, select the cell, row, or column you'd like to split and choose Table | Split Cells to display the Split Cells dialog. From there, you can select whether you want to split your selection into columns or rows (and how many you want to split them into).

CAUTION

As any Web programmer will tell you, mastering tables takes a lot of time and practice. Many advanced techniques available with FrontPage Express are beyond the scope of this book, but don't be afraid to experiment to your heart's content.

As far as content goes, you can type, paste, insert, and format any element into a table cell just as you can anywhere else on your Web page. You can resize cells for different effects and to display information for maximum appeal. Think of a table cell as a little Web page within a page.

JUST A MINUTE

You can also set custom colors or background images for tables, rows, columns, or cells. To do this, simply select the element you want to set the background for, open the appropriate Properties dialog, and go for it.

23

Summary

In this hour, you learned how to create many types of lists on your Web page. Additionally, you were taught how to include images and hyperlinks in your page. Finally, you found out how to create and modify tables to display information more effectively.

Q&A

Q You mentioned that I should use `.jpg` or `.gif` images on my page. What's the easiest way to do this?

A Well, there are two ways. One, you can use noncopyrighted images already on the Web. Lots of clip art and image libraries on the Web have free images in the proper format. Two, you can convert images to the proper format using an image such as `LView`, which is located at `ftp://ftp.simtel.net/pub/simtelnet/win95/graphics/lview1d2.zip`.

Q How much more is there to creating complex tables?

A Would you believe "a lot"? For instance, you can click and drag table cells to put a cell inside an existing cell. Really, though, the biggest trick is to get a large table with several rows and columns all containing different numbers of cells. Although it may seem difficult to make these complex tables with FrontPage Express, imagine how hard it would be to do it by hand!

Quiz

Take the following quiz to see how much you've learned.

Questions

1. Which of the following graphics file formats cannot be viewed on the Web?
   a. TIF
   b. GIF
   c. JPEG

2. It is generally a good idea to set your table width to a percentage.
   a. True
   b. False

3. Can you create a link from a Web page to a file on your hard drive?
   a. Yes
   b. No

23

Answers

1. a. TIF

2. a. True. Setting a table width in pixels (especially if you make it big) can make it hard to read by many users.

3. b. No. This is a trick question. Hyperlinks must point to files or resources that are always connected to the Internet. Because your hard drive won't generally be accessible to the Internet, this type of link won't work.

Activity

This is the Rubik's cube lesson. See if you can duplicate the following table in FrontPage Express:

20	40	20	20
20	40	40	

Hour 24

Advanced Topics for FrontPage Express

In the last hour, you went beyond the basics. Well, this hour will take you *way* beyond the basics. FrontPage Express has even more features and capabilities that the truly adventurous might want to use in their Web pages, such as the integration of sound and video, WebBots, and more.

The following questions will be answered this hour:

☐ How do I put sound clips in my Web page?

☐ How do I put video clips on my Web page?

☐ What are WebBots and how do I use them?

☐ How can I use Java and Visual Basic Scripts?

☐ How can I use forms in my Web page?

Hear Ye, Hear Ye

FrontPage Express enables you to embed a sound into your Web page so that it is played when a Web browser first opens your page. However, most of the time you will include a hyperlink to a sound file that you allow the user of your page to hear. To embed the sound as a link in your Web page, use the techniques you learned in the previous hour. Creating a link to a sound file is no different than creating a link to a Web page.

The Web Is Alive with the Sound of Music

Before continuing, it might help to have an overview of the most common types of sound files you can find on the Internet. The following list describes several popular sound file formats:

☐ AU—Audio files are the most common sound files on the Web. Most Web browsers play them in the browser without the assistance of a helper application. These files are small and of reasonable quality. Their file name ends with .au, for example, sound.au.

☐ WAV—These sound files, pronounced "wave," are the second most common sound file type and closely tied to the Windows operating system. You can create WAV files right from Windows using Sound Recorder in the Accessories folder if your computer has a microphone. A WAV file might be called sound.wav.

☐ MPEG-Audio—MPEG stands for moving picture experts group. This is one of the newer formats and may not be supported by an older browser. MPEG-Audio claims CD-quality music with a small file size for faster downloading. It's file name might end with .mp3.

☐ MIDI—Musical instrument digital interface is commonly used for recording electronic musical instruments. MIDI files are small but that's because MIDI files contain instruments and no voices. MIDI file names end with .mid.

When you create a link to a sound file on your page and a user clicks on the link to hear it using Internet Explorer 4, the ActiveMovie control panel will open and play the sound. Figure 24.1 shows what happens when a sound link is clicked in Internet Explorer. Other browsers may not have the capability to play your sound clip without the assistance of a helper application. However, most modern browsers come equipped with helpers to handle these files.

Figure 24.1.

ActiveMovie automatically plays sounds for Internet Explorer.

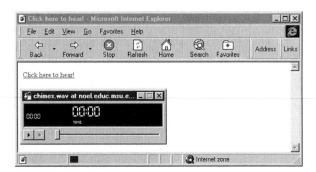

Greeting Your Users

As mentioned, you can also embed a sound in your page to be played whenever someone first opens your page. This type of file can be a greeting that is played once or a file of background music that plays continuously while your page is being viewed. Let's put a background sound on a page now.

To Do: Insert a Background Sound

1. Start a new Web page or use one you've already created.

2. Choose File|Page Properties (or choose Insert | Background Sound).

3. Under Background Sound, click the Browse button and select your sound file. (If you don't have one handy, go to `c:\Windows\Media` and select one.)

4. Decide whether you want the sound to play once, twice, a number of times, or forever.

5. Click OK.

6. After you upload your page and the sound to your Web server, load the page into your browser and see what happens!

24

Getting the Right Sound

You can get sound files in several ways. You can record your own if you have the right hardware and software on your machine (but that's another book!). Many CD-ROMs come with sound clips that you can copy to your Web site. In addition, lots of sites on the Web have music and sound samples for your use.

JUST A MINUTE

Be considerate of copyrighted material. Just because you can record an entire music CD to a sound file doesn't mean you can post it on your Web page. Usually, only small clips or samples are allowed.

Who's Listening?

You should remember a couple caveats when putting sounds into your Web pages. First, sound files can be quite large. As a result, people who access your page using a modem or other slow connection may not want to wait for your sound to download to their computer before it's played.

Second, not everyone will be using Internet Explorer and a modern, multimedia computer to access your page. Older browsers and slower hardware-poor computers may be unable to play your sound. Never create a Web page that is dependent on sound files to make it work. In other words, sound files should be a "value-added" element on your page and not the main portion of your page.

And Now, Our Feature Presentation

Video clips, which you can find online or on CDs or create with multimedia equipment, are sprouting up on Web pages all over. But if you thought sound files were large, you ain't seen nothin' yet. A typical video clip can easily be four or five (or more) megabytes.

CAUTION

As with sound files, some Web browsers don't play movies in the Web page. Usually, a helper application is called by the Web browser to play the movie, so it's seen in a separate window. Some older Web browsers can't play them at all.

Common Movie File Formats

Only a few different video file formats are currently on the Web. The following list describes the more common video file formats:

☐ AVI—Audio Video Interleaved is the most common format for video data on the PC and is common on the Web. FrontPage Express works well with AVI movie files. AVI file names end in .avi.

☐ QuickTime—A rival of AVI, and common on the Web, QuickTime movies boast better quality video than AVI with smaller file sizes, and generally offer better compatibility. You will almost always see Web sites with video clip files of AVI and QuickTime together. QuickTime movie file names end in .mov.

☐ MPEG—MPEG is the up-and-coming standard of movie formats on the Web. Many mini-movies on CD-ROMs use this format. The file name of an MPEG file ends in .mpg or .mpeg.

To be safe, you should stick to AVI format at first. FrontPage Express works well with this format. As you become more advanced, you can play around with some of the other formats.

TIME SAVER

It might be helpful to have a few movie clips to start with. A great place to find some different types of movies is Jesse's Movies, at http://www.uslink.net/~edgerton/index.html.

Putting in the Flick

After you have a few clips, you're ready to put one in your page. After uploading the video clip to your Web site, follow these steps.

24

To Do: Insert a Video Clip

1. Position your cursor at the beginning of a blank line where you want your video to be viewed.

2. Choose Insert | Video. The Video dialog appears.

3. Enter the URL where the newly uploaded video segment is located.

CAUTION

> Some people will tell you to go ahead and embed a video clip on your page that's located on someone else's server. Quite frankly, this is rude. You are, in essence, using their server time and space for free. Take the time to put the clip on your own Web server and be considerate to others.

4. Click OK. The first frame of the video you just inserted (AVI only) appears in your document.

5. Right-click on the image and choose the Image Properties option from the resulting pop-up menu.

6. With the Video tab selected, tell FrontPage Express whether VCR-type controls should show up with the video clip in the browser window, whether the video should play over and over (loop), and whether you want the video to play when the Web page is opened or when the mouse cursor touches the video clip.

7. Save your page to your Web site.

Display your new page in Internet Explorer. Figure 24.2 shows what a typical movie clip in a browser window might look like.

Figure 24.2.

Here is a video clip right on a Web page.

24

Those Wascally WebBots

Elmer Fudd would have a much easier time with these mini-programs than he would with that long-eared wabbit. WebBots enable your Web page to perform complex tasks that would otherwise require extensive programming skills. For example, one WebBot provides a form to search your page for key words without your having to write a CGI script.

 CGI script: CGI (Common Gateway Interface) scripts are small programs that run on a Web server and usually perform some complex function. CGI scripts require programming knowledge and aren't for the beginner.

When using WebBots, it is important to remember that these programs aren't in your Web page; they're on the Web server that your page is on. WebBots leave a little marker on your Web page telling the server to perform a specific WebBot action.

 CAUTION

> If your FrontPage Express Web page won't be on a server that has WebBot functionality, none of what is described in this section will work for you. Check with your system administrator to see whether WebBots are supported.

Following is a list of WebBots included with FrontPage Express:

- ☐ Include—This feature enables you to place another Web page inside your Web page. This is handy, for example, if you want to include the ESPN SportsZone Web page in your Web page to have instant access to sports information.
- ☐ Search—A search form enables a user to find words on your Web site using a simple one-line text box. When the form is submitted, it creates a list of links to pages containing one or more of the search words.
- ☐ Timestamp—This feature adds a date and time that the page was last edited or automatically updated. You'll want to place timestamps at the bottom of the page so that your readers know you've been regularly updating your page. (You have, haven't you?)

New WebBots are being written all the time. Check Microsoft's home page for new ones or look in Microsoft-related newsgroups. For more WebBot functionality, FrontPage offers a greater variety with more advanced features, but you have to pay for this professional version.

24

Wot's a Bot Do?

The *Bot* in *WebBot* is short for *robot;* its purpose is to do something automatically for you and your users. Including the different kinds of WebBots into your page is basically the same for each of the three kinds of Bots.

To Do: Insert a Search WebBot

1. Position your cursor at the beginning of a blank line, where you want your Search form to begin.

2. Click the robot icon on the formatting toolbar, or choose Insert | WebBot Component. The Insert WebBot Component dialog appears.

3. Choose Search. You have several choices for your search input form, such as button labels and the label that prompts users for the search term.

4. For now, accept the default by clicking OK. Your search form might look like the one shown in Figure 24.3.

Figure 24.3.

This is what a Search WebBot might look like.

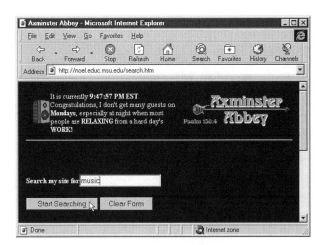

Using the search form is easy. Just type the words you are searching for in the text box, and then click the Search button. A Web page with hyperlinks to the words you searched for is displayed.

When you move your cursor over a WebBot in FrontPage Express, notice that it turns into a robot icon. This indicates that you can alter the settings for the WebBot after you've created it. Simply right-click on the WebBot, and then choose WebBot Component Properties from the resulting pop-up menu. A dialog appears, from which you can change the WebBot settings.

Scripting Your Page

WebBots are simple scripts that FrontPage Express includes on your page; to run, they require special software on your Web server. However, other scripts (such as Java and VBScript) require you to write code that is included in your page's HTML. These scripts will run without additional software on the server, but you have to write (or borrow) the scripts.

CAUTION

> Borrowing scripts without the author's consent is considered pirating someone's hard work. If you do borrow a script, ask first or be sure that the author has given permission to use it.

FrontPage Express recognizes two primary types of scripts: Java and Visual Basic (also called VBScript). Of the two, Java is used far more on the Web. Also, some VBScripts need to be run on the server. (A check box in the Script dialog covers that eventuality.) Again, check with your server administrator to see whether you can include these special types of VBScripts on your page.

Hot Page O' Java

The techies say that Java is the next big programming language. Created by Sun Microsystems, Inc., JavaScript can be used on any computer. Java is also free, so you don't have to ask to use it. (However, you do have to ask permission of the authors of Java *scripts* to use their scripts.)

To Do: Insert a Script

1. Position your cursor at the beginning of a blank line where you want your script to begin.
2. Choose Insert|Script.
3. In the Language box, choose which type of script you will use. This example assumes Java is the script being used.
4. In the Script box, type or paste a script formatted in the Java programming language. (See Figure 24.4 for what such a script might look like.)
5. Click OK.

The Java script used in Figure 24.4 is located at `http://www.valdosta.peachnet.edu/vsu/dept/aux/animation/cool.html`. As you can see in Figure 24.5, it is a script that automatically calculates how many calories a person burns by running, based on body weight.

Figure 24.4.

*Not something most
people want to do
themselves!*

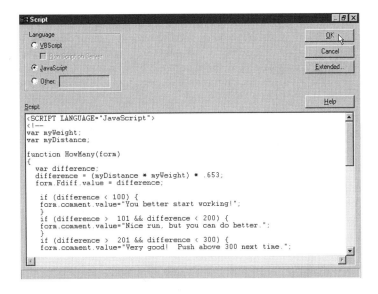

Figure 24.5.

*This version of the script
is much easier to
understand.*

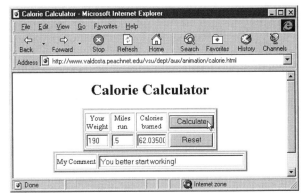

Good Form!

You've probably seen forms on Web pages by now—places where you can type data on a Web
page and click a button to get some information or accomplish a task. An example of a form
is the simple search form described previously. Other forms (such as a stock quote service)
take comments or requests for information and return a Web page with the answer.

As tired as you are of seeing these cautions, here's another one. A form doesn't work unless a script or a WebBot on the Web server knows what to do with the data being entered. You'll have to check with the server administrator to find out how (and whether) to use forms.

A form can have several types of boxes, buttons, and pull-down menus. The following describes the form fields that FrontPage Express creates. These buttons are found on the lowest toolbar button bar.

 One-line text box. You can set its length and make it a password field (which means the characters a user types will not show up in the window).

 Scrolling text box. It can be many lines high and as wide as you like.

 Check box. Its starting value can be set to checked or unchecked.

 Radio button. These are like check boxes, except usually only one radio button in any particular set of radio buttons can be selected at one time.

 Drop-down menu. It has predefined data that a user can select, such as a list of states or products.

 Push button. It's usually the item a user selects to send data to a database, a CGI script, or a WebBot.

Time Saver

Like WebBots, a form field can be double-clicked to change its properties. These properties can range from the size of the text box to the text that will appear on a button. There are many possibilities. Try them all!

Plan your form before you create it. The form should clearly show what a user should do with each button or pull-down menu. It helps to draw the form out before you begin.

24

To Do: Build a Form in Your Web Page

1. Position the cursor where you want the form field to appear, probably at the beginning of a line. (You can put a form field anywhere, even in a table cell.)

2. Select from the formatting buttons the form item you want.

3. Click on the form field or button and change the settings to meet your needs.

When you're finished, your form might look something like the one shown in Figure 24.6.

Figure 24.6.

This is a typical form.

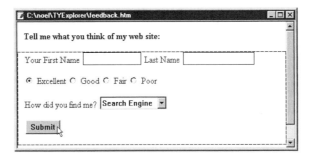

FrontPage Express offers several more options, which are beyond the scope of this book. However, you are encouraged to explore them as you gain knowledge and confidence. If you are ready for some adventure, you might also want to consider purchasing FrontPage.

Summary

This hour started with an overview of audio and video files and how to integrate them into your Web pages. Next, you learned how to use WebBots for even more functionality. You were then shown how to include scripts in your HTML. The hour ended by showing you how to quickly and easily create an interactive form for your page.

Q&A

Q Is there an easy way to record simple sounds for inclusion on my Web page?

A The easiest way to create your own simple sounds is to use the Sound Recorder program that comes with Windows (as long as your computer has a sound card and a microphone). Sound Recorder lets you record sounds in several Windows formats that can be placed or linked to your Web page. Many Web sites feature software that enables you to create and edit audio. This software is often distributed as freeware or shareware. You might want to go to http://www.download.com or http://www.shareware.com and look around.

Q I put an MPEG movie in my Web page instead of an AVI file and it doesn't seem to be working. What's up?

A FrontPage Express works very well with AVI files and displays them as they should be. But FrontPage Express is not quite as good with QuickTime or MPEG. With AVI files, you can see the first frame of the video on your Web page in FrontPage Express and also when that page is loaded using Internet Explorer 4. With QuickTime and MPEG, you can place movie files in your Web page but you won't see the first frame of the movie in FrontPage Express. Instead, the video clip is represented by a small box. However, go ahead and save the page. When it's displayed in Internet Explorer, it will work.

Quiz

Take the following quiz to see how much you've learned.

Questions

1. Which of the following is not a video file format?

    a. AVI

    b. WAV

    c. MPEG

2. WebBots are very flexible in that they will work on any server.

    a. True

    b. False

3. What are the two types of scripts that FrontPage Express will allow you to automatically include in your page?

Answers

1. b.

2. b. False. Remember, WebBots are very reliant on servers.

3. JavaScript and VBScript

Activity

One of the easiest and least server-reliant ways to spice up your Web site is through the use of Java scripts. Go out on the Web and search for an interesting public domain Java script and embed it in your Web page.

24

PART VII

Appendixes

Hour

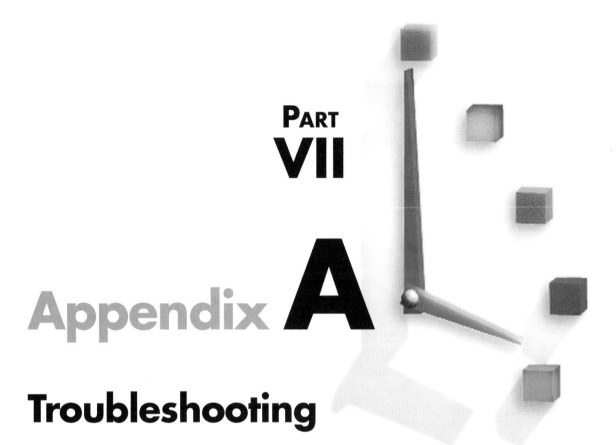

Appendix A

Troubleshooting

The information listed in this Appendix is designed to help you through some potential trouble spots you might—I repeat, *might*— encounter using Internet Explorer 4. Remember, just because there are warnings here on some potential trouble spots does not mean you will experience these problems.

Q I can't find some of the Internet Explorer 4 components—such as NetMeeting or FrontPage Express—in my Start menu. Is there another way to open them?

A If the components don't show up on the Start menu where this book says you'll find them, you haven't installed them. When you installed Internet Explorer 4, you had the option of selecting Minimal, Standard, or Full installation; only Full installs all components.

To learn how to add components now, see Hour 3 or Hour 11.

Q I have a 33.6 Kbps modem, but my Internet connection dialog says I'm connected at 28.8 Kbps.

The speed at which a connection runs is determined by the slowest of the modems involved. If your ISP does not support 33.6 Kbps access, you'll run at the ISP's modem speed (probably 28.8 Kbps), no matter how fast your modem. Some ISPs use different dial-in numbers for different speeds; contact your ISP and ask how to get 33.6 Kbps access.

If you're already connecting through a 33.6 Kbps modem at your ISP, your modem may be configured for 28.8 Kbps operation. Open the Modems icon in Control Panel, and reconfigure your modem for its top speed. Consult your modem's manual for configuration details.

Also, note that a poor phone connection or a "noisy" phone line makes accurate modem communications more difficult. To compensate, most modems will automatically slow down to a speed at which they can communicate reliably over the line. If you've eliminated the other potential causes, and you still see your modem communicating below its rated speed, you may have a noisy phone line. Contact your local telephone company to find out what can be done about the problem.

Q I know that Internet Explorer 4 and its components are supposed to connect to the Internet automatically, when necessary. But sometimes, Internet Explorer tells me it's offline when I know I'm online.

A This feature works pretty well, but not perfectly. Sometimes while you're online, Internet Explorer thinks you're off. It's quirky, and there's not really anything you can do to correct it, other than keeping up with new Internet Explorer 4 files (see Hour 11) in case Microsoft corrects the problem.

But it's no big deal. If you're online when Internet Explorer thinks you're off, when you try to do something that requires a connection, it asks whether you want to go online. Even though you're already online, just humor Internet Explorer and click Yes. Internet Explorer will immediately detect that you're online, and continue the operation you started.

Q Before I installed Internet Explorer, my graphics editing program opened whenever I opened an image file icon. Now Internet Explorer opens, instead.

A When you install Internet Explorer 4, the installation program edits Windows's file types registry (see Hour 11) to make Internet Explorer the default program for lots of different file types, including Web page (HTML) files and most image file types. This is so Internet Explorer can display most types of files you encounter on the Web quickly, right in the Internet Explorer window, without having to open another program first.

A

If you want a certain image file type to always open in your graphics program instead of Internet Explorer, you can open the Windows file types registry (open any folder and choose View | Folder Options | File Types), select the image file type in the list, and click Edit to change the program used for opening that file from Internet Explorer 4 to your graphics program. Alternatively, you can simply reinstall your graphics program, which may automatically update the file types registry to make the graphics program the default for opening images.

If you do change the file types registry, note that images that are part of a Web page layout—*inline* images—will still display in the Web page, in the Internet Explorer window. But if you click a link that opens an image file of a type registered to your graphics program, the image will not appear in the Internet Explorer window. Instead, your graphics program opens to display the image.

Q Sometimes when I enter a URL, use a favorite from my Favorites list, or click a link, I get a message saying that Internet Explorer couldn't find the server, or that it couldn't find the file.

A When Internet Explorer reports that it can't find a file, it has successfully reached the server but can't find the specific file the address points to. The file may have been deleted, renamed, or moved, or you may have typed the part of the URL that comes after the address incorrectly. Try entering just the server portion of the URL —everything up to and including the first single, forward slash (/)—to access the server's top page, and then see whether you can navigate to what you want by clicking through links from there.

When Internet Explorer reports that it can't find the server, you may have typed the server address portion of the URL incorrectly. Or the server may have changed its address or gone out of business. However, when you get this message, the server may just be experiencing temporary technical problems. Double-check the URL, and if you still can't get through, try again in a few hours, by which time the server may be back in action.

Q When I click the Back button, nothing happens.

A Is the Back button "greyed out"? If so, you've already reached the page at which your current session began. Back no longer works because there's nowhere to go back to.

If the Back button is not greyed out but seems to do nothing when you click it, you're probably looking at a page that uses frames. Remember, when you view a frames page, Back and Forward move you among the frames. If you keep clicking Back, though, you'll eventually move to the page you visited before the frames page.

Q **I've noticed that most Web server addresses begin with www.·. Is this a universal naming convention?**

A There is no chiseled-in-stone rule on using www.·. Just as using WWW as the name of a Web server is a practice and not a hard-and-fast rule, the same practice applies to naming FTP sites. One popular example of an FTP site that is not named FTP is gatekeeper.dec.com. To access this FTP site, you enter the URL ftp://gatekeeper.dec.com. Remember, where names are concerned on the Internet, there are no exact rules.

Q **If I choose to send someone an HTML e-mail message using Outlook Express, and the recipient is not using an e-mail client capable of displaying HTML, won't the recipient's e-mail program just spit out the part it can't read?**

A Yes, that is true. If you receive a message containing HTML and your e-mail client can't read HTML, the program will simply ignore the part it can't understand.

That means you can send HTML e-mail to anyone. But it also means that you must be sure that all important information in the message is contained within the text itself, and is not dependent on any images, text formatting, or other HTML features the reader will not see if his or her e-mail program is not HTML compatible.

Q **My friend told me about this great newsgroup, but when I try to subscribe to it, I get a message that it's not on the server.**

A Not all newsgroups are available on all servers. Some newsgroups are private and are maintained on servers accessible only to those with permission to use the newsgroup.

Also, each ISP maintains its own news server. While most ISPs keep all 14,000+ newsgroups on their servers, some do not. For example, some attempt to minimize sexual traffic by not including the alt. groups on their servers. Others try to save space by including only newsgroups their members have requested. In case that's the reason you can't get through to the newsgroup, try sending an e-mail to your ISP, requesting that the newsgroup be added to the server.

Q **I instructed my service provider's news server to display all newsgroups; I've been waiting for several minutes, and nothing seems to be happening.**

A Because of the sheer number of newsgroups on the typical news server, it may take several minutes to display all newsgroup names, so don't panic if it appears that nothing is happening. Just be patient. Also keep in mind that the speed of your Internet connection also affects how long it takes to display all those newsgroups.

Q Are there any precautions I need to take before downloading files from newsgroups?

A Before you start downloading files from newsgroups, make sure you have a functioning, up-to-date anti-virus program in operation, because files attached to newsgroup messages may not have been scanned by anyone. Keep in mind, too, that all files and photos on newsgroups were not placed there by Disney and Mr. Rogers. Many of the photos you will find posted on Usenet are pornographic, and some are quite explicit. Fortunately, the newsgroups containing the porno photos are usually easy to identify by their names (such as `alt.binary.pictures.erotica`, and so on,) so you aren't likely to just stumble across them.

Q I'm trying to create my home page, and I'm experimenting with different background and text colors. Maybe I've been working too hard for too long, but it seems that some colors are harder on the eyes than others. Am I imagining this?

A No, not at all. Be careful in the color combinations you select for your fonts and your page background. The human eye is not capable of focusing on all color combinations. Also, some color combinations can be focused on but are uncomfortable to look at for any length of time.

Q My friend called me up and said he visited my home page (which I created in FrontPage Express)—and said it looks sloppy. The text colors make it hard to read, he said, and the placement of graphics and text looks haphazard. The page looks okay to me in FrontPage Express, so what gives?

A The same Web page looks different through different browsers. Some browsers handle certain kinds of formatting instructions differently than others, and some don't support certain kinds of formatting. For example, some browsers don't support backgrounds, text alignment, or most image-positioning options. When you've applied these techniques in your page, it will look dramatically different to someone using that browser than it does to you.

When you work on your page in FrontPage Express, what you see is generally what you'd see if you viewed the page online through Internet Explorer (version 3 or 4) or any recent version of Netscape Navigator. Most folks online who use a graphical browser use either of these two browsers. Your tactless (but reliably frank) friend must be using a different browser. If you want to make sure your page looks great through any browser, keep the formatting simple, and test the page by viewing it through as many different browsers as you can get your hands on.

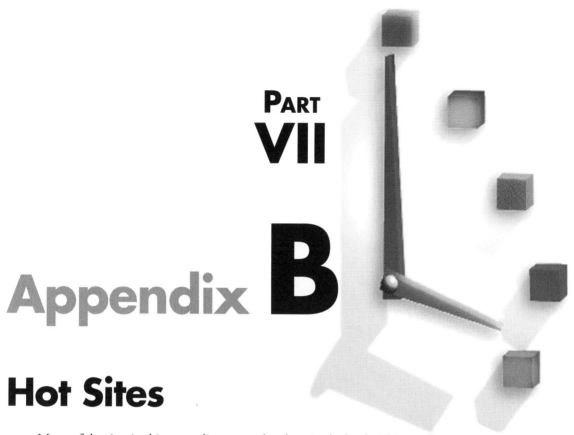

Appendix B

Hot Sites

Many of the sites in this appendix appear elsewhere in the book. This simply represents a quick reference of sites you might find most useful or entertaining.

Computer- and Internet-Related Sites

These sites take you to some of the major producers of computers, computer systems, and related hardware and software.

Computer Systems

☐ IBM

www.ibm.com

☐ Apple Computer, Inc.

www.apple.com

☐ Sun Microsystems, Inc.

www.sun.com

- ☐ Digital Equipment Corporation (DEC)

    www.dec.com

- ☐ Compaq

    www.compaq.com

- ☐ Gateway 2000

    www.gateway2000.com

- ☐ Dell

    www.dell.com

- ☐ Toshiba

    www.toshiba.com

Printers

- ☐ Hewlett-Packard

    www.hp.com

- ☐ Brother

    www.brother.com

- ☐ Canon

    www.canon.com

Modems

- ☐ U.S. Robotics

    www.usr.com

- ☐ Hayes

    www.hayes.com

- ☐ Practical Peripherals

    www.practinet.com

- ☐ Microcom

    www.microcom.com

- ☐ Zoom

    www.zoom.com

- ☐ Global Village

    www.globalvillage.com

B

Major Software Corporations

☐ Microsoft, Corp.

www.microsoft.com or home.microsoft.com

☐ Netscape Communications, Corp.

www.netscape.com or home.netscape.com

☐ Novell, Inc.

www.novell.com

☐ Claris

www.claris.com

☐ Adobe Systems Incorporated

www.adobe.com

☐ Quarterdeck

www.quarterdeck.com

Internet Sites

This section contains Internet-related World Wide Web sites.

Browsers and Plug-Ins

☐ Netscape Communications, Corp.

www.netscape.com or home.netscape.com

☐ Netscape Navigator plug-ins

www.netscape.com/comprod/mirror/navcomponents_download.html

☐ Microsoft Internet Explorer

www.microsoft.com/ie/

☐ Using Netscape Navigator plug-ins in Microsoft Internet Explorer

www.microsoft.com/ie/challenge/comparison/plug.htm

☐ NCSA Mosaic

www.ncsa.uiuc.edu/SDG/Software/Mosaic/

Search Engines

☐ Excite

www.excite.com

☐ Yahoo!

www.yahoo.com

☐ Infoseek

www.infoseek.com/

☐ AltaVista

www.altavista.digital.com/

☐ Magellan

www.mckinley.com/

☐ Lycos

www.lycos.com/

☐ Open Text

www.opentext.com/

☐ WebCrawler

www.webcrawler.com/

☐ MetaCrawler—searches by geographic region

metacrawler.cs.washington.edu

☐ shareware.com—Searches for shareware

www.shareware.com/

☐ Catalist—searches for listservs

segate.sunet.se/lists/listref.html

People Finders

☐ Four11

www.four11.com/

☐ InfoSpace

www.infospace.com

☐ WhoWhere?

www.whowhere.com

☐ America Directory Assistance

www.lookupusa.com/lookupusa/adp/peopsrch.htm

B

U.S. Government Sites

The following are a few of the more popular government sites on the Web:

- [ ] The White House

  www.whitehouse.gov

- [ ] The U.S. Senate

  www.senate.gov

- [ ] The U.S. House of Representatives

  www.house.gov

- [ ] The U.S. Library of Congress

  lcweb.loc.gov

- [ ] FedWorld

  www.fedworld.gov

Broadcast Media

This list of sites covers everything from network TV to cable to the movies.

Network TV

- [ ] ABC

  www.abc.com

- [ ] CBS

  www.cbs.com

- [ ] NBC

  www.nbc.com

- [ ] Fox

  www.foxworld.com

Cable TV

- [ ] Cinemax

  www.cinemax.com

- [ ] HBO

  www.hbo.com

☐ The Disney Channel

www.disney.com/DisneyChannel/

☐ ESPN

www.espn.com

Movie Studios

☐ MCA/Universal

www.mca.com

☐ Metro Goldwyn Mayer

www.mgmua.com

☐ Paramount Pictures

www.paramount.com

☐ Sony Pictures

www.spe.sony.com/Pictures/SonyMovies/index.html

☐ Twentieth Century Fox

www.tcfhe.com

☐ Walt Disney Studios

www.disney.com/DisneyPictures/

☐ Warner Bros.

www.movies.warnerbros.com/

B

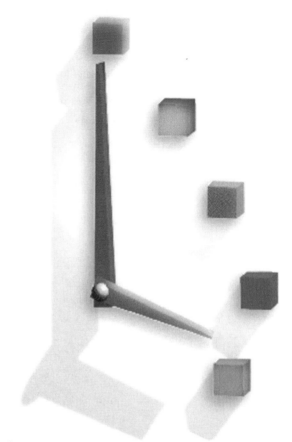

Glossary

Active desktop. A catchall term describing the many changes Internet Explorer 4 makes to the Windows interface, such as single-clicking to open file and folder icons. Sometimes also called *Web integrated desktop* or *Web desktop update*.

ActiveX. Microsoft's answer to Netscape's plug-ins. ActiveX components act like plug-ins but claim to be more dynamic because they can be downloaded along with the page that uses them. Note that Internet Explorer 4 supports both Netscape plug-ins and ActiveX modules.

address book. A feature of Outlook Express that holds personal information (for example, name, e-mail address, phone number) for reference and to make addressing an e-mail message easier.

aliases. Also called a *nickname*, an alias is a shortcut that represents a real e-mail address.

attachment. A computer file (graphics, text, program, or any other type) sent with an e-mail message.

authoring. The process of writing a Web page.

BCC (blind carbon copy). When e-mailing, it is a way to send a copy of an e-mail message without letting the other recipients know you are sending a copy.

Big Seven Hierarchies. Newsgroup hierarchies established years ago and are still in effect today. They make up what is known as the Big 7 newsgroup hierarchies. These seven hierarchies contain a majority of all newsgroup traffic: comp, soc, rec, sci, talk, news, and misc.

binary. Any non-text file, such as a picture or program.

Boolean operators. These operators are designed to put conditions on a search. The most common Boolean operators are AND, OR, and NOT.

browser. A software program that requests, interprets, and presents World Wide Web documents. Frequently used browsers include Internet Explorer, Netscape Navigator (a part of Netscape Communicator in its latest version), Lynx, and Mosaic.

cache. The storage area on a person's computer that has copies of original data stored so that the computer doesn't have to go to a remote server to get information every time it is requested.

CC (carbon copy). A copy of an e-mail message, sent to someone other than the message's principle recipient.

CERN. The European Laboratory for Particle Physics and the birthplace of the World Wide Web.

certificate. A file used in secure connections to authenticate the server to a client. It is used when two parties want a third party to certify that a file is authentic.

CGI (Common Gateway Interface). Allows a Web server limited access to other programs or data on the computer. Often CGI scripts are created to automate the transfer of data to and from the Web server.

channel. A special Web page to which you can subscribe with Internet Explorer to receive automatic updates whenever the page's content changes.

client. All the computers and software that make up the Internet are either *clients* (which receive and translate data) or *servers* (which provide and translate data). Thus, client software enables you to get information from the Internet.

Codec. Short for *compression/decompression*, a mathematical algorithm responsible for encoding an analog signal into digital form. It also decodes a received digital signal back into an analog signal.

Communicator.   Also known as Netscape 4.0, it is the newest suite of Internet tools from Netscape Communications Corp. Like Internet Explorer, it includes a browser (Navigator), e-mail (Messenger), newsreader (Collabra), Web authoring (Composer), conferencing (Conference), and other Internet tools.

cookie.   A collection of information that a Web site can leave on your computer for later access.

cross-posting.   A method by which you can post a single article to multiple newsgroups.

desktop item.   A special kind of channel that always appears on your Windows desktop.

domain name.   The name given to any computer registered on the World Wide Web as an official provider of information and files. Domain names are usually two or more terms separated by periods. A couple of examples are aol.com and www.msu.edu.

download.   Transferring a file from a host computer to your computer.

drag and drop.   A process where you use your computer's mouse to click and hold on icons on the monitor, move them around while continuing to hold the mouse button, and release the mouse button when you have moved the icon to the desired location.

e-mail address.   Consists of a user ID, followed by an @ sign and a domain name. For instance: tom@candlestick.com.

emoticons.   Short for *emotional icons*. These character combinations are one way of trying to get across a little emotion in what you say. For instance, :) is a smile.

encoding.   Sometimes referred to as *encryption*. A method for turning binary data into textual data for transmission over the Internet. Binhex (used on Macintosh computers and the Eudora e-mail client), UUDecode (used by UNIX and some other e-mail clients), and MIME (used on the Web and by a few other e-mail clients) are standard encoding schemes.

encrypt.   Changing the appearance of data using a logical formula to protect the data's integrity. It requires a key to allow a person to read the encrypted material.

FAQs (frequently asked questions).   Many times, newcomers to a newsgroup will ask questions that the old-timers have heard over and over again. FAQs are written and posted periodically to reduce the number of redundant questions.

favorite.   A way that Internet Explorer keeps a permanent record of Internet sites, folders, and files you like to visit often, so you can revisit them easily.

filter.   Simply a way that an e-mail client looks at e-mail message header information to determine what to do with the message. Filters are applied by Outlook Express's Inbox Assistant (see Hour 14).

firewall. One way to protect information on an internal computer network from people outside the network.

flame. An Internet message that often uses profanity or otherwise berates and belittles the recipient.

frames. A feature available on the World Wide Web that presents text, links, graphics, and other media in separate portions of the browser display. Some sections remain unchanging, while others serve as an exhibit of linked documents.

FrontPage Express. The WYSIWYG (what you see is what you get) HTML (Web page) editor built into Internet Explorer.

FTP (file transfer protocol). FTP is a set of rules for transferring files on the Internet.

full-duplex. Referring to a type of sound card, a full-duplex card allows two users to speak simultaneously while using an Internet phone application such as NetMeeting.

GIF (graphics interchange format). An image format, typically smaller in size than other formats, that allows users to exchange graphics electronically.

half-duplex. Referring to a type of sound card, a half-duplex card allows only one user to speak at a time while using an Internet phone application such as NetMeeting.

header. See *message headers.*

helper application. Programs that run or show files that aren't part of a Web page and don't appear as part of the Web browser.

hits. When conducting an Internet search on the Web, each result of a particular search is called a hit. *Hit* also describes each time a Web site is visited by someone.

home page. Frequently, this term refers to the cover of a particular Web site. The home page is the main, or first, page displayed for an organization's or person's World Wide Web site. *Home page* also describes the page a Web browser is configured to access first when you go online, or anytime you click the browser's Home button.

HTML (Hypertext Markup Language). HTML is the coding language for the World Wide Web that informs browsers how to display a document's text, links, graphics, and other media. This language forms the foundation for all Web pages.

HTTP (Hypertext Transfer Protocol). The way information is exchanged between HTTP servers and their clients

hyperlink. Sometimes called *link*, a pointer within a document that, when clicked, transports you somewhere else.

image map. A feature available on the World Wide Web that allows users to click on various locations in a graphic image to link to different documents.

IMAP (Internet Message Access Protocol). The process through which a person can access e-mail messages on a mail server rather than on a local computer.

inbox. The place people go to get their incoming messages within their e-mail program.

Internet. The global network of computers that enables people all over the world to electronically communicate with each other.

Intranet. A network of computers set up like the Internet except only certain people, such as those who work for a company, are given access.

IP address. An address used by Internet Protocol (IP) to identify each computer on the Internet. This number consists of four numbers between 0 and 255, each separated by a period. A typical IP address might be 35.8.7.92.

IRC (Internet Relay Chat). A very large network of servers that allows users to communicate in real time to one another via the keyboard.

ISP (Internet Service Provider). An organization or company that provides users access to the Internet.

JavaScript. A compact, object-based language for developing client/server Internet applications.

JPEG (Joint Photographic Experts Group). A graphics file format.

launch. To start an application on a computer.

listserv. An e-mail address configured to forward every message it receives to the e-mail addresses of those who have subscribed to it. You can think of it as an electronic interactive newspaper.

login name. The name you type into your computer when you log onto a network or an account you access via your computer.

lurking. Reading a newsgroup without posting to it.

mailing list. See *listserv*.

message headers. The part of an e-mail message (or newsgroup posting) that contains basic information such as sender, receiver, and subject. Message headers act much like the information on the envelope of a letter.

micropayments. A method by which companies can keep an "electronic charge account" for customers. Micropayments offer an affordable way to charge from one-hundredth of a cent to one cent as payment for services or products offered over the Internet.

modem.　A device that allows your computer to talk to other computers using your phone line. Conventional modems range in speeds up to 56.6 Kbps (kilobits per second). Modems designed to communicate over lines other than regular phone lines (such as ISDN or cable) can achieve even higher speeds.

moderated listserv.　Just as a debate has a moderator to make sure both sides stick to the rules, so too do some listservs have a human moderator who makes sure the rules of the listserv are being followed. These listservs are called *moderated listservs*.

moderator.　Anyone who moderates, or filters, the content on a listserv or newsgroup.

netiquette.　The acceptably polite method of talking via electronic communication.

NetMeeting.　A client developed to provide real-time conferencing over the Internet. It includes live audio and video transmission, text chat, a whiteboard, and other tools.

newsgroups.　Topical areas of Usenet that operate much like bulletin boards for the discussion of topics regarding recreation, society, culture, business and—of course—computers. Currently, more than 12,000 newsgroups are available.

.newsrc file.　A file that contains information about your newsgroups, such as which groups you subscribe to and how many articles (both read and unread) are in each group you subscribe to.

NNTP server (Network News Transfer Protocol).　An NNTP server transfers news to your client using the language of Usenet.

offline.　The state of being disconnected from a network.

operators.　Anything that modifies a term or equation. In the equation $2 + 2 = 4$, the plus sign is an operator. When searching on the Web, you can often use special symbols or words to build a search "equation" that is often more effective than searching for a single word or phrase.

outbox.　The place within an e-mail program where messages are queued before they're sent.

pathname.　Identifies the location of a file on a server or other computer.

plug-in.　A small file that increases the capabilities of a Web browser. Plug-ins enable browsers to display file types beyond images and text.

POP server (Post Office Protocol server).　A server that processes incoming mail.

post.　A message to a Usenet newsgroup. When you submit messages (also called articles) to newsgroups, you are said to be *posting*.

protocol.　A set of rules. On the Internet, this translates into the set of rules computers use to communicate across networks.

public key encryption. A key given to those whom you want to be able to unencrypt a document.

publish. The process by which Web pages are put on a server connected to the Internet so others can see the page.

search engine. A computer program that indexes a database and then allows people to search it for relevant information available on the Internet.

server. Any computer that delivers—serves—information and data.

signature. A small text file that contains information your e-mail or newsgroup client automatically attaches to the bottom of every message you send.

SMTP (Simple Mail Transport Protocol). SMTP is a technical name for the way e-mail messages are sent.

spam. Any mass-mailed material meant for self-promotion, advertisement, or pure silliness. Spam, or electronic junk mail, is probably one of the most offensive aspects of the Internet.

SSL (Secure Sockets Link). Used to make Internet transactions secure from unauthorized access.

streaming audio/video. The capability of multimedia to begin playback as the file is being downloaded.

subscribe. Adding a discussion group to your subscription list.

tables. A feature available on the World Wide Web that presents document text, links, graphics, and other media in row and column format. Table borders may be visible in some documents and invisible in others.

thread. A series of newsgroup articles all dealing with the same topic. Someone replies to an article, and then someone else replies to the reply, and so on.

thumbnail image. An image that is a smaller version of a larger one.

traffic. A term used to describe how much activity there is on either a listserv or a newsgroup.

trash. A folder containing unwanted messages that can be emptied when the person desires.

upload. Transferring a file to a host computer from your computer.

UPS (uninterruptible power supply). A backup battery supply that allows you to safely shut down your machine as the result of a sudden power loss.

URL (uniform resource locator). A URL (pronounced "You-Are-El" or "Earl") serves as identification for all Internet servers and documents.

userID.   Every person with an e-mail address has a user identification of some sort. This is usually something very simple, like johndoe, but could be quite a bit more enigmatic.

username.   The name a person uses as identification within electronic communications.

Web desktop update.   See *Active desktop.*

Web integrated desktop.   See *Active desktop.*

Webmaster.   The individual responsible for maintaining and updating the content of a World Wide Web document. Webmasters are the creative force behind the World Wide Web.

Web page.   An HTML document that can be browsed and edited.

Web site.   A collection of World Wide Web documents, usually consisting of a home page and several related pages. You might think of a Web site as an interactive electronic book.

World Wide Web.   The graphical interface portion of the Internet.

WYSIWYG (what you see is what you get).   Refers to a program that shows you on screen exactly the way a document will appear when published. For example, Microsoft Word shows you exactly the way a document will look when printed, and FrontPage Express shows you a Web page you're creating exactly the way it will look on the Web to others.

INDEX

Symbols

in chat room lists, 260
20th Century Fox web site,
362

A

ABC television web site,
361
accepting calls
(NetMeeting), 278
Active Desktop, 5
changing background,
68-69
changing wallpaper, 68-69
customizing, 111-121
deleting, 120-121
enabling/disabling items,
116-117
enabling/disabling single-
clicks, 74-76
links, 7, 69-71
overview, 67
Web page styling, 80
Active Desktop Gallery, 170
ActiveX, 363
ActiveX files, 158
Add Channel dialog box,
102
addictions, 244-245
address bar, 11, 80, 84
address book (Messenger),
363
address toolbar, 83-84, 93
addresses
e-mail, 191, 365
IP address, 367
ISPs, 37
Adobe Systems Incorpo-
rated site, 359
Advanced options (Internet
Options dialog box),
60-61
advertising on newsgroups,
226
aliases, 363
alignment
headers, 314
images, 330
text (marquees), 319
alt newsgroups, 225

The Information SuperLibrary™

Bookstore	Search	What's New	Reference	Software	Newsletter	Company Overviews
Yellow Pages	Internet Starter Kit	HTML Workshop	Win a Free T-Shirt!	Macmillan Computer Publishing	Site Map	Talk to Us

CHECK OUT THE BOOKS IN THIS LIBRARY.

You'll find thousands of shareware files and over 1600 computer books designed for both technowizards and technophobes. You can browse through 700 sample chapters, get the latest news on the Net, and find just about anything using our massive search directories.

All Macmillan Computer Publishing books are available at your local bookstore.

We're open 24-hours a day, 365 days a year.

You don't need a card.

We don't charge fines.

And you can be as **LOUD** as you want.

The Information SuperLibrary

http://www.mcp.com/mcp/   ftp.mcp.com

MACMILLAN COMPUTER PUBLISHING USA

A V I A C O M C O M P A N Y

Technical ----, ---- **Support:**

If you need assistance with the information in this book or with a CD/Disk
accompanying the book, please access the Knowledge Base on our Web
site at **http://www.superlibrary.com/general/support**. Our most
Frequently Asked Questions are answered there. If you do not find the
answer to your questions on our Web site, you may contact Macmillan
Technical Support **(317) 581-3833** or e-mail us at **support@mcp.com**.

Teach Yourself Dynamic HTML in a Week

—Bruce Campbell and Rick Darnell

In this thorough tutorial, you'll learn about all the technologies collectively referred to as dynamic HTML, including Microsoft Internet Explorer 4 and Netscape Communicator. Detailed instructions are provided on how to use dynamic HTML and Web scripting languages to create Web pages and Web applications that change in response to user actions. New dynamic HTML tags, as well as concepts such as the document object model, are presented in a clear, step-by-step manner with lots of practical examples.

Price: $29.99 USA/$42.95 CDN   *Casual–Advanced*
ISBN: 1-57521-335-4   *500 pages*

Laura Lemay's Teach Yourself Web Publishing with HTML 4 in 14 Days, Second Professional Reference Edition

—Laura Lemay and Arman Danesh

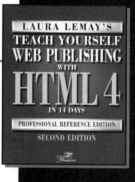

A thoroughly revised version of the best-selling book that started the HTML/Web publishing phenomenon, *Laura Lemay's Teach Yourself Web Publishing with HTML in 14 Days, Second Professional Reference Edition* is easy enough for the beginner yet comprehensive enough that even experienced Web authors will find it indispensable as a reference. This edition includes 16 more chapters than the softcover edition, plus a 300-page HTML reference section. You'll find coverage of the new Cougar specification for the next version of HTML as well as new Netscape and Microsoft technologies such as style sheets, absolute positioning, and dynamic HTML. The CD-ROM includes an electronic version of the reference section, plus additional Web publishing tools for Windows and Macintosh platforms.

Price: $59.99 USA/$84.95 CDN   *Casual–Accomplished*
ISBN: 1-57521-305-2   *1,100 pages*

Laura Lemay's Web Workshop: Advanced FrontPage 97

—Denise Tyler

As the follow-up to the national best-selling title *Laura Lemay's Web Workshop: Microsoft FrontPage 97*, this clear, hands-on guide shows you how to create and maintain Web sites and successfully use Microsoft's image composer. The book is organized into small, task-oriented chapters with real-world examples. The CD-ROM, designed to be an interactive workshop, is filled with all the tools and materials you need to follow the book's examples to create new Web pages and scripts. The CD-ROM also contains an electronic version of the text.

Price: $39.99 USA/$56.95 CDN   *Accomplished–Expert*
ISBN: 1-57521-308-7   *700 pages*

Teach Yourself Active Server Pages in 14 Days

—Sanjaya Hettihewa, et al.

In just 14 days, you can be creating dynamic and powerful Web-based business solutions. *Teach Yourself Active Server Pages in 14 Days* is your guide for discovering how to develop sophisticated Web applications using scripting languages such as VBScript, JScript/JavaScript, and Perl. You'll learn about the fundamentals of Active Server Pages, which enable server-side scripting for IIS with native support for both VBScript and JScript.

Price: $29.99 USA/$42.95 CDN   *Accomplished–Advanced*
ISBN: 1-57521-330-3   *500 pages*

Add to Your Sams.net Library Today
with the Best Books for Internet Technologies

ISBN	Quantity	Description of Item	Unit Cost	Total Cost
1-57521-335-4		Teach Yourself Dynamic HTML in a Week	$29.99	
1-57521-305-2		Laura Lemay's Teach Yourself Web Publishing with HTML 4 in 14 Days, Second Professional Reference Edition (Book/CD-ROM)	$59.99	
1-57521-308-7		Laura Lemay's Web Workshop: Advanced FrontPage97 (Book/CD-ROM)	$39.99	
1-57521-330-3		Teach Yourself Active Server Pages in 14 Days	$29.99	
		Shipping and handling: See information below.		
		TOTAL		

Shipping and Handling: $4.00 for the first book, and $1.75 for each additional book. If you need to have it NOW, we can ship product to you in 24 hours for an additional charge of approximately $18.00, and you will receive your item overnight or in two days. For overseas shipping and handling add $2.00. Prices subject to change. Call between 9:00 a.m. and 5:00 p.m. EST for availability and pricing information on latest editions.

201 W. 103rd Street, Indianapolis, Indiana 46290

1-800-428-5331 — Orders   1-800-835-3202 — FAX   1-800-858-7674 — Customer Service

Book ISBN 1-57521-233-1